The Wild Wandering Arc:
A Journey Through Vanlife, Nature & Love

MORGAN KHALSA

Copyright © 2022 Morgan Khalsa Nichols

Wildmuse Portal Publishing

All rights reserved.

ISBN: 9798499889503

ACKNOWLEDGMENTS

Thank you to Sally-Shakti Willow for being an early reader, editor and supporter of this book.

Thank you to everyone who supported me to know that my story is worth telling. You know who you are.

Thank you to Mahadeva Volt Cottrell for everything.

PROLOGUE: THE ECLIPSE

Cambrian Mountains Reservoir, Wales, August 2017
3 months before moving into the van

I know he is out there, feeling hurt, but I must have this time. The urgency of it, after only two days together in the van, is like a spear in my side. The panic of being so enclosed has become unbearable.

Being alone brings immediate relief. I sit at the water's edge, letting the hush of the water over the stones reach into my chest and lap at my heart.

After a few minutes of basking in freedom and silence, staring at the blue mountain, the water, the sky, I become sleepy and lie back on my sarong. It's the blue and yellow one salvaged from Aunt Diana's bedroom in 2015 when she died, feeling unloved by the man who cried after her death, regretting that he hadn't given her the marriage and security she craved.

Feeling the pebbles under me as a kindness, I drift into a half-sleep. Just as I emerge, a distant shout travels to my quiet spot. It's got to be him: we haven't seen anyone else for days. I weigh fear against excitement, hold disappointment at having my space disrupted alongside a half-guilty concern: Is he OK? Has he lost the plot? Is he really crazy after all, like Dylan said? Is he angry?

When my dad was angry, it felt like the sun was being eclipsed. Whatever play, laughter or peace was moving through our home, his mood could change everything in a split second.

Now, I'm part of a duo rather than a quartet. Simpler. More intimate. My dad played out his stuff in an intricate dance between me, my sister, my mother and my grandmother.

But maybe the safety is an illusion: yes, this man will not hit me, but his hurt could turn to anger at any moment. It's also scarier because it is more intimate, and because we're in the middle of nowhere. And there's nowhere to hide.

He appears with his staff, running down to the water a few metres from me. He's close enough for it to seem like an intentional proximity, but he doesn't look at me. He strips down and goes full tilt into the water with his staff. I watch him throw it up in the air, catch it, throw it again, over and over.

The fear in my throat is as hard as the pebbles. What will happen next? Will he throw it at me? Will he shout at me? I've only known him for three months. This is insane. What was I thinking?

I remember my closest friend, Kristen, warning me that I might find some of Thor's behaviour strange. This was despite the fact that both she and her partner Graham were huge fans of our relationship, and far preferred him to Dylan, my previous partner.

Kristen told me that they'd seen Thor in some deep 'shamanic trance states' around the fire at a free-spirited Rainbow Gathering, expressing himself with a lot of wild animal noises. "I think you're quite self-conscious, so you might be embarrassed by it. But," she added, "he's clearly a good guy."

Now, I place my stomach on the stones and let their friendly warmth enter me. In the background, I can hear his shouts; inside me, the uncertainty bubbles. Finally, I turn on my back.

With a sudden resolve, I spring up and strip off, then run into the water without looking at him. Its icy coldness reprimands me; I step out after only a couple of minutes and walk back to my spot on the pebbles with what I hope is dignity.

This time, he meets my eye as I walk towards his line of vision. But it's as if he doesn't know me. As if I'm looking at a man from some archetypal story: the wizard with his staff. The seer. On a human level, though, the desire works its way into my blood. The way his ribs are outlined so clearly, the cave underneath them that I know so well. His breastbone extends out from his body: it started growing when he was eleven. I'm so used to it now – in fact, I've become fond of it, seeing a proud stag rather than the deformity that made his teen years so full of insecurity.

His cock, even though not erect, stirs the very tip of an eruption in me.

"Come here," I say, taking a risk.

"No." His answer is firm but neutral, not cold or angry. He carries on twirling the staff. I feel both rebuffed and oddly turned on by his assertiveness. I start to roll around on the stones, offering up surrender in the only way I can right now.

Then he's running through the water, shouting again, cathartically. My fear vies with fascination. He is so utterly unselfconscious, so free in his expression. My own cavorting on the stones feels so tame by comparison.

I watch him kneel on the stones in front of me. Pulling them up onto his body, covering himself with them. Soon he's buried up to his waist, his cock hidden. He is making the animal noises that I've also become accustomed to. I remember being startled by these sounds the first time we were in bed at my house. Now, they are just part of the texture of numerous things that make him known and loveable to me.

I'm oddly touched by this solemn ceremony. I cannot see his cock. It's as if he has become harmless, gentle, a boy and not a man, not a scary man who can hurt me. His masculinity redeemed.

Finally, he joins me. We lie entwined on top of the pebbles. It's as if we are both children and adults at the same time. Some kind of ritual has been completed – one I was invited into, resistant and scared. I have found a kind of healing of what my father broke.

THE ANNOUNCEMENT

When the blow comes, I've just arrived back from the last big festival of the summer: Into the Wild, a 'conscious' festival where I have held writing workshops for the past couple of years. I've danced and sung myself into a state of bliss, but I'm also raw from sleep-deprivation. Thor is part of the take-down crew and has stayed on at the festival, planning to join me at my house in a few days.

We're about to begin a new phase: he's going to bring his summer travels in his live-in van to an end and base himself in Lewes, the small Sussex country town where my nine-year-old son Jay and I have lived for nearly half a decade. And in the longer term, we're planning to look for a place to live in rural Sussex for the three of us.

This is stirring both excitement and nervousness in me. Because our relationship started in early summer, it's been conducted largely at festivals and on roadtrips, sidestepping the nitty-gritty day to day of school runs and dinners. I'm thrilled to be moving into a more settled, committed phase, but also scared that we'll lose the romance or that Thor will be put off by the less carefree, non-summer me, with all her moods and stressed-out moments.

Thor has met Jay a few times: they've got on well and we've all enjoyed hanging out together. But I know that sharing a house – and sharing me – in a more ongoing way will be a whole different thing.

At first, we thought we had plenty of time to make this move, and we intended that in the meantime, Thor would regularly go to his van when we all needed space from each other. It was going to be a gradual shift to more full co-habitation.

Then came the eviction notice.

It was nothing personal: the landlords simply needed to do some vital maintenance and, no doubt, wanted to rent the property again at a higher price. A big part of me felt relieved: there were many aspects of the house I was unhappy with. A vague, unidentifiable damp smell, a noisy, dirty street without a pavement, a small, awkwardly shaped kitchen. I knew that having a three-month deadline would make me get my act together and take concrete steps to follow my long-held dreams of living more rurally.

So, the eviction notice was a catalyst, rather than the crunch that comes now, when Jay has just returned from his alternate weekend at his dad's. In my loved-up post-festival state, I'm happy to see him and keen to reconnect. Jay chatters cheerfully to me about Lego and games and I listen with the focused attention that comes easily after a few days' break from mothering.

I am totally unprepared for his next words.

"I've been thinking, I'd like to try living with Dad when we move out of this house."

After days of following my flow in the strong August heat, dancing for hours with hundreds of people, singing around the campfire, making love in the woods, I'm open and thin-skinned. Immediately, the hot tears rush to the surface. I am wordless.

"Are you OK, Mom?" Jay springs into concern at once. I nod, still unable to speak, and go into the kitchen, where I start to clang pots around to get dinner started. A million things are rushing through my head, and I can't let any of them out of my mouth. It's just so, completely, unexpected.

Now, he follows me into the kitchen and looks at me worriedly, expectantly. "I'm just ... surprised. It's a big decision," I say finally.

"You look upset," he says, frowning at me, and my heart clenches. *He shouldn't have to worry about me.*

"Well ... it's a big thing. It's going to take me a while to take it in. But we'll talk about it more."

"It's just that I've never tried it before, living with Dad," he bursts out, the excitement coming through in his voice. "I want to see what it's like. I could go to a new school and make new friends. It would be fun. It's just that I'd be in a different house in the week. I'd still see you every second weekend, and Dad said he could take me to you in the week as well."

I force myself to look at his eager face. But my mind is already leaping ahead with the financial implications: without the help I get from the government to top up my earnings as a lone parent, there's no way I'll be able to rent in this expensive area anymore. Who knows how far away I'll end up living, and his father won't facilitate access regularly if I'm not local.

"Was it your idea?" The words come out, inadvisable pebbles from my dry mouth.

"Well, Dad and I were talking about it in the car. He said that I could always come live with him, and I said, yes, I want to do that."

Helplessness and grief war with anger in my stomach. "But when we talked about it before, you and I … when you weren't sure about the idea that we might have to move out of Lewes because it's so expensive now … and I said you could always stay with Dad if you wanted – you said you would still want to stay with me."

He's quiet for a moment, looking down at the floor. "Yes. I know. But that's because I hadn't thought about it. Now I've thought about it."

"Okay." My throat is tight, but I feel a sudden respect for him, and with it, a rush of affection. He really is growing up. I take a deep breath and hug him. "It's okay. I want you to do what feels right for you and what makes you happy. What do you want for dinner?"

*

Over the next weeks, in the maelstrom of emotions that ensue, I still find it impossible to express to Jay anything of what I'm feeling. I just don't know how to be open about my feelings of loss without burdening him with adult emotions he shouldn't feel responsible for.

Thor, who, of course, I've been crying down the phone to, asks me several times, "When are you going to talk to him about it?" But it's a block I can't get past. I just want Thor to get here – I'm struggling to hold this all alone.

I'm aware of the risk of not speaking about my feelings: that I might be giving Jay the message that I don't really care. That I am letting him go without a second thought.

And my guilty secret is this: in amongst the grief and incredulity is the unmistakable rise of relief and excitement. Maybe, after ten years of motherhood being the altar of my life, the sacrifice is coming to an end.

PARALLEL UNIVERSE

"I wonder where we would be moving to if I wasn't moving in with Dad now."

I look up from my breakfast of seeds, nuts, and dates in surprise. Jay is dipping Marmite soldiers into eggs I've boiled just right, after much practice. "You mean like if we were in a parallel universe, like you talked about yesterday?"

"Yes." On the way home from school yesterday, he waxed lyrical about all the inventions he'd create in this parallel universe. For instance, instead of being green, the field we were walking across would be orange.

"Hmm," I chew on this. Nothing more comes from him.

So I go on, tentatively: "Remember when I said you could always live with your dad if you want to stay in this area?"

He thinks for a moment, then: "Yeah."

"Well, I sometimes wonder what would have happened if I hadn't said that. If you would still be moving in with Dad."

His thoughtful expression deepens. "I don't know."

It feels good to get the unspoken thoughts out in the air in an 'imagine if' sort of way, rather than the angst-ridden emotional outburst I kept visualising and refraining from. I haven't been able to allow that because I'm so scared of guilt-tripping him into changing his mind. I want him to do what he feels is right, not stay with me out of a sense of loyalty.

But I still don't say it all, still don't reveal another parallel universe of mine: that I also wonder if it would have happened if I hadn't been near to tears talking to his dad on the phone a few months ago.

That evening, his father had picked up Jay's sullenness and distance on the phone and asked to be put on to talk to me.

"Is he OK?" Usually consistently level and quick to shrug things off, Luke sounded more concerned than I had ever heard him.

I nearly burst into tears simply at being asked the question. It had been a tough week.

"Well, I've been finding Jay's behaviour very difficult at times, to be honest. It's really hard to get his co-operation with a lot of things. I'm wondering if he might benefit from some more masculine guidance on a regular basis."

I waited anxiously for Luke's response, feeling nervous about revealing this vulnerability to him. I half expected him to laugh at me or downplay my feelings.

But to my surprise, he said, "I'd be totally up for Jay living with me. I could work my job hours around it. My parents would help." Luke had moved back in with his parents a couple of years before.

Suddenly, after ten years of doing 90% of the parenting alone, I saw a gap of possibility. And underneath: an unmistakable fear, even then.

Was that what set it all off? Did it plant a seed in Luke's head that made him unable to resist making a suggestion to Jay when we got our eviction notice? I never have been able to get the clear story of who, out of the two of them, had broached the subject first. When I'd asked Luke, he said Jay had raised the subject – the opposite of what Jay had said.

After my conversation with Luke, I spent a near-sleepless night obsessing about what it would be like if Jay did change households. A desperate melancholy clutched me as I imagined what the house would feel and sound like without his exuberant, insistent presence. No, I don't want that. I realised that having the option made real for me, rather than holding it as impossible, made me feel that I now had a choice.

Rather than it being forced on me by circumstances, I was choosing to continue as the residential parent and to hold everything that entailed. In the weeks that followed, I felt more appreciation for Jay. The weariness of juggling my freelance work, mothering, and domestic management with the constant backdrop of fatigue, came into the perspective of love again.

*

After dinner on the evening of Jay's announcement, I'm reading his favourite Tom Gates book to him, featuring the everyday modern adventures of a boy exactly his age through comical drawings and words. I suddenly burst into tears, an unstoppable and embarrassing flood.

I tell him simply, "I'm sad," as he puts his arm on mine with that carefully practiced concerned expression. He's fairly used to this sort of thing from me, after the numerous relationship breakups where I've been unable to keep my tears fully locked up for private times. Next morning, at breakfast, the tears are gone but something has broken in me. I get him up with silly voices and it's like when he was younger. I tell him that when he moves to Dad's I will miss his grumpy face and his silly face, his happy face, and his sad face.

CONFINED SPACE

As I sit down in my garden on a warm September Saturday for a phone call with Thor, the sun has already left most of the back yard, but it's still warm and I'm excited to be talking to him. Our conversations always seem to go deep, uncovering new discoveries and connections, even breakthroughs.

Over the past week, I've roller-coastered my way from shock and sadness to excitement, quickly shifting into a good dose of the manic as, never comfortable sitting in the unknown, doing nothing, I frantically research how and where I can live and support myself.

Thor and I have already spoken a lot about the changes to come. He's been a patient listener, saying I can talk about it as much as I needed. In my loss of residential parenthood, he feels an echo of his own circumstances eight years ago, when he moved out from his marital home and faced the sadness of not living with his two sons anymore.

But it's in this conversation, sitting on my wooden garden chair staring at the ivy on the too-high wall, that he finally names what has been buzzing gently around in my background awareness. The thing I've been too embarrassed to ask.

"You've not mentioned my role in all this ... if I can be part of your plans at all."

I pause, suddenly aware of my heart rate. His tone is warm and gentle and I allow it to sink in that he might genuinely want to be part of my next move.

I realise that underneath my surface survival-mode, I've been feeling vulnerable around the question of how we'll go forward now that things have changed so radically. My wondering about where he'll fit in has been shoved to the back of the queue of practical considerations and the ongoing processing of my grief around losing Jay.

I know that the part-time programming job that fits perfectly into his frugal life on the road would never stretch to renting a property in the expensive South-East. So, I've been thinking of my housing situation as solely my problem to solve. As a single mother, I'm so used to managing everything myself that I haven't quite taken on board that I now have a proper partner.

"What about if you move into the van with me for a while and we look for somewhere to live together?" he goes on.

My heart thuds in my chest. Can he really be saying this? He's always maintained that the van is only suitable for two for a maximum of a week. "Anything longer than that, and you'll drive each other crazy."

But he's going on, "It's small, and we would probably make each other nuts sometimes, but it could be a good base for a while. Remember how we talked about living in a cabin in the woods one day? Well, maybe this has just accelerated the process of us finding a set up like that. I did wonder, sometimes, if we should just go straight for it and take the leap."

I've wondered this, too. In our original set of plans, we considered the move to a rural house as a stepping-stone to eventually living either in an offgrid-ish community or using Thor's bare bones of a geodesic dome to build our own home in a field or in the woods. I loved all these ideas, but I also found it harder to believe in them since my previous relationship with a yurt-builder, when I came within a hair's breadth of living in a yurt – another dream of mine – before it all went wrong between us.

I'm also all too aware of the draconian laws governing land use in the UK – "this benighted isle", as a boat-dwelling acquaintance put it – and how difficult it could be to find somewhere where we were allowed to live as we wanted. Even people who have pots of money to buy their own land have to run the gauntlet of strict planning regulations. I've seen this scupper the dreams of several of my earth-loving Sussex acquaintances.

But something about his words, "take the leap", hits me right in the heart. In the last year, my extended community lost two inspirational women: Tanya and Ren. Tanya, an outspoken breastfeeding advocate and a sacred sexuality teacher and therapist, was tragically killed in a motorbike accident in Bali, along with her unborn baby, leaving her young son, his father, and her current partner behind. Ren was a passionate and powerful Irish female health advocate and educator. She was also a poet and the mother of a toddler, and died from a painful, viciously invasive form of cancer.

Both Tanya and Ren were in their mid-to-late-thirties and both should have had many more years of sharing their wisdom and love of life with their families. They would have been the wise Elders of our local 'tribe'. Although neither was a close friend, they made big impressions on me the few times I met them, and I grieved the loss of them in our community. They were unconventionalists who lived life on their own terms. The message struck home: live your life now because you may not have 'til you're 90.

"That sounds really good," I find myself saying now, the excitement in my heart and throat warring with voices of doom in my head. "I mean, it is tiny, and I know it won't always be easy, but I feel really good hearing you say that." I'm so touched by his support for me, the way he's offering me what he has, even though by the standards of many it's so little.

Now that I think about it, for some time there have been clues that this was the way I'd go. I remember getting a lift to a festival – the one where Thor and I met – with a hardy dreadlocked woman in her live-in purple van.

She was an extremely resourceful and skilled long-term nomad who, as well as having foraging and forest school abilities, impressed me with the fact that she made accessories out of roadkill she collected herself. I remember looking at the rabbit skin headdress that wound through her dreadlocks and thinking, "I could never do that." I couldn't imagine dealing with the gore.

Soon after my pivotal conversation with Thor, I receive a message from Dorothy, a woman I met at community camps. When I read over our previous correspondence from a year or two back, I'm surprised and delighted to find a conversation where she told me she was now living in a van in Devon and I responded: "Oh, that's great, I'd love to live in a van, if I didn't have Jay".

Her reply: "I'll live in it for you for now."

I'd completely forgotten about this exchange and the fact that I wanted to live in a van – even if it was just a passing thought. I feel exhilarated. And then, that phrase, "if I didn't have Jay" strikes the pit of my stomach. It's a sad, even shameful, thing, but I wonder: have I subconsciously created this situation so I could be free?

*

A couple of years ago, an astrologer told me that according to my birth chart, I should make sure my time with a lover is confined to weekends. "Your independence is vital to you," he emphasised.

So far, apart from my highly co-dependent first love relationship, I'd always had partners who were either equally free spirits or absent through their addiction to something else: alcohol, weed, music-making, porn. This was particularly true of the two men I had lived with in long-term relationships. So, I didn't think too deeply on my astrologer's advice; I seemed to be able to live with partners without us being on top of each other.

Now, I'm seriously considering moving into the most confined space possible with my partner, for an unspecified period. I have to question whether this is a good idea.

I've experienced far more genuine emotional intimacy with Thor than any other man. We have a connection so intense that I know, deep inside, that I'll not be able to get away with the distance built into previous partnerships.

We'll only get a breather from each other every two weeks when I go to visit Jay. And that won't be space for me: not only will that time, of course, be focused on my son, but it will also involve staying with friends, adapting to their needs and preferences – very different from having Jay come and visit me in my own home. Space is a staple of my sanity and something I've been used to having in my life when Jay is at school or at his dad's.

But even though I know all this about myself, something in me sounds a big yes when Thor gives me his invitation. A living tendril of hope, which, against all logical sense, tells me this is the right thing to do.

*

I'm walking past the local playpark on my way home from Tesco's when I see Rose, a well-known, much-loved member of my local alternative community. She made a documentary with her partner Carl based on their truck travels around intentional communities and off-grid experiments. I feel my heart beating: I'm drawn to her like a magnet. Rose knows something of the journey I'm considering embarking on – this crazy, possibly ill-advised break out of the known.

We've only spoken a few times before, and mostly in the context of Red Tent women's circles, but she greets me warmly. In-between her checking on her blonde, excitable four-year-old daughter, who's playing with a couple of other children on the climbing frame, I tell her my plan.

She isn't surprised. "It's cosy and lovely," she says. "I would do it again if I didn't have a child. I loved it – all sitting in one room together with the stew cooking. And in the winter, you just read a lot, just sit and read."

"What are the downsides, though? What did you struggle with?"

"You have to be very interdependent. Like, if your home is moved – you need to know. You need to work together."

The word 'interdependent' lands in my system with a frightening thud. My childhood of dealing with the unpredictable and threatening moods of the adults around me trained me to fear being dependent on anyone.

"You might sometimes have to pee in front of each other, and things like that," she adds with a little laugh, and I laugh too, omitting to mention that we are used to that already from our road trip.

We watch the children together: two girls and a boy, exuberant in their joy. I feel the ache that is fast becoming familiar, the longing to see my son little again, playing like these three.

Rose's daughter is clearly signalling for her attention. "Feel free to contact me and talk about it more," she says, before she moves away.

"Thank you," I say, and turn back into the sunshine, walking up the hill towards my house for one of the last times.

THE OTHER FACE

Stonehenge, with its ancient stone circle, copious woods and huge arcing sky over fields dotted with burial mounds, is Thor's spiritual home. It's where he comes to connect to his ancestors, a big part of his spiritual practice, and it's also the place where he has parked up most often in his six years of vanlife; he even spent one entire winter there when his van needed extensive repairs. So, there is enormous weight in me joining him here for the first time: one of pressure as well as excitement.

It's my third substantial van visit: the first was our ten days at Buddhafield Festival in July, and the second was our Wales road trip in August, a month ago. The pressure is heightened by the fact that we are about to make a big move. We're going to get handfasted.

At a handfasting ceremony, based on the Celtic tradition, a couple commits to each other for a year and a day. These ceremonies are popular at the pagan holidays, or 'sabbats', celebrated at Stonehenge – such as Solstice and Equinox – and I've long dreamed about having one of them when I met the right person.

I've never been one to daydream about a big white wedding, even as a little girl. The idea of making a commitment in front of a lot of strangers, being on display in that way, was uncomfortable even as I yearned for the indefinable 'thing' that it could offer – the feeling of being chosen.

But in recent years, particularly after witnessing a few handfastings, I've developed a fantasy about having my own ceremony like this.

We were lying together on the van sofa one summer night, when the conversation turned to our romantic fantasies. I can remember nothing of any fantasies he shared, just him saying: "Go on then, what's yours?"

I hesitated for ages before finally saying, "My fantasy is that we have a handfasting ceremony at Beltane," with a big lump in my throat. Beltane is the first of May, when neo-pagans celebrate the beginning of spring.

To my surprise, Thor immediately responded: "Yes, I'd be up for that." My heart leaped. "Let's do it sooner. We could do it at Stonehenge for the Equinox. I know some druids who could hold the ceremony for us."

I instantly felt the kind of anxiety you get when something you long for comes into close view and you realise you never expected to get it. Beltane was comfortably far enough in the future to feel safe and slightly abstract –

this was frighteningly real.

But I didn't name my nerves to him. After we agreed to go ahead, I spent days researching online, asking a pagan celebrant friend for advice, and getting more and more knotted and jumpy.

Fast forward to September and, of course, my period arrives just before I travel from Sussex to join Thor at Salisbury station. I'm in an inward, thin-skinned zone, unable to connect as deeply as he wants me to, and we immediately start getting into arguments.

This is not the first emergence of this issue in our relationship, and we've explored why my withdrawal is so painful for him. The roots go back to his early childhood, when his teenage mother would hand him over to his grandmother or simply detach emotionally when she couldn't cope. I'm empathetic, but I'm also being strongly triggered; when he's hurt, he often gets angry, and that reminds me of my father.

Now, I'm pushing away the knowledge that I'm having a massive case of cold feet about our ceremony. I also don't feel a 100% yes about the druid he's chosen for the ceremony, Phil, who, with his chain joint-smoking and London accent just doesn't strike me as the kind of druid I'd imagined.

Always sensitive to undercurrents, Thor knows that on some level I'm not up for it. Time passes as we process what's going on between us in endless discussions, and we still haven't got our materials together for the ceremony. In the end, we decide not to go ahead, telling Phil that 'stuff' has come up. Although I'm relieved, I also feel bitterly sad and disappointed that we haven't been able to overcome our challenges and reconnect. I can't shrug off the sense that we've failed an important test to our commitment.

*

It's the first time I've visited the stones: these ancient, mysterious reminders of another time. The power in their presence during the Equinox sunrise is palpable, shining even through my pain.

As we enter the site, let through with a big crowd of people by the security staff, I join Thor in his ceremonial way of being with the stones, walking three times with him around the perimeter. Then I go inside the stone circle and sit with my back against one, closing my eyes and trying to get into it. It's challenging, with all the noise around. The druids are doing a ceremony in the centre and others are milling around taking photographs. I feel separate from all of it, fragile with all the intensity and lack of sleep.

And then I open my eyes and see, across the circle, a couple being handfasted, dressed in green, gold and red. I can hear the words they are saying to each other and see the smile that lights up her face as he stares into her eyes, the druid wrapping their hands together with a big multi-coloured cloth. The tears stirring just under the surface break free. I get up without thinking and move towards Thor, who is standing with his staff not far away.

He immediately senses what I need. He hugs me for a long time, and then says, "Let's do our own private ceremony, just the two of us outside the stones." I nod, the constriction still hard in my throat. We go to one of the stones that sits a way outside the central structure, away from the tourists with their flashing cameras and the rowdy singing in the centre.

As we sit down, I suddenly feel terrified. This is really happening. Not in the way I imagined it, not publicly, but still – it's a big commitment. I had started thinking about my vows when we were planning the ceremony, but I hadn't planned anything concrete, and now my mind goes blank. I insist he speak first, and the words he says choke me up further, as he commits to our relationship for the year ahead and to being intimate only with me. I can barely take it in – I hadn't expected it to be so powerful, to hear these simple words.

He symbolically puts a piece of his heart inside mine and I become so emotional I can't do the same back. I feel so moved by the power of his intention towards me. Eventually, I manage to summon my own words and speak them into the space between us, where nothing but our love exists, for just this moment.

*

On the way back from Stonehenge, we stop at an estuary in Bosham, West Sussex, a favourite spot Thor has been keen to show me for some time. "It's got loads of good water energy," he says, "good for us since we're both water signs."

But in my menstrual zone of self-protective criticism, I hate it immediately: there's no privacy, we're parked right up close to the water on what isn't even a proper layby, and people crane their necks at the van as they walk past, giving what I'm sure are judgmental frowns.

It seems that my need for space hasn't disappeared, and it soon brings the thorny doubts thick and fast.

I stand outside the van, looking at the estuary and the last fading pink of the sunset.

I can't stop brooding on my worries: how on earth are we going to live in the van together pretty much full-time if I need that much space? How will both of our needs be met if it's so painful for Thor when he wants connection that isn't available?

The extremities of the ups and downs we're going through are all too familiar to me from previous relationships. Yesterday, in a honeymoonish reprieve from the drama, we lay together in the sun on top of a burial mound at Stonehenge while I stroked his warm, naked back. We ate cacao nibs and drank chai tea from a flask, laughing and kissing each other all over. Today, hours of processing and tears because I, again, could not connect in intimacy. I feel the pain of the boulder in me that has been there ever since Jay left.

I feel like I'm drowning: worn out from tears, trying, and the repeated necessity of letting go. Tired to the bone from years of hoping, waiting and getting excited over and over again: This time it will work! This time I can make a proper family with someone – only to have the other face of my partner revealed time and again. The judgment, the message that I'm not OK as I am, the message that echoes every bit of bullying, rejection and abuse I endured as a child.

This other face is mine, too. The part of me that sabotages loving and being loved. Who needs to feel herself outside of an intimate relationship, to know her own outlines. Why would this be any different from the way I needed space away from Jay, to be free of the demands and expectations that come when someone needs you – even if you need them too?

Will I ever be capable of a mature relationship? Or am I doomed to repeat the play of power, control and despair so beautifully modelled by my parents?

Like the encroaching tide, my self-pity turns quickly into disgust and boredom with myself. Only minutes ago, I wanted to end this relationship. Now, I am devastated that Thor doesn't want to hug me. I want only to be held and for him to make everything right again.

I hear an owl call and Thor remarks that he's not heard one for ages. At first, I'm so stuck in my misery that I don't care. But there is also a comfort in being reminded that there's a world out there, beyond this van and our pressure cooker of issues.

It feels like I'm being asked, over and over again, to let go of every plan and every idea of who and what I am, of what my life is about. And at moments, I feel like I'm losing the thread.

THE SPELL

When I caught my first glimpse of Thor, I was feeling lost and more than a little dark. It was the descending part of the wave I ride at every festival, even after I'd left my drug-fuelled psychedelic trance days behind me and attended only conscious festivals with tantra, drumming workshops and world music. Usually, my mood eventually came up again – I'd learned to trust this process.

But for now, I was wandering bleakly around, looking for my friends, seeing nothing but clumps of intimates huddled together and wishing my boyfriend, Dylan, was there to cuddle up with around the fire. We'd only been together officially for a couple of weeks, but as friends had flirted with each other on and off for years in-between relationships. He was at another festival where he had already committed to lead workshops, while I'd arranged to run workshops here.

As I walked past the Community Kitchen, a crew meal area doubling as a gathering place for impromptu jams, I heard the familiar sounds of kirtan, a devotional chanting practice that almost never failed to put me into a state of ecstatic connection. The comforting chant 'Om Namah Shivayah' reached out like tendrils of smoke to my matchstick-girl. An earnest 70's-moustached guy was leading on the guitar, joined by several others on banjo, djembe and flute. I saw my closest friend, Marion, sitting between the legs of her friend Sara. With enormous relief, I joined them and received their welcoming smiles.

The chanting quickly absorbed me into the rising energy. After a while, I opened my eyes to notice a bearded, long-haired, forty-something guy opposite me, singing with his eyes closed a lot of the time. He looked really serious and into it. There were so many 'hippy Jesus' guys around that at first he didn't strike me in any particular way.

But after a while, his mysterious aura started to draw me in a little – as well as make me feel vaguely intimidated. The seeds of our entire relationship dynamic, right there.

Marion and I got into conversation and, as it continued, I started to feel more and more uncomfortable. I just knew that the serious bearded guy would disapprove of our chatting, that he would find it disturbing to the sacred atmosphere. I even found myself apologising to him in a knee-jerk way when he glanced our way, assuming he was irritated. He didn't respond, only looked at me without any change in his expression, no polite smile, nothing.

Marion, as was her way, was totally in the moment and oblivious to any annoyance she might be causing, while I felt increasingly self-conscious. Eventually, we dissolved our chatter and returned to singing; I relaxed and forgot about the bearded guy. Marion, Sara and I moved to the teepee café, where we chatted over hot chocolate and a smorgasbord of cakes until past midnight. I was on the upswing again: connected and happy, and only vaguely missing Dylan, who was now a distant presence in my awareness.

But there's another aspect to the 'up' stage of the wave ride: getting almost *too* happy. The next day, at a 5Rhythms movement meditation workshop, I danced myself into such an expanded, open state that I felt painfully raw and uncontained afterwards.

Festival workshops aren't safely held spaces like those you might attend on a weekend in a community hall or someone's home. You have to go into the process and trust it when plenty of others dancing around you seem totally un-present, their eyes darting nervously around – or worse, voyeuristically watching from the sidelines, clutching a latte. "It's not a spectator sport," the teacher gently teases, but they still hang around. To go into a deep state, connecting with your own experience, is more vulnerable in such a space; you do it despite yourself.

After the workshop, I wanted to hug someone, to be held, but the only hug I was offered felt dutiful and meagre, leaving my vulnerability stretching out of me and into the space, searching. I had no real idea yet how to hold myself, then. As I walked out, I checked the time on my phone, conscious that in forty-five minutes I would have to run a workshop myself, a writing and sharing circle for mothers. I needed to get into a 'together' space by then, able to hold other people's emotions and needs.

I walked past a group of people cuddled together in front of another workshop venue and was immediately drawn in. The usual part of me that judges and edits everything before it comes out was quick to say, *No, don't be silly, walk on past.* But because I knew two of the people in the cuddle puddle, it felt possible to override that and say, "Is this a spontaneous gathering or part of a workshop?"

And they all invited me over with warmth and smiles, explaining that they had been in a workshop together, but anyone was welcome. With a huge sense of relief, I allowed myself to be enveloped, soothed, welcomed.

I became aware that another person had joined the cuddle puddle, slipping in behind me. As soon as I felt his hand on my back, I was aware of the strength of his presence. Beginning to melt at the sense of warmth flowing from his hand, I eased back into his holding. A worry niggled at me: maybe this wasn't fully appropriate, since I was in a relationship. But festivals are full of these borderline situations. Cuddle puddles are harmless – and besides, it isn't personal, I justified it to myself.

After some more delicious time in this group embrace, I thought to ask what the time was and realised I had to go prepare for my workshop. As I gently extricated myself, I saw that the person doing healing on the back of my heart was the mysterious bearded guy from the kirtan. Only he didn't seem intimidating anymore, but warm and open.

"Which workshop is that?" I asked the group, pointing at the small, round marquee we'd all been sitting outside. "It's going to be Adam's Tantra workshop," answered Tara, an elven, sweet poet with long dark hair and big eyes who always wore flowery dresses and walked barefoot. "Aah, pity I have to run one of my own now." I had always been curious about Adam's workshops – he was an eccentric, flamboyant and amusing character and I'd heard he was a good Tantra teacher.

But although I'd had a good turn-out at yesterday's workshop, this time no one showed up. I imagined they might have been drawn to the family dance workshop that was scheduled at the same time. I sat alone on my sheepskin feeling peaceful for fifteen minutes, then took myself off with a building sense of excitement to the Tantra workshop, hoping they would let me in late. I realised it was what I'd wanted to do all along.

As it turned out, I wasn't the only late arrival and I easily segued into the workshop. People were dancing around the room as Adam, the facilitator, prompted us to stop and interact with different people briefly. He was almost as camp and outrageous seeming as he was on stage as a festival compere, but in this workshop setting he also had a touch of groundedness, a loving and accepting vibe which made me feel safe.

In one exercise, we were invited to do a finger dance with the next person we came across. "You're only going to touch your index fingers to the other person's. Start by looking into each other's eyes, then close your eyes and just allow your fingers to guide the dance." I felt excitement suffuse me from the waist up when I saw who my partner was for this exercise: standing in front of me was the hippy Jesus guy. My stomach erupted in butterflies. Shit. I liked him more than I'd realised.

I had done my fair share of eye gazing in intimacy workshops and 5Rhythms classes; I'd experienced everything from boredom to tear-raising compassion to fascination. This was different. I had never imagined that touching index fingers or simply making eye contact could be such an intense, overpowering experience. It was as intimate and captivating as sex but also completely innocent.

As our fingers danced, we were completely in sync, flowing together as if in a choreography practiced for so many years that it had become effortless. The air between us crackled like wildfire. When the exercise came to an end, I forcibly let go in my mind so that I could be present with the next person and the following section of the workshop. *It's just a workshop exercise*, I reminded myself. Strong connections sometimes happen.

But my whole body had come alive.

Next, we were divided into 'Trees' and 'Butterflies'. The butterflies flew around the trees, who were blindfolded and remained stationery, treating them to different kinds of specific touch as directed by Adam, including stroking with feathers. Experiencing sensuality in intriguing new ways, often unable to guess whether the person touching me was male or female, I soon forgot about the bearded guy. When it was my turn to be a butterfly, the guy who was the tree in my arms convulsed in sobs as I gently cupped his hands, which were placed over his genitals. I felt moved and honoured to be trusted in this way.

At the end of the workshop, my heart stopped again: I could hardly believe it, but the bearded guy was coming up to me. As he stood in front of me for a silent moment, I think I stopped breathing. When he said, with complete seriousness and not a trace of irony or smile: "That was beautiful. Shall we do it again?" I realised it was the first time I had heard him speak. When I nodded, we dropped immediately into that wordless deep space shared between our eyes and so much more. Time stretched into meaninglessness.

Eventually, the workshop leader shooed us out and we went outside with a silent acknowledgment to continue somewhere else. We sat on a blanket outside the marquee and carried on eye-gazing, only this time we brought some touch in – stroking hands, then arms. It was all very slow, gentle and non-sexual but nevertheless intense. I made myself ask him his name although it seemed irrelevant. "Thor," he answered, and I gave mine.

"Shall we have a code word?" he suggested. We agreed on a simple "stop" if either of us was uncomfortable with anything.

After what could have been anywhere between fifteen minutes to an hour, I heard a man clearing his throat at my ear. "Um, I know you guys are planning your future kids and all that, but I need my blanket back."

I felt myself blush and Thor smiled. We got up and let the guy reclaim his blanket, his girlfriend giggling beside him. "Shall we go get a blanket from my van?" Thor offered, and it wasn't even a question in my mind that I would go with him.

As I followed him to the live-in vehicle camping area nearby, I realised I was in a completely altered state, but I couldn't make myself care. As far as Dylan was concerned, I felt fine – we'd agreed that cuddling and non-sexual touch was fine with others, and no doubt he was doing the same at his festival – and probably with his ex-girlfriend too, for that matter, who was leading kirtan sessions with him.

I didn't think anything much of the van when I first saw it, noting only that it was white and had a sign saying "Free Reiki healing and attunements" on the side. It was only much later, that night, sitting and drinking the delicious hot chocolate Thor had made me, that I felt into it more: and I recognise now that there was an unmistakeable sense of rightness, even of home.

I followed Thor and his blanket into the woods. "I want to show you a yew tree," he said, and it felt like an exciting invitation into some kind of mystery. As we walked, we did the usual getting-to-know-you conversation, though it felt strange after so much connection in the deep wordless realms. In his surprisingly ordinary London accent he told me he had two teenage sons and that astrologically, he was a Cancerian; he was very interested when he heard I was a Piscean. "I've been needing some Pisces energy in my life." He even asked me my specific birthdate.

In an attempt to keep myself out of the cheating danger zone that I realised I was rapidly approaching, I mentioned my boyfriend as soon as possible. I answered his questions about my relationship, such as whether Dylan was my son's father and then how long we'd been together. My reply, "2 ½ weeks but we've known each other nine years", sounded lame even to my ears.

"You look too young to have a nine-year-old," he said.

"How old do you think I am?" I smiled, liking this, but he said, "Let's not talk about age."

We reached the yew tree, where he spread the blanket out and guided me to sit opposite him. Again, we fell into a silent connection through our eyes, only this time I seemed to be going into another space entirely, altered brainwaves turning into a full-on trip. It was as if the tree and everything around us became the setting in an Arthurian legend; the magic was so thick in the air I could hardly breathe. "What do you see?" I asked him eventually, and he said, "So much beauty it takes my breath away."

When he returned the question, I responded, "King energy. And something softer too."

We relaxed into a pose where I was lying back, resting in his arms, and it felt so delicious, it was almost orgasmic. "You feel good, Morgan," he sighed, and I realise this was probably crossing the territory of platonic touch that Dylan and I had agreed.

But it was too late: I was gone.

I leant my legs against the tree. The Queen song, "I want to break free," boomed out from the dance marquee just on the other side of the trees, and I found myself singing along. A moment of incredulity: I was singing in front of a man I'd just met, lounging around in his arms, totally sober, and I felt completely comfortable.

*

Later, when Dylan and I had split up, Thor told me that the yew tree we lay under was one he'd connected with early in his time at Into the Wild, when he was doing festival set-up. It had told him to "bring her here" – trees, I was soon to find out, communicated with him directly.

He'd considered a few women for this pathway during the festival but each time, when he sensed into the energy of the yew again, he knew she wasn't the right one. When he met me, he checked in and there was a "yes" from the tree.

It's just as well he didn't tell me this when we first met, because I would have thought he was a bit crazy and just trying to lure me in. By the time I heard the story, I had learned that I, too, in my own way, could talk to trees.

We spent the next two days joined at the hip, only separating to sleep and eat. At the Martha Tilston gig, he lay on my lap and we stroked each other constantly as Martha sang about giving all of her poetry, all of her words, all of her songs, to feel 'like that again'.

"I prayed for you in a church," he told me. "I asked the Universe to send me a woman who had all these qualities. And it's you."

THE LAST BIRTHDAY PARTY

I'm not sure what my place is, here at the Pizza Express table at Jay's tenth birthday party.

As the boys kick each other under the table and snort with laughter, I'm achingly aware of only pretending to be a responsible adult. A woman with glasses and short hair walks in with her son, wearing a big T-shirt pronouncing 'Choose love'. We catch eyes and smile. She is one of my kind.

That little moment of connection somehow lets me off the leash and I find myself surrendering to being one of the kids, spontaneously joking with them. It comes more naturally than I expected. Is this because I'm becoming untethered, all too soon, from my parental role – from the rigidity of the sensible mother at the school gates? Could I be the Cool Mom all the way now, the way Leora, my friend Kristen's daughter, sees me, declaring regularly that she wishes I was her mum instead?

I will be the holiday and weekend mom, I muse as the four boys pore over their kids' menus. One of them insists on having an adult size pizza and I frantically calculate in my head to see if I can afford it, then decide to let it go. This is, after all, the last birthday party I am likely to organise for Jay, at least until adulthood (his twenty-first looms, impossible-to-imagine). The tenth and the last.

I'm suddenly aware that Jay has chosen to sit next to me and not across from me. Every fifteen minutes or so, he leans in and gives me a spontaneous hug or drapes his arm across my shoulder. Surprised at how unselfconscious he is with doing this in front of his friends, I soak up the affection with a new permeability.

I remember when he was younger, and I was so worn out from being constantly required for hugs; picking up and carrying until my back hurt. The lifeline-strength thread of physical contact he used to need has thinned, but it's still very present, and now I'm grateful it remains. He is certainly far more affectionate with me than I ever was with my parents. Whether that was because of their natures or my own, I'm not sure. I'm told I was 'not a huggy child' but maybe that's because I was already mistrustful of adults by then.

But I can only go so far: when I say, 'my love' at the end of a sentence within hearing of his friend Rowan, he hisses, "Mom!", putting me in my place. I plod through my pizza, which is delicious but too big, and eaten over a backdrop of fear that the boys will grow bored. Eggs Fiorentina, with spinach and olives and gluten free dough. I wince as the boys order more drinks, totting up the bill – I had stuck to my own bottle of water – and again mentally let go, though my thoughts keep returning to worry at the money issue.

Soon, I will be living literally on the breadline. For now, for this month, because of the timings of my single parent benefit payments and my rent, I still have a comfortable margin and don't really have to worry. And my costs will be so minimal, living in the van, that I will be OK. But I worry anyway – the habit of years of living month to month and watching every penny.

At last, the meal is finished and it's time for cake. Jay cringes as the waiters sing Happy Birthday to him, which I've allowed them to do despite his aversion to being sung to. One of the boys gets silly and puts his face repeatedly in the chocolate cake crumbs, while the others tackle him and start roughhousing. Anxious at the prospect of disturbing other diners, I shift into disciplinarian mode, always an uncomfortable role for me.

I round them up after paying the whopping £67 bill – breathe, release – and trail after them to the local toy shop, where Jay has elected to spend his birthday money from his dad with the cheerful agreement of the others. At the counter, he spends what's left over from his chosen toy on animal-shaped erasers for his friends: I feel proud of his generosity.

I enjoy seeing the bond between these boys, who spend many more hours together each week than Jay and I do anymore. I watch them laughing at the top of the stairs in the shop, trying and failing to imagine them as future men, feeling the bittersweetness of their poised fall from boyhood into adolescence.

PATHS NOT TAKEN

A year before moving into the van, I was dating a guy who had two teenage children. He frequently told me how much he missed his son, who he used to hang out with all the time and called his 'best friend' in a way I'm not sure is entirely healthy. But now that he was older, the son was mostly out with his friends. This boyfriend would urge me to appreciate Jay and wouldn't listen to any complaints about how hard a day I'd had with him. He'd constantly check his phone for text messages from his son, which at the time felt a bit pathetic to me.

I dismissed his warnings because I was still in the thick of hands-on parenthood and had an eternity to go before I had to face any such feelings, or so I thought.

After Jay made his choice, there were many times when I wanted to retrace my steps to the forks in the road that came before, speculating endlessly about what could have been.

If I had continued to home educate after the first year, despite the active opposition of his father and my ex 'in-laws' and despite my chronic fatigue issues, would he have been the kind of free-spirited hippy child I could live a nomadic life with, like the women I met at festivals with their big vans and little dreadlocked kids?

If I'd kept him out of the mainstream, would he still be with me? Would saving him from state school have staved off whatever eventually made him scoff at the veggie food stalls at festivals, shouting loudly in the earshot of every vegetarian around, "Where's the meat and milk? I want steak!"

Comparing myself to my friend Marion, who home educates her young son and leads an alternative lifestyle in many respects, constantly confronts me with this sense of lives unlived. Untethered by school runs and term times, she's able to travel around the world teaching Tantra and be fully present with her son when she's home, even taking him with her sometimes.

I have the uncomfortable and unresolvable suspicion that giving up home ed unravelled the tapestry I could have woven, leaving gaps for a takeover from Luke and his folks. What if I'd stuck to my path, to what I thought was best for Jay? Would he still be with me?

Or perhaps Jay would have chosen his dad and grandparents' lifestyle anyway, simply because he feels more of an affinity with those values. Maybe it was all down to his normal, age- and gender-appropriate, identification with his dad, whose values are in so many ways diametrically opposed to mine.

Luke and I are both politically liberal and music-loving, but there the similarities end. While I'd been vegetarian (now a lapsed one) for thirteen years, Luke is an avid meat eater, and my 'hippy' interests were met with teasing and sometimes outright derision. He liked to watch BBC war documentaries with a bottle of wine and listen to Radio 4 while chain smoking; I preferred to dance 5Rhythms and sing earth chants.

The enormity of our differences hit me most starkly on New Year's Day, 2007. We were walking along the seafront when we passed a guy playing a djembe drum. Luke's vitriol was so prolific that it totally killed my euphoric New Year vibe. My head echoed with the thought, *What the fuck am I doing here?*

I started the process of moving out of our shared flat soon after, only to discover I was pregnant. Since I wasn't yet a British citizen, the financial implications of being a single mother would have meant having to move back to South Africa, the last thing I wanted to do – and also meant no possibility of my baby having his dad in his life. I resolved to make things work and spent the next two years battling on with the relationship.

I also wondered if following my pull to move to Devon or Norfolk, where I had made some soul-nourishing connections, would have changed things. If I had been able to move into a community, as I had tried to do for so many years, maybe home education would have been possible to continue because I'd have had the support of other adults and children around. And Jay would have been exposed to more alternative-thinking people as part of his everyday life.

But in the end, I couldn't face living so far away from his father and having to travel so much to allow them to see each other regularly. Over and over, I chose facilitating his relationship with his father, and the support I so desperately needed through the guaranteed childcare breaks he provided, over my calling to follow my own path in life.

Sitting painfully in my gut was one key question: what if I had worked more, made more money, been more 'successful'? If I'd been able to buy as much Lego as Luke, who always seemed to have new gifts for Jay every time they saw each other, would the outcome have been different?

From around six or seven years old, Jay's interest in having 'more' seemed to grow. Although I was sometimes worn down by the involuntary simplicity (i.e. poverty) of our lives, it was important to me that Jay knew what was important in life, and was clear that commercialism was not the way to go.

It had always been more important to me to be there for Jay than to be a high earner; to pick him up from nursery and eventually school, to have the emotional energy for him that I knew I wouldn't have if I was working forty hours a week. But I know that to him it looked like his dad was the more 'fun' one, able to give more Yeses than Nos – and, of course, he also wasn't the one tasked with the day-to-day discipline.

Even though I know these wonderings are a form of torture, sometimes at three in the morning I can't resist going down the rabbit hole. Thor tells me not to blame myself; that this is happening for a reason, and that it could be healing for my relationship with Jay. I want to believe him.

THE ROOTS

"By the end of it, I can tell you, I was so happy to be back in a house, with doors and walls and space," my friend Naomi told me over a joint at a party at Zu Studios, a local hippy hub, after relating the story of her seven weeks in a van over the summer.

Later, when I've been in the van for a little while, she checks in with me to see how it's going. She meets my gushes of enthusiasm with the observation: "Maybe you're more of a natural nomad than me. You don't seem to need your comforts as much."

It's true that, although I'm crap at DIY and generally – due to my dyspraxia – very impractical, I have the main requirement for being a vandweller. I'm pretty hardy, with a high tolerance for physical discomfort and low luxury requirements. I have community camps to thank for that.

I was surprised to find out how much I loved camping. Although I always felt at home in the peace of the forest, as a child I was violently allergic to dust, horses, dogs, and cats. Eventually, I got notes excusing me from the annual school camp because I suffered so much. I hated the itch of sand and avoided the beach like the plague despite growing up with a sea view from my garden, the beach accessible by literally walking down a few steps.

Then things changed. When I was twenty-nine, after half a decade of tripped-out trance festivals, and in the wake of my split from Luke, I spotted a random flyer at a 5Rhythms class inviting me to what, even then, I knew would be home. The photo showed people sitting around fires, dancing outdoors, sharing hugs and smiles. It was called Midsummer Camp and even though it was many miles away and I didn't know anyone who was going, I was immediately determined to be there.

I travelled for six hours by train and bus, lugging my breastfeeding toddler and all our stuff. When I arrived on that field, Tuttington, in the middle of nowhere in Norfolk, where I didn't know a soul, I immediately exhaled in relief at the sight of the oak tree like a beacon in the middle of the field.

I was welcomed into the roundhouse with tea and hugs by a plump middle-aged woman who gave me the low-down on how everything worked. Jay loved the roundhouse on first sight, running around and climbing on the seats, sliding down the mattresses. When he discovered the wheelbarrows outside, his joy was even more uncontainable.

After obliging him with a few pushes around the field in the wheelbarrow,

I proceeded to choose a circle to camp in and to put up my tent. A woman with short curly hair and a little girl at her side poked her head out of her bell tent and said, "Where have you come from?"

When I'd explained, she looked very impressed. "I can't believe you've come all this way on your own."

To me, though, it was nothing. I simply followed the call. That is what I do.

Midsummer Camp was revelatory. For just over a week, I, the perennial black sheep both at school and at home, found myself part of a group (called a 'circle') of twenty people who accepted without question my right to be there and to be one of them. They were my family for those eight days. I also felt held by the larger group of the full camp of five circles, about a hundred people in total.

We sang around the fire, just like on the flyer. Bob Dylan and the Beatles and Joni Mitchell – all my favourites. There was talking late into the night in hot tubs and saunas and on the sweet grass. Fire-based cooking was shared in a co-creation full of laughter and fun, rather than the monotonous chore it was at home. We moved effortlessly in a space where everyone could all simply be.

Yes, there were dance workshops and structured ceremonies, celebrating the summer solstice as we dressed up flamboyantly to honour the height of the year, but that wasn't even the point. It was about the complete sense of freedom and permission to be who you are. It was a place of belonging.

People supported me with Jay, playing with him so that I could avail myself of what was on offer. Having borne the brunt of the parenting on my own for two and a half years, I'd never had an experience like that in my life. I saw Jay soak up the attention from new and different adults who had the energy and enthusiasm to play with him wholeheartedly. I felt the truth of the saying "It takes a village to raise a child".

Every night after dinner, we had sharing circles around the fire, where we each had a turn to hold the talking stick and speak without interruption about how we were feeling and what our day had been like. On the last night, I burst into tears, saying "I want to live like this always". Two of the group members – a couple who I camped with subsequently – came and held me. My outpouring of grief was understood and met, even as I felt embarrassed at being so vulnerable.

I fell so deeply in love with that field and those people that I made the long journey three times that year to other camps held there. I attended the Midsummer Camp annually until it stopped running because of a dispute between the landowners.

I even went to a Winter Solstice camp, staying in a freezing cold borrowed caravan in the snow with Jay so that I could come and say goodbye to 'The Field', as it was known. Tuttington, and the folk I met there, was the reason

I considered moving to Norfolk, even spending a week with friends in Norwich to try it out. But in the end, I decided to try and find more community in Sussex, where living was much easier on a practical level.

I discovered more camps in other areas – all far from my home – and lived the lifestyle of community, simplicity, freedom and closeness to nature for a precious few weeks every year. I came back to the atomised, dark, and dingy feel of my flat and the necessity of coffee dates for connection, with a heart that felt like it was being stuffed back into a cage.

I would tell my friend Fiona, a camp convert who I'd 'turned on' to camps two years after I started going, that I wanted to stay on the field, to run away. The year before my van move, we discussed being a nomad in a text conversation: "But would you return in the winter to a nice warm home," she asked, "or be *truly* nomadic?"

My answer was: *Truly*.

After Jay went to school, my relief at having more time to myself was soon tainted by frustration with the limitations of fitting community camps and festivals – what felt like my 'real life' – into the school term. By the time he was nine, I was very close to registering as a New Age Traveller so I could take Jay away without being fined according to the stringent attendance rules.

A friend, who often worked at festivals, had taken this route, but I felt like I'd be faking if I did it because I didn't really rely on festivals for work – just for sanity. Little did I know how soon I would actually become what I was about to fill in on the forms.

Discovering 'home' on The Field' was like opening a lid on my dissatisfaction with isolated urban life. There was no going back, no pretending that things were OK. Ironic, then, that I should end up being a nomad, instead of finding a communal home: but it never was about a building, or about security. It was a feeling, a state of being.

And now it turned out that 'camp' was more than just an escape from life. The camps had equipped me for nomadic life in many ways. They trained me in living in all kinds of weather and in being extremely flexible: working around others, sharing resources, letting go of timetables and structure to go with the flow of the day and with the needs of the whole.

They educated me in what is really important to me in life: waking up to birdsong, listening to trees, creating together with others in the beauty of the natural world. I will always be grateful for that.

LETTING GO: THE SIGNS

Six weeks after his announcement, Jay leaves for his first residential school trip on a brisk cold October morning.

Although making my way through the never-ending packing list from the school is a little stressful, the two-night separation itself doesn't feel like a big deal. I can see it's huge for many of the other mothers, who stay anxiously close to their children right up until the moment the coach leaves. Jay, accustomed to alternate weekends at his other home and to regular sleepovers with friends, is happy for me to go, and I feel both superfluous and relieved to be released so easily.

It's so unlike when he started nursery school at the Buddhist Dharma School that I had chosen for its gentleness but which smelled just like any other school – stale socks, sandwiches, faint urine. Then, I felt utterly bamboozled by the fact that he was doing things I would know nothing about. Reading the school reports, I was amazed that he apparently liked dressing up as a doctor and listening to people's heartbeats with the toy stethoscope, an interest I had never been witness to. I was just so used to being part of every aspect of his day, from brushing his teeth in the morning to the friendships I helped him develop and maintain, that the idea of him being at nursery, doing stuff that I wasn't part of, was really alien.

It's not that I lack curiosity about what he'll get up to on the trip, which involves a lot of outdoor adventure activities that would have filled me with horror as the bookworm child I was, but which he is excited about. I know I'll be a little frustrated at the monosyllabic answers he'll provide on his return. But the sense of panic and bewilderment at being excluded from his lived experiences, so prickly when he started nursery school, is now absent. What *is* present is excitement and pride, which feels good.

After the drop-off, another mum at the school, who I'm mildly friendly with, gives me a lift home. She tells me that she's been watching Jay walking home each day as she drives past. He's recently started doing the walk alone, something he's been wanting for a while but I didn't allow him to do until I was confident about his road safety.

"I can see him so deep in thought, the cogs turning. There's loads of wisdom waiting to burst out from his boy-self into manhood," she says, her blue eyes lighting up with excitement. "The other day, I had this conversation with my son Michael about what his grandchildren might be like. I mean, the future generations will be born hard-wired for community. It will all be completely different."

I don't know if I fully believe that, but to think that Jay could be on the spearhead of that shift fills me with awe. The unknowability of the world his descendants (and mine) will inherit is exciting. I love the fact that he's going beyond where I can go, even if it does also make me tearful.

LIMINAL

Journal Entry, October 2017

Lines are drawn on the surface of clear water. The branches are like halos, reflecting each other as if they were magical requests.

Let the time fall, captive, gentle, dropping into the river. Let the water fill slowly with our demons, hopes, holdings of love.

Let it swallow the sky's waiting white, these trees that have been here much longer than the interminable toddler years took to pass, the aching hours of walking at the pace of a slug along the pond – seeing everything anew, yes, but also demonic with impatience, held in an arc of sheer frustration.

Wanting fluidity, to touch the precious intimacy of life, but having to be somewhere at three o'clock every weekday. Now, I can sit on a bench and watch no clock, look instead at swans gliding past as they nibble busily at weeds, remembering that day walking in the New Forest when you told me I was your swan, only we never had to fight to find our way to love like swan pairs do. Like you had to in that other Big Relationship. No, this isn't any other love. This is the love I fought my own personal battles for. This is the journey that will test me to the limit even as it gives me everything I always wanted.

STRIPPING BARE

Getting the contents of an entire house down to suitcase-full of stuff to fit in the van is the monumental task ahead of me.

I'm in that last, horrific couple of weeks before moving house. Because I've been here so long, the mission of getting the property up to scratch for the inspection – crucial, as I'm relying on getting most of my deposit back from the rental agency – is gruelling and seemingly never-ending. By the end, I'm pulling twelve-hour days. I don't know how I'd have coped if Jay were still here.

It has been decided that he would move to his dad's during half term week so that he can start at his new school at the beginning of term. I absorb the shock of the suddenly bare and quiet house in furious scrubbing and loud *Florence and the Machine*, but most of the time I'm too stressed to feel any real grief yet. It hasn't sunk in fully.

I'm desperate to be in the van, to be in that cosy cocoon with its soft fairy lights and the woodburner going, away from this chaos. I know Thor has been on his own stripping down mission, working hard for two weeks to make room for me in the van, adapting the electrical set up to hold my needs as well as his, and I'm touched by this sign of his love.

There's a glimmer of respite, though, amidst the endless decluttering and the intense scrubbing of an oven I must have cleaned twice in four years (which Thor reluctantly helps me with, stripping down to his pants and getting right in there). Today, I quit my very part-time job as a virtual assistant/ PA for a healing academy.

It's the only bit of solid ongoing income I have – my freelance copywriting and editing work fluctuates wildly – and letting go of it feels vaguely financially suicidal. But as I put down the phone, I'm euphoric. There is now nothing standing in the way of my complete freedom. No job. No school run. No child to cook meals for. No tethers!

A few moments ago, I heard myself explaining to my employer, a sympathetic man who is a healer, after all, that I needed to be free to listen to the trees. Well, I said I needed to be connecting with nature deeply without interruption and without mobile phones for days at a time in order to write my next book. That I needed to deeply trust this process, not knowing what the hell is happening next. Letting go of productivity and the need to do something tangible. Trusting the soft whispers.

And he understood.
But part of my brain is still screaming, "Are you crazy?"

YOU'RE A WRITER. THAT'S SWEET

On one of my last weekends in my Lewes house, after Jay's been gone for a couple of weeks, I attend Carl's fortieth birthday party in the local youth hall transformed for this occasion. Carl's the husband of Rose, the friend who gave me encouragement to try out vanlife as a couple. Since he's an important member of the local hippy and environmental activist community, all the stars of the scene are here in full force, chatting at the long table with their dreadlocks, earthy-coloured many-layered skirts and earnest crochet projects.

It's my weekend with Jay so I've brought him along, slightly guilty, since now that he no longer lives with me I should, theoretically, have all the time in the world to meet my adult social needs. I have the idea that I should be focusing solely on him during our time together. But I knew it would be a child-friendly party and there are indeed a few kids floating around. Besides, I'm aware that when I move into the van, I'll have a far less accessible social life. Being out in the sticks without my own vehicle, I won't be able to just go to a 5Rhythms class or pop along to a local café to meet a friend whenever I feel like it.

I feel sad that I won't be able to easily participate in some of the staples of my current life, like women's circles. It feels ironic that now that I am leaving the concerns of arranging childcare behind me, I still won't have the freedom to partake fully of what's on offer. So, it feels important to be here, to connect in with this community that was the main reason I moved to Lewes in the first place.

The difference between this party and the few others I've brought Jay along to over the past decade is that now I don't resent his request for frequent cuddles or his wanting me to sit beside him on the sofa when there are people I want to talk to and mingle with. I'm soaking up every moment of contact with him. Eventually, he detaches and curls up on his chosen favourite sofa and I feel vaguely uneasy again – *I should be tucking him in at home with a story book, not gallivanting around and expecting him to adapt,* goes the critical inner voice.

At that point, an eccentric older guy wearing a beret decides to get to know me. A few minutes into the conversation, it's clear that he has had a few glasses of wine. He tells me that he's the owner of a famous fringe bookshop in Brighton, one of those I must have walked past hundreds of times but never entered.

When I answer his question as to how often I see Jay with "every second weekend", he pronounces "Fuck that". I immediately correct him. "Actually, it was the other way around for eight years, since I left his dad, and this means I can work whenever I like – I can start work at five p.m. if I want to."

I have no idea why I'm emphasising my freedom to work over any other kind of freedom, but I suspect it's some weird internalised patriarchal bullshit masquerading as equality. "What's your work?"

"I'm a writer."

"Oh, you're a writer. That's sweet."

I feel I should be more annoyed by this than I actually am, but he is taking far more interest in my life than most men I talk to casually.

"You should meet my son. He's a writer," the bohemian bookseller goes on. Uh-oh. I hope I'm not being matchmade here.

Eventually, after the food – most of which Jay refuses to eat as quiches and hummus are far too 'hippy' – it's time for Carl's birthday ceremony. Everyone gathers with excitement and reverence.

Carl makes a heartfelt speech about all the shadow aspects of himself he's faced and transformed in the past year, supported by Rose and his male friends. I'm captivated by his openness and honesty. Then, his friends – who, like him, are members of a woodland-based men's group – make speeches about him, naming the qualities they see in him and what they wish for him in the next chapter of his life: creating a conscious earth-based community.

One of his friends, a bespectacled guy I recognise from other parties, invites him to step across a line of sand in the middle of the room to symbolise the step he's taking into this new mission. Before Carl can step over the threshold, he has to answer five questions from five men from his community, testing his commitment to his journey. It's simple but powerful: my eyes tear up as he's welcomed and praised on the other side. I can sense Jay, rigid and bored beside me.

We all gather in the centre of the room to give him a group hug and he's picked up and passed through the crowd. I can't imagine being able to gather so many people in one room for my own birthday.

The most poignant part for me, as mother of a son, is when his mom reads a poem about his whole life. It's clear from her words how very well she knows him, in a way I'm sure my parents have never known me. Against a backdrop of Jay's comments, "What's the big deal about turning forty? My dad's forty-three," I'm struck by the importance of my son having these kinds of initiations and communities around him from a young age. I feel the weight of my own powerlessness to create that for him now that he lives with his other family.

LISTENING

"Pay attention. Be astonished. Tell about it." ~ Mary Oliver

My listening experiment with the trees begins in the last week of November, after it's all finally over and I move my one-shelf-full of clothes into the van.

We don't go anywhere 'exciting' yet, as others expect us to, but it doesn't matter. This is definitely an adventure: I'm seeing Sussex, my home county for the past fourteen years, through different eyes.

I both love and am terrified by the fact that I wake up every day and have no idea what to expect. I surprise myself with how quickly I get used to not knowing where I will be each night or the next day. Sometimes, when I wake up, I don't remember where I am and need to think about where we've parked up.

We take it on the wing where we will go and when, adjusting to the weather and to random signs. We take our cues from a North-Westerly coming in, then a high tide approaching when we park up at Bosham Harbour, where the water comes right up to the van wheels and it's a little like being in a boat. Another time, we follow a road sign merely because of its shape.

Biting winds accompany us to Arundel in West Sussex, and when we pass a 'Comfort Inn' sign it looks highly appealing. I have a soporific head cold and want nothing more than to lie in bed with a hot water bottle.

But as soon as we park up next to the tranquil Swanbourne Lake, I fall in love, forgetting all about my cold. We watch the mother swan with her cygnets swimming behind her and Thor says, "They're learning how to be majestic but they haven't quite got it yet, that tilt of the neck."

Today, I sense that I'm re-learning and remembering how to be majestic; I got a little bit frumpled up during my recent weekend in London, visiting friends. But I'm fascinated to notice for the first time since forever that I don't have PMT. I definitely felt sensitive to the hustle and bustle of the big city — but there's been no moodiness, no profound depression, no pickiness at Thor, no suddenly wanting to break up.

Is it the security of living with him now? Is it hormonal? After all, hormones are affected by stress and my life is now starkly stress-free. Or maybe it's because now that I no longer have to hold the fort for another person – Jay – I don't get that emotional build-up anymore: I can just let my feelings out as they come up, right then and there.

As we walk along the lake, thickly surrounded by trees that climb far up the banks on either side, we discover heart-like pink berries neither of us has ever seen before. I feel a deep bliss of relaxation in my body. There's nowhere I have to go and nothing I have to do today except what I'm doing in this very moment, and the connection to nature is already as strong as I hoped for when I chose this move.

In my urban life, 'Being in Nature' used to be another item on the self-care list: "OK, I need to walk in the woods, it's good for me." But while I was doing it, my head would frequently still be in the to-do list. Now that that endless document barely exists, I can really be here, I can truly listen. I'm learning to receive the medicine from the land.

I'm also learning to wait until it comes. Even when I'm lost in my head, if I just sit down on a log and wait, I will eventually feel the impact of the trees through the screen of my thoughts. If I stay there long enough, they break through; I will hear them. My thoughts will drop like useless pebbles onto the ground.

If I sit there long enough, with the clouds and the sky and the birdsong and the sun, I will feel grateful to be alive.

Now, we stop at an elder tree. "What do you feel the tree is about?" Thor asks me. And, before I can answer: "Ask your yoni."

Asking my yoni – the yogic word for the womb and the female sexual organs – is a new practice of feeling into myself and my truth of the moment that I have been experimenting with, and I've been touched by his support for this. It's the kind of thing I've read and heard about for years in women's groups but never really took on as an inquiry myself. At first, I feel self-conscious as people walk past and stare at us, standing there. Thor's encouragement to not worry about them is only partially effective.

As best as I can, I drop into my pelvic bowl and all that it holds. I receive: echoes of the burning bush of the Bible and a half-burning, half-glowing tree that guards the entrance to a magical faery realm. Then, I have a sense that the elder takes in the sadness of the world and grows new roots from it. I translate this into words for Thor and ask him what he senses. "The elder is a faery tree," he says simply. Walking back to the van in silence as dark falls, we hear a new owl song neither of us recognises.

The next morning, when I wake up, I feel a bit anxious, which is typical for this time of my cycle, winding down towards my period. I want to get on with things and it feels like there isn't enough time – the pesky, habitual to-do list creeping back in. I take myself for a walk by the lake, alone, knowing that this will re-set me.

I sit with a tree and allow the view of the lake, the swans, and the surrounding green to open up a space inside me. The stress about time instantly dissipates and I find myself held by a deep trust in the process I'm in, even though I have no idea what it is. It's suddenly clear to me that I can do things that are quantifiably 'nothing', but in fact, what I'm doing is profound: this letting go, this simply being. Particularly in this, the autumn of my cycle, the shedding that comes before I go into the dark of my monthly bleeding time.

I remember a podcast I listened to recently with Kate Joyner, who created a travelling theatre production called 'The Blood Tales' based on poetry she channels during her bleed. I burst into tears listening to her talk about the Hopi proverb that says: if all women everywhere gave their blood to the earth, it will heal.

I have been partaking of this practice for a little while now. Sometimes, I give my blood to the windowsill pot plants – the little yew tree that has white fluffy mould from the rice that accidentally once fell on it – and sometimes I give it to an oak, or the yew at Stonehenge. Next, I intend to give it to a river.

Now, on the hill with the trees, the immensity of Kate's words fills me. I know that generations of women have suffered because of their monthly blood, experiencing inconvenience, pain, and even shame. Our power has been cut from us, and the anger and sadness of that is so big that I don't even want to touch it. I don't know how to go into it – it's so sad, so overwhelming.

And I let this feeling move through me in waves, and the tears come again, collecting on the soil, landing in a knowing that I am doing the right thing, right now, not only for me, but for all women.

I have a vision of myself going wild in the woods, raging, screaming, like an animal on the ground. I've had a persistent discomfort in my throat for days, requiring me to clear my throat almost constantly. I know that this wildness would get it out of me, as well as express the rage and sadness I feel at the disempowerment of women. But, of course, I can't bring myself to do it – I hear the voices of walkers nearby.

As I sit quietly for a while longer, an excitement surges in me, and with it, a new certainty. I feel clear that my part of the puzzle is to empower women to listen to their yonis and to access that power, the power of their womb blood, directly. The knowing of it throbs through my body like a pulse. Listening to the birds circling softly, I know that all I need to do is keep softening into this journey.

*

After watching streams of people head into town all day, we walk in to see what all the fuss is about, intrigued by posters everywhere for the Arundel Festival of Lights. We've already been once into the quaint town with its winding streets and cobblestoned quarters, visiting the cathedral, doing some Christmas shopping, and dropping into the little bookstore. It felt good between us: natural, cosy, partnered, in a way it never did when we walked through Lewes together. Maybe it's something about visiting a place rather than living in it. Lewes always felt like my home rather than our joint home.

I've been continuing to experiment with yoni magic. Thor's encouraging me to try shining the light out from my yoni as we walk into town and to keep that up no matter what's happening. "Men would really have to step into their power if all women were doing that all the time. Otherwise, they'd be annihilated."

We trundle through the crowds of families clamouring for mulled wine and hot-chocolate and I wonder what we're doing here, out of our cosy nest of peace. We arrive at the central hub just as a singer named Annabelle is being introduced and I have that instant cringey sensation of feeling pressured to like something. But the moment she starts singing, I am enraptured: she inhabits her song fully and takes us all with her.

But after two songs, I am worried about Thor getting bored, so I turn to ask him if he wants to go. We push through the milling families to the top of the road, just as she starts to sing a song about 'The power of love'. My heart drops: I know I should have stayed with it.

And indeed, later Thor tells me he was moved by the song and wanted to share it with me. Why do I always do that – worry so much about getting it right that I drop away from the rightness that's already there?

*

On the way home in the moonlight, I confess something that I think is a light thing: that I have been avoiding sex lately because I feel the energy between us to create a baby is so strong and I don't trust myself to use protection when the moment comes.

For me, this baby creation urge has emerged at some stage of every one of the intimate relationships I've had since Jay's birth. It's as if crossing the frontier of motherhood for the first time makes it somehow easier to open to the experience again. I've long since let go of my dream of having a family with two children, but the strong love between Thor and me has sometimes evoked this longing.

To my surprise, my casual revelation evokes anger in him. Instead of focusing on the fact that I trust him enough to want to have a baby with him, he hones in on the idea that I don't want to make love and might have been doing it at times without wanting to. Back in the van, we spend hours thrashing it out, getting nowhere. It's not exactly an argument, but it's far from pleasant.

Eventually, he goes to the yew tree outside to seek guidance. I wait, listening to the wind howling outside, feeling defeated and empty and misunderstood.

When he comes back, he tells me the yew instructed him to "Drop it. It's a power thing".

The tension's still there between us, so we eventually agree to have a healing tantric session, using a practice we spent time perfecting during our Wales trip in the summer. It involves simply joining our bodies and moving very little, allowing the only movements to be spontaneous rather than habitual ones while focusing on our breathing and inner sensations. It's about dropping the need to 'get' anywhere or for anything in particular to happen.

We have had both difficult and breakthrough experiences with this practice: because it challenges so many conditioned responses around sex, it tends to bring up insecurities, but it's also brought us much closer and created a deep sensitivity and intimacy.

To my surprise, tonight, we go in a completely different direction from the usual stillness of this practice. I find myself going wild in a way that I never have before – and in a way he says he's never seen in a woman before. I'm on all fours, growling, licking his face with total abandon. Afterwards, it feels surreal: did that really happen?

The odd thing is, it's not entirely unfamiliar: it's an expression of what, yesterday, sitting with the trees and the lake, I had such a vivid image of myself doing, but couldn't bring myself to.

REQUIREMENTS FOR VAN LIFE

Extreme flexibility

Be prepared to be moved on at any time by local council officials, the Forestry Commission or the National Trust. This could happen as early as nine a.m., so be ready to put everything into 'move mode' – put the mugs in the sink, anything spillable on the floor, turn the gas off – and go. In my year in the van, though, we only have a couple of knocks on the door. The secret is to keep moving.

A typical scenario is this: we park up somewhere and realise that the mobile signal is not good enough to do our online work. Just as we've started brewing some tea and thinking about putting on the wood-burner to get warm, we have to batten down the hatches again and drive on in search of another spot. Or we get to a place that looks great on the map, only to find it has metered parking that closes at six p.m.

Another aspect of flexibility is the physical ability to manoeuvre one's self around another person in a small space. For example, Thor is sawing wood, completely naked except for one trainer to protect his foot, and there's about three inches between his bottom and me sitting on the toilet. Needless to say, it's crucial that I not bump him in any way.

A dose of the rebel

You need a willingness to deal with breaking the law on a daily basis, since technically, you're not allowed to sleep in your own vehicle in the United Kingdom. Probably the only reason it's largely overlooked by the legal system is that there are not large amounts of people doing it.

A lot of people have the mistaken perception that all vandwellers are skiving benefit scroungers. I start off ultra thin-skinned with people's disapproving frowns, but become more immune over time. After a while, I can put bags of rubbish into public bins without a worry. Still, on one occasion the fears prove to have substance when we are 'egged' by locals in the New Forest and forced to move on at midnight.

Tolerance

It goes without saying that sharing a small space with someone 24/7 means you're going to see each other in all moods and modes. When tension is high, you can't simply go to another room or even, in the depths of winter, just go for a long walk. We improvise solutions such as using curtains to separate the bedroom and living areas. But privacy is an ongoing challenge.

Organisational skills

There's no space for dishes to pile up and chaos quickly becomes intolerable, so things need to be washed and put away immediately.

Because you can't store a lot, you have to plan and stock up on provisions, always ensuring there's enough food and water for a few days. This becomes particularly crucial when the weather is severe in winter, and you could find yourself stranded for some time.

Making resources last

One of the first things I need to learn in my new lifestyle is water conservation, washing up with the barest minimum of water using very specific methods. Our washing water supply is reliant on nearby garages – and not all of them have free water – or occasionally public toilets or graveyard taps. When I visit my homeland of South Africa after four months in the van to find Cape Town amid level six water restrictions due to nearly half a decade of drought, I'm astounded that even in this dire situation, each person is allotted fifty litres of water daily, an amount that lasts a week between the two of us.

I guess it's safe to say I've mastered this one: after a few months, Thor jokes that I get 8.5 out of 10 for washing up skills.

Then there's the art of one-pot cooking: making stews that last for three days. The plus side: you can live so incredibly cheaply, which frees you up to do more of what you want with your time.

Lowering your standards

First: cleanliness. I've learned how to make do with washing using heated water and take my showers when I can get them. Washing hair every 2 weeks instead of twice a week has become the norm.

(A confession: Some days, I feel deeply unattractive. This is usually when my hair goes past the ten-day mark of the last wash, my skin feels itchy, and my hands are raw with the eczema that seems to plague me most in winter and when having to handle cold water a lot. But to my amazement, Thor is always telling me I'm beautiful. He takes little videos of me and shows them back to me and I can see that my blue eyes are vivid, and my smile shows a certain unfamiliar happiness. That I don't look like a scruffy, disgusting hobo.)

Then there's the tolerance for the lack of dignity that results from no privacy and the restricted amenities. I feel the inconvenience of my female anatomy acutely. One period, it turns out that my blood has been getting stuck in the front of the improvised Thunderbox – a small funnel at the front of the toilet that he's adapted for me.

Another time, when we have a food stop at the carpark of a rural castle, Thor discovers that the toilet has been leaking piss all over the 'bathroom' floor and he has to take it all out and clean it with bleach while I desperately cook an omelette because my blood sugar has chosen that precise moment to crash badly. I feel terrible because it's my fault – I must have missed a few times when trying to get my pee in the exact right place. The entire van stinks of piss.

I enthusiastically get a Shee-Wee when I first moved in, but Thor warns that even the tiniest spilled drop will cause havoc, so I give it up. Keeping the toilet from smelling becomes another thing for Thor to have to attend to in his never-ending list of van tasks. And he warns ominously that in the summer I'm just going to have to pee outside in the day and use a bowl at night – the rising warmth will make it impossible to use the Thunderbox.

This brings us to the *pièce de résistance* – there is no door on the toilet. Well, to be precise, there is, but since the toilet goes right up to the door there's no way of closing it and having room for your feet at the same time. Thor 'trained' me for this reality very gradually and carefully. When we first went on roadtrips together, we would each leave the room when the other needed to use the compost loo. Then, when the weather was bad or it was nighttime, the non-pooing person would sit in the top cab with their head out the skylight.

Eventually, as we live together, these measures are consigned to the dust heap and, incredible as it sounds, we're able to have full conversations while using the toilet within view of each other. I never thought I would see this day. I used to feel utter horror and revulsion if a partner ran in to use the toilet while I was in the shower, no matter how desperate they were.

To spare Thor the unpleasant task of emptying the toilet too frequently, we always avail ourselves of any woods we were parked up at. Thor is convinced it's good for the trees. But once we start taking toilet trips to the woods together– digging pits just a few metres from each other – the whole issue becomes amusing and entertaining rather than embarrassing. I realise it was all childhood conditioning anyway.

Weather ruggedness

Weather is, of course, the number one factor that you co-create with when you take on living in a van. Luckily, my capacity for weather-discomfort has already been developed through years of extended camping, including in torrential rain and wind.

As a vanomad, you have to pre-empt the weather constantly so that you know where it's safe to park up: such as considering north-westerly winds buffeting the van and keeping you up at night (even tipping you over). And sometimes you can't check the upcoming weather online because there's no signal, so it can get complicated.

The most frequent question I am asked is "How do you keep warm?" Particularly when the snow hit – five times over the winter. While the wood-burner keeps us toasty, it's true that severe weather can up the ante.

One night, the weather is dodgy when we're exploring Devon. We have to change intended park up spots at the last minute when the weather forecast shifts to heavy rain and strong winds. The spot we've chosen is too close to the river, making floods a risk.

Just 1.5 miles away from the new park up, driving up an extremely steep and winding road, it starts to snow. While Thor stays calm, it's the longest mile I'd ever experienced as a passenger: I'm terrified by the suddenly poor visibility and the skiddiness of the road.

When we visit the stunning landscape of Dartmoor, we don't see a single other van for five nights. On the sixth night, as we drive into view of the layby at ten-thirty p.m., we spot two other vans there, taking all the space. Back to square one.

Eventually, we manage to get the van flat in a different spot nearby, with the use of various bits of wood under the wheels. It's eleven p.m. and I'm exhausted. It hits me just how much work it is to have a home for the night, and I feel the truth of what Thor's vandwelling friend Lisa says when we bump into her in the Barcombe car park. "Van living takes a lot of energy. I need that energy for other things, to create something in my life."

Safety awareness

Don't kill yourself with carbon monoxide. It's a confined space, after all. Don't leave the gas flame on too high on the hob. Open windows when using two hob plates. And for God's sake, check the hob is turned off before you drive.

One time, we leave for our sleeping destination in a bit of a hurry only to realise when we arrive, forty-five minutes later, that Thor has left the cooker on with potatoes still boiling away (I'm so relieved it wasn't me). It's s a narrow escape: the cooker flame could have easily caught on our coats hanging nearby and the whole van caught on fire. We are shocked, relieved, scared, and newly dedicated to safety first.

Optional extra skills

Ability to find your way back on a walk, using your instinct and internalising the van as a homing device. For someone with absolutely no sense of direction, who can get lost using Google Maps route direction and has been known to end up in the middle of a council estate when headed for a street protest march, this is no mean feat.

I do this for the first time when we park up in Ashdown Forest and go for a walk together. Thor lets me 'bundu bash' through the most unlikely paths and somehow, we end up back home, more to my amazement than his. Then I do it on my own in the Quantock Hills, making my way back just as it starts to rain and before dark hit.

I credit slowing down and listening to my intuition more, uncrowded by the busy-ness of my former life, as well as Thor's encouragement.

THE PHASE OF THE MOON

Kingley Vale, Surrey

I'm looking out the window at an oak that might be six hundred years old. Dogwalkers and strollers get out of their cars, and I duck behind the curtain in my fluffy white dressing gown with its bunny rabbit hood, the one we laughed about buying at Tesco a couple of weeks ago – "It'll never be cold enough to wear this – it's ridiculous!"

Last night, we took a sunset-dusk walk to visit 'The Watchers', the oldest yews in the forest here at Kingley Vale. Some of them are up to two thousand years old. I would have been too nervous to be there alone as dark fell, but together, it was an adventure. We sat with the trees and felt their wisdom as an unsayable yet bone-deep reality. There was definitely a spookiness to it, too: I could easily imagine the spirits of witches and druids floating around.

In my new life on the road, I feel welcome with the trees and rivers, but with the people, there's always the sense that I don't really have the right to be here. A realisation that, in their eyes, I'm a tramp of sorts. I'm nervous in the mornings and late at night, alert to car door slams. I listen out for people who might tell us we have to get out, to move on, or who would harass us in some way. I'm amazed at Thor's calm about all this; but then, he's done it for six years.

It's not so much that I don't have a home anymore, as that everywhere is my home: in a way that wasn't possible when I was confined to one house. Kingley Vale is my home today, these trees are my home, and it's a very different feeling from when I'd simply visit these places.

But other people pay for this land and maintain this and I'm just riding off the back of that … I don't have my own, comes the thought, and then I notice the clouds moving by through the cracked window and I realise how ridiculous it is to even think about that stuff. Who cares? Right now, this is what's given and I'm going to receive it with gratitude. When I was living in my little Lewes house with most of my rent paid by the government, it wasn't any more mine than this is. None of it is mine; even people who 'own' their houses – pay a mortgage – are living an illusion.

I remember one of my heroes, Chris McCandless, whose story was told in Into the Wild, a movie I've watched at least ten times. He left his privileged American upbringing to take to the road in the early 90's and had all kinds of crazy adventures. He tragically died in Alaska, alone in a bus he'd been using as a home.

In one of my favourite scenes, a couple of hippy van-dwellers befriend him. "You're a leather tramp – we're rubber tramps," they tell Chris, referring to the difference between being a vandwelling nomad and a nomad on foot. In another scene, Chris shows his pride in his tramp status by writing his new, self-chosen name, 'Alex Supertramp' in lipstick on a public bathroom mirror.

I pour chopped dates into a bowl for our raw breakfast. Thor is the breakfast alchemist but I'm getting my own stride with it: adding orange oil, mixing in the chia seeds so they look like frogspawn. We've been working out who does what in our new domestic arrangement, an exciting endeavour for me after not living with a man for eight years.

His jobs are to get the coal and tend the woodburner, which is an art beyond me (he claims it took him years to get it right); collect and change the tap water (too heavy for me), manage the electrics, do all the driving (not an option for me, with my dyspraxia), repair the van when it needs it (which is regularly), empty the toilet (also too heavy for me), and doing most of the washing up. I do all the cooking and keep track of the finances, and we share recycling and rubbish management and disposal.

I realise that probably doesn't sound like an equivalent division of labour. But I feel comfortable with the fact that it's based on our respective skillsets. I soon learn that Thor has immense efficiency capabilities, and that me fumbling along only slows us down.

When it's time to put the van into motion, he is ready and in the front seat within ten minutes. He can lie in bed for hours and then suddenly leap into action: a sleeping naked beast emerging into full power mode, battening down the hatches and drinking a cup of tea with a trucker cap on as he puts the van into gear. "Mega efficiency 101," he calls this mode, jokingly.

Besides, the amount of time our jobs add up to is roughly equal. Cooking, after all, is something I do every day, whereas his jobs are mostly more sporadic. And cooking is more than just sticking things in a pot; it's menu planning and ingredient awareness and being organised. This is about the only thing I feel competent to do in my new life as a 'vanomad', a word for my adopted lifestyle that I've picked up from following other vandwellers on Instagram.

But Thor is 'training me up' to do more, a process in which I quickly resign myself to getting it wrong much of the time. One day, I somehow use the wrong water for tea: the water intended for washing, not drinking – collected from less sanitary sources like public bathroom taps. Another evening, I create a cooking disaster, burning the pan with undercooked pork sausages, and fail to keep the woodburner going effectively. Of course, it doesn't help that I'm attempting to do yoga while cooking, trying to ignore the chips of coal under my knees as I extend into cat-cow stretch on the thin bit of Indian carpet between the cooker and the sofa.

One night, Thor gets me out of bed at midnight to train me in putting on the gas heater (a backup to the woodburner) so it can be done safely and without waking him up in the morning. But although, with his logical, mathematical brain – he once studied physics – these things are effortless for him, he's cottoned on to my dyspraxic need for clear, repeated instruction and is kind about it. After all the times I've been ridiculed or misunderstood because of my struggles with practical tasks, it's a relief to find that I can make a mistake and still be accepted, that I can be trusted to keep learning.

Putting the metal teapot onto the hob, aware that it's eleven a.m. already, I glance fondly at the plants that live on the windowsill: the unidentifiable ivy-type one curling around the kitchen window, the moss gathering at the corners of the living room window, which Thor tells me is repellent to mould but I still can't resist picking off.

I think of the poetry that's released in me by not having to hold a structure for a child every day. I imagine Jay's grandparents and father doing the cooking, the homework, the timetabling, for him instead. Maybe I was too free for that.

Guilt tugs at my edges.

*

During the first few weeks, I regularly swing from the extreme contentedness of the teapot moments to a clear "what were we thinking? We can't do this!" Then I come down with the stinking cold I fended off in Arundel, and with it comes a low mood; I wonder if it's a clearing out of sorts.

One of the low points is a failed, stressful attempt to settle for the night at the gorgeous Stanmer Park just outside Brighton, which used to be the most beautiful and popular East Sussex spot for vanlifers. It's quickly clear that the rumours of anti-travelling restrictions are true: things have changed. When asked by hi-vis jackets at the gate if we're visiting people in the Village, we lie and say 'yes', but as we drive in, we see the signs everywhere: a Public Service Order is in full force, which means that we cannot legally stay there overnight.

We drive into the tiny estate village itself but are both unsure whether we can stay here without dangerously offending people. It's bitterly cold but we can't start the woodburner because we might have to suddenly move again, and we can't drive off with it still going. Thor says, "I'm not used to being responsible for someone else. I normally just have to make it OK for me…" My stomach lurches with responsibility, worry and guilt.

We decide that it's a lost cause. It's very late by the time we find somewhere else for the night, and the mood between us is heavy.

*

After the initial high of moving in, I often feel anxious and insecure about whether I'm truly welcome in the van in Thor's eyes. I start to worry about not being able to pull my weight equally because I don't have all the skills. We revisit our task division and explore whether we want to deal with this through Thor teaching me the skills I need, or through me contributing more in the ways that come naturally to me, such as reading him extracts from my writing or decorating the van and making it more aesthetically pleasing. In the end, it's a combination of both that emerges.

I start to develop the ability to gather fresh herbs, flowers and berries for tea and to make concoctions intuitively, like a medicine woman. I guess city-dwelling vanomads, who can just pop into Neal's Yard don't need this skill so much, but for me it's integral to the 'back to nature' element of the vanlife I've chosen.

Thor has bags of freshly gathered herbs hanging from the ceiling, which he encourages me to make use of by picking what I feel drawn to for each pot of tea: chamomile, marjoram, rosehips, hawthorn. I surprise myself with the delicious and nourishing combinations I come up with and find myself learning about plants along the way – something I've been curious about for years but never applied myself to. When we go for walks, Thor also shows me which flowers are safe to eat and which ones can decrease pollen allergy in the spring.

As someone who has had chronic ailments throughout my life, I could easily panic about not being able to access a doctor's surgery quickly. Learning to use essential oils as healing remedies, consulting the encyclopaedic book on the van shelf, proves enlightening. But I never do figure out how to sew a hem onto the curtain in the bed area.

Before the move, I remember Sally, the mum of Jay's best friend, saying, "There will be days when you'll be cold and fed up and missing Jay, but you'll also know what phase the moon is in and what the weather is doing. You'll feel and see the dew on the grass."

And it's true. Sometimes I wake extremely cold: in the early hours, it's typically four degrees outside and not far off inside the van. One night, I dream that I've failed to organise sandwiches for Jay's lunch and get lost driving them to his school. Another night, in another nightmare, I'm unable to work out how to get a simple train with him – where the platform is, what time it departs. I lose Jay on the platform and scream repeatedly for help, but I can't get the sound out; I'm left with an endlessly echoing silence.

But once the woodburner is going, the warmth is divine ecstasy itself, and it's like being in a sauna. Vanlife is patterned with many of these once 'little' pleasures – there's an almost unbearable cosiness if I let it in.

On my first night in the van, on Firle Beacon, I poked my head out of the bedroom skylight and looked at the big round disc shining in the sky, letting the wind into my hair and watching the tiny lights of Lewes far below. The freedom was like nothing I'd ever felt before.

THE LAST REMNANTS OF LILA

The continual contrast in our relationship is momentous. I'm so impressed with this man and how he is totally there for me. But the triggers and arguments are also frequent. At times, I wonder what the hell I'm doing because there's so much about him that's extremely difficult for me – but I know he finds some things challenging about me too.

I discover a stomping, furious small child inside me, who hasn't felt safe to come out in other relationships, where I struggled even to bring out my soft, vulnerable side. It's taken me nearly six months of us being together to feel fully comfortable with that part of me, and now that we're together 24/7, it's on the rise.

I feel that this angry part is not just my past – my history with my father, my school bullying experiences – it's much more. It's the ancestral line of abused women and disempowered women; it's collective, it's global.

Maybe it's just a case of accepting each other's madness, since we're all mad in one way or another. By the time we go to sleep on our second day in the van together, we have traversed some of the most painful territory of our relationship so far.

As part of my process of settling into the van, the mission for today is to create a new, unified altar, up in the top right-hand corner of the kitchen area. At the moment, the shelf looks to me like a rather chaotic hodgepodge of various feathers and memorabilia that Thor has collected over the years. I've been given artistic license to remake it, incorporating certain items from my previous altar at home.

At first, I enjoy discovering little snippets of Thor's life, clues to his journey: drawings, cards and notes from friends and people he's encountered at retreats. Then, while Thor is on a work call, I discover what I think is another note from a friend and begin, innocently enough, to read it.

The note is in the format of a printed, shop-bought tick list, vaguely cheesy, reading "Dear ___. I appreciate your ___". When I see that the blank spaces have been filled in with "warm hands" and "wild man", it quickly becomes apparent that this note is from someone far more intimate than a friend. The giveaway is "I remember when …" which is filled in with "we kissed under the moon".

Then, the clincher. "I'm looking forward to…" is filled in with "making love at Stonehenge." As I read these words, I remember our own disastrous experience at Stonehenge. I feel physically sick. Of course, it was his special place and so he would naturally have shared it with his other special women.

I realise with a plummeting stomach that I'm holding in my hands a love note from 'B', who I know must be the woman he was with two girlfriends ago, the woman he told me he thought was 'the one': Lila. She's 'B' for Butterfly (or Bitch, I think furiously now), his pet name for her because butterflies were their love 'spirit animal'. I know all this because we've had a lot of conversations about Lila.

It doesn't matter how many times he's held me in his arms and told me I am his 'favouritest girlfriend', or that he's said he's never liked being around someone so much; that he's never been so comfortable with anyone. Every single mention of Lila has triggered this same feeling in my solar plexus: a fear that I am not special, that he loved her just the way he loves me, or even more. I'm deeply ashamed of these feelings.

The butterfly has become something of a totem for us, too: a butterfly landed on his arm when he was letting me go after I chose to stay with Dylan, and he told me it reminded him of hope and love. But this is another reminder that *she* is where it started: where his spiritual journey of connecting with the energies of nature began.

I put the note aside and carry on arranging the altar, but there is lead in my gut. I realise I probably am not in the right space to be doing this any longer, but I don't know what else to do.

When Thor gets off the phone, I put the sword through my solar plexus in front of him and say casually, lightly, "I found this on your altar".

His face registers nothing and it's clear he doesn't recognise the note. I watch the truth dawn as his eyes move down the page. "Did you read this?" he asks, looking up.

"Yes. I didn't know what it was ... I thought it was from a friend, like the other notes. I'm sorry, I should have stopped reading it when I realised."

"You should have." He looks at me carefully, searching my eyes for my reaction. "I don't even remember this. It must have been early in our relationship because she never said stuff like this after the first three months. She was always criticising me." Now, his expression is almost amused. "This just doesn't sound like her at all."

"What about the Stonehenge bit?" I blurt.

"I don't think that even happened," he says. But he can see I'm struggling. "How do you feel?"

"Well, triggered, to be honest." I sigh. Retrospective jealousy has afflicted me ever since my relationship with Matthew, who talked too much about his ex and flirted with other women in front of me, somehow brewing up a complex, illogical internal mixture of being threatened by both past and present. I used to trawl through his Facebook account looking at photos of his ex-wife, sticking the knife into the wound.

But it was my most recent relationship with Dylan that really activated this plague of irrational, shameful jealousy. He always insisted he was over his ex, who he'd had a tumultuous on-and-off relationship with for four years. As it turned out, he couldn't resist Nina's lure and got back together with her within minutes of us breaking up. When they sang together on a stage at a festival I attended days later, I could only bear to watch for a couple of minutes. Since then, I've found it difficult to believe that people ever fully move on from their past.

Thor already knows I feel jealous of Lila, that I sense there was a strong bond between them, even if at this point, they've been out of contact for at least a year. When Thor and I first connected at Into the Wild and were inseparable for twenty-four hours, he said his connection with her was 'like this' – like he felt about me – but that they broke up because she wanted kids and he wasn't ready to take that step.

When we later got to know each other better, I found out that things were a bit more complex than that: they had actually been trying to conceive together. Fortunately, they never had. But having a baby with someone is, for me, the ultimate in commitment; even if your relationship ends, the person you create a baby with will leave a lasting legacy in your life. It always stuck in my mind that he'd been willing to do that with her.

"What do you want me to do with it?" he asks. "Shall I burn it?"

I look at him numbly. "I don't know. I just don't want it on the altar." A pause, then the hurt words fall like hot stones from my mouth: "But actually, why would you keep it? Why would you want to?"

Without looking at me, he goes to the storage cupboard and takes out a black A4 notebook. "I wrote about our relationship in this. I'll burn the note, and I'll burn this." He sits down and starts tearing stacks of pages out of the journal. I watch, wracked by a strange guilt and shame. "I don't know if I should be doing this," he says, but he carries on.

As the pages curl up in the flames of the woodburner, he drops this bombshell: "It's only your suspicion that would even make me consider going back to her. I wouldn't imagine my feelings coming back if you hadn't mentioned it."

I don't know what to do with that, and my eyes fill up with tears again. "But you know," he goes on, taking me in his arms, "The sex was always disconnected and shit. Everyone told me we looked uncomfortable with each other. After the honeymoon period, it was more pain than joy." At hearing these words, I feel something in me release. I wish it were otherwise: I wish I could reassure myself without needing this from him.

Maybe this is an opportunity to love each thing that arises, each bloody bruised home-seeking missile of jealousy, terror of abandonment, each attempt of my lost child to be heard. But, fuck, it hurts.

Later, I take up my tending of the altar again. I place our objects of importance next to each other: my pinecone from the field in Norfolk where I first experienced the love and holding of the community camps; his owl feathers; my Red Tent pendant from Brighton women's circles, his shamanic rattle; my Wiccan mini-cauldron; our dream catchers, mine multi-coloured with turquoise, pink and yellow feathers, his earth-coloured.

The next morning, I wake up with a busy head, as I often do. My mind immediately journeys into the territory of Lila and the toxic *mélange* sticks its claws in as I remember specific things she'd said she loved about him. The mistrust is back.

Beside me in the bed, Thor senses my energy going into a downward spiral. He puts his hand on my yoni over my pyjamas and brings the energy up to my head. I feel warm, pleasurable, powerful. The pain is gone.

Later, I ask my yoni what is going on with my jealous paranoia and if I am sabotaging the relationship as Thor and I reach deeper and deeper levels of closeness. She brings me images and memories of Matthew, who I had a six-month intense relationship with two years ago.

I thought I had done so much work on healing that relationship, which had ended so painfully with his sudden rejection of me – but it seems that now, another layer is emerging. I get in touch with the sadness for the beautiful times Matthew and I had together, allowing myself to feel the loss. I see that I never owned the happiness and beauty; I pushed it all away in my attempt to recover from the pain of the breakup.

I realise that the last time I felt really close to someone and wanted them to be around all the time, things crashed to a devastating end, with anger, criticism and a total cut-off. Matthew got together with someone else only a month later, someone I had introduced him to while we were still together. Someone he now has had a baby with.

My hopes and dreams for my relationship with him were high. And while I'd like to think I'm just going with the flow with Thor, I know that the stakes are high here too. That I want this to be 'the special one'.

WILD

My mom asks for pictures of the van. Fair enough – she wants to see where I'm living these days. I'm nervous: my mom is a product of late 40's apartheid South Africa, accustomed to an affluent style of living; she's also a security-minded, conservative person, who usually speaks her mind when she has a judgement. But when I finally send her some photos, her response surprises me: "The van looks great – it looks like it has everything one needs."

I don't know if this is genuine or if she really thinks it looks shabby and is just being polite because it's such a big deal to me. In fact, it feels strange that she hasn't said a single negative thing about my lifestyle change so far. I expected a lot of bafflement and concern when I first announced my decision. But she seemed to see it as a logical extension of Jay moving out, a reasonable next step.

Only after a couple of weeks does she ask me one of the most common questions I recently find myself fielding: does the van have a toilet and a shower?

Well, no. I remember that when Thor first came to visit me, I found his odour pretty strong, outside of the festival context where everyone is a little musky. He asked me if I liked the cedarwood oils he'd used, and I did, but underneath was still an unfamiliar bass note that daily showers tend to banish from existence. Later, he told me that often he'd connect with a woman at a festival, where everyone is in wild unwashed mode, but as soon as they met in an urban café, his smell became an issue for her. So, it was an area of some sensitivity to him.

Prior to vanlife, I was a woman who didn't shave my armpits in the winter but was more or less religious about removing leg hair all year round. I used natural deodorants but was scared to go without them altogether, and daily showers or baths were my norm. So, despite my general hippy-ness, there was an undercurrent of fear that I wouldn't adjust to Thor's odour.

He was understanding about how I felt. "It's because you're used to men who cover up their natural smell with aftershave and stuff." It was true. Whenever he dropped Jay off, Luke would waft in on a cloud of Brut and our son would stink of it for hours afterwards.

I slowly acclimated to the raw man scent. I started to realise that the masks and veils we use to hide our natural animal self are a choice, not a necessity.

I even discovered the aphrodisiac properties of that musky odour. He preferred me '*au naturel*' and I let go of my deodorant (except on visits to the sweaty city) and grew all my body hair in the summer – a big deal for me, since my hair is long and dark and was always a source of shame as a young girl.

After I moved into the van, I was perfectly happy to top up my daily tea tree and lavender washes with bi-weekly showers, though I still hoped I'd never smell as rank as the vandweller who I chatted to one day in a Lewes café – that sour, neglected stink.

But when my mom asks me about the hygiene set up in the van, I'm not feeling quite ready to tell her all this. I explain simply, matter-of-factly, that there's a toilet but no shower, that we just wash with heated water. To my surprise, she doesn't express any disgust. Maybe my parents are getting more of a clue – and releasing their grip on me, becoming more realistic about who I am. Maybe everyone *doesn't* always expect me to do things 'their way'. This could be a story I've clung on to for far too long.

After all, even Luke, who I've so often cast in the role of judgmental oppressor in the eight years since our split, surprised me when he said, "We can finally be more ourselves now. Jay's under my roof, as I've always wanted it, and you get to travel and be free."

MORGAN KHALSA

WE ONLY WANT HARDWORKING PEOPLE AROUND HERE

I will not surrender my smooth slow silver rhythms to this city staccato. It is intolerable to always be rushing, to feel adrenaline pumping, to overschedule because of the fear of missing out. I want measured field-time, camp-time. When we held each other on the field, time slowed to the length of the earth's long orbit around the sun.

~ *Journal Entry, pre van days*

Before Jay chose to move in with Luke, when Thor and I were looking for a place where the three of us could live together, I viewed a cottage near Forest Row, an area popular with both alternative types and wealthy property owners. Thor had given me permission to make a decision in his absence, if I came across a place that felt really right.

And this one did: it was charming, in a peaceful area with plenty of trees, and had the perfect amount of space for the three of us. The landlady, along with her husband, owned three properties on that road. When she explained that she would need to look at my bank statements to make sure I was good for the rent, I had to be transparent that as a lone parent, I was in receipt of housing benefit. "If it's just a top up, it's OK," she said, tight-lipped, "but we only want hard-working people here."

I wondered whether £700 a month would be seen as a top up. Probably not. Both Jay and I loved the cottage and wanted to move in – and Thor was up for it too, especially when he heard it was on Yew Close, given his strong connection with yews. But although I impressed upon the landlady how reliable and keen we were, we never heard from her again.

When I told the story to my artist friend Charity, who had seen me through the writing of my first book and my attempts to create a coaching business for mothers while juggling part-time copywriting work and full-time motherhood, she declared emphatically and angrily, "You are so hardworking, Morgan. It makes me so angry."

But the truth is that now, as a vanlifer, I couldn't be regarded as hardworking by any stretch of the imagination. My newfound euphoric liberation has been tempered by a realisation that my energy levels are still very low. After going for a thirty-minute walk, I'm often ready to return to the van for a nap. Partly, it's adjusting to our different sleep rhythms; I've ended up going to bed at the same time as Thor, who is a night owl, leaving me exhausted the next day even though I sleep just as late as him.

I realise that I'm in recovery from ten years of putting another being's needs first, from a decade of relentless intensity. It's a bit like when you go on holiday after months of pushing yourself at work and immediately get ill.

I remember an occasion years ago when my chronic fatigue was at its worst. I was visiting my parents in my home country, South Africa, and my mom said, "What you need is just a complete break. From work and Jay and everything." Of course, I thought, "Yeah right, how's that going to happen?"

Yet, that's exactly my situation now: Thanks to getting back most of my hefty rent deposit, I have enough money to work minimally for a few months and have no responsibilities apart from visiting Jay every couple of weeks. This could be an opportunity to rest, recover and heal and not just take on a whole load of new stuff, the way I usually do when a gap appears.

At first, this is the best thing about vanlife for me: the utter lack of structure. I want to marinate in my own essence and in what Thor and I create together, stepping into doing only when I need to. It's bliss.

In the interests of self-care, I try to maintain my usual yoga routine, but it's easier to stay warm in bed till late in the morning. The frequent honeymoon-flavour lovemaking often keeps me in bed for hours after I would usually be doing Sun Salutations. And the Indian rug squeezed between the fridge and the sofa – the only possible yoga space – is usually covered in crumbs and bits of coal, that re-appear as quickly as you sweep them and are hardly inviting to my knees. Besides, I want to enjoy being able to sleep late for the first time since I became a sleep-deprived mother – I never recovered from the two years of broken sleep, remaining easily-woken and jumpy.

After a while of all this being, though, I strike a restlessness in my mind. I want to do something. It's not too long before the clash of my conditioning and the call of the present moment starts to create tension in me.

Is it important to honour this need? Or is my antsiness just conditioning, born of my sense of identity being based on achievement from school age onwards? It's as if my inner Pusher or Slavedriver rebels every now and then and tries to claw back who I thought I was.

But it's more than that. Now that the novelty of my newfound freedom is beginning to wear off, I feel frustrated at the fact that I don't seem to be able to do all the things I imagined I'd be free to do in my new life. Released from the endless work of keeping a ravenous ten-year-old boy and a two-storey house alive and well, I thought I'd write a lot. I thought we'd be playing and writing music together daily. But somehow, this isn't happening.

I guess the saying that "wherever you go, there you are" must be true. Because this "I don't have enough time" trope is very familiar. It's been my perpetual companion, wherever I go and whatever I do.

In my mid-twenties, I went part-time in my job so that I could write more, but spent most of my time on the beach or socialising instead. When I became pregnant, I thought that compared to work, maternity leave would give me more time (I don't think we even need to discuss the ridiculousness of that concept).

Now that I've moved from the head-scrambling mission of juggling precarious part-time freelancing with full-time single parenthood to this spacious lifestyle, I still find myself saying "there's not enough time to write".

On my good days, I would say that the days flow by in a joyful stream of rivers, trees, lovemaking and hot chocolate. On my bad days, it feels like just living life takes up far too much time: finding park-ups and driving to them, cooking on the basic gas stove, keeping the wood-burner going, staying on top of the clearing up so that the small space doesn't become unmanageable, and going to the supermarket every three days because we can't fit a week's supply of groceries in our limited storage space.

One of the things I struggle with is being able to work on my book in the small space. We soon realise that if one of us is working, it takes over the whole space and the other doesn't feel free to move around and do as they feel. Thor also struggles with the sound of my fast typing; "It's like a hamster on a wheel." Sometimes his energetic sensitivity, so useful and beautiful when we're making love or he's holding space for me to process something, feels like a hindrance to me simply getting on with stuff.

On Day 8 in the van, we finally discuss the work issue openly, with a view to finding solutions. We agree that I need more time to work; that there should be an equal importance in both of our minds between my writing and Thor's work. We decide that I'm going to make time for my book in a disciplined way at the same times as Thor works. We also agree that sometimes, when he's doing 'van stuff', I can take that opportunity to work as well.

He takes his role as my writing cheerleader very seriously. He kicks me off the internet hotspot so I can't distract myself with Facebook. He doles out chocolate as a reward when I have banged out a certain number of words.

What I soon realise is that it's our relationship itself that is capturing most of my days. So much stuff seems to come up when you put two intense, sensitive people with childhood trauma and issues into the pressure-cooker of such a tiny space together.

It's like being in a twenty-four intense retreat or intimacy workshop with no breaks.

TRUE UTOPIAN

One day, struggling with my inner battle with time and the lack of it, I suddenly remember the words of an abundance coach who once gave me a free introductory session. She told me: "Just keep walking in nature and being in nature. Instead of all this busyness and hustling, trying to make things happen, make your connection with nature the basis of your life. Only do those things that really feel aligned with your spirit. The things that will feed you and bring you what your vision is."

It's as if I've forgotten the seeds of my vision of close communion with nature, first planted at community camps and abundantly watered on my first roadtrip with the van., three months before I moved into it full-time.

On that summer trip, there was no need to account for every moment. There was sitting, and looking out of the window, and being present with a leaf or a bird. Watching the sky celebrate the sun's ascent and descent.

Thor had just spent six days on an Enlightenment Intensive retreat, where spiritual inquiry is the route into connecting with the deeper truth of who we are, beyond our roles and personalities, bringing ecstasy and liberation.

It was as if he transmitted this experience to me by osmosis: I got a strong taste of what it would be like to be free of my restlessness, to drop into the essence that has no words, no drive, just pure being. We spent hours just sitting gazing into each other's eyes on the sofa, each moment a portal into a deep stillness.

On our last stop, we parked up beside a tiny lake near the Cambrian mountains that Thor was excited to show me. The sun had made a rare Welsh appearance and as we walked up close to the lake, the water felt so good on my feet, washing away the pebbles and the remnants of urban life.

As we picked our way through the cracks of clear water, almost like a stream, and the muddier pools, it felt like we had all the time in the world.

Thor started to spin me a tale seeded from a single thought: if we were the only humans left, would we just start having babies? Would we want to keep this human race going?

My feet were occupied but the bit of my brain that didn't need to watch them spun out into this scenario. The profound emptiness of a landscape free of humans; how long it'd take for all the wild things to proliferate once again, to reclaim their homes; how many decades or centuries the abandoned cars and laptops and random parts would last; how long we could live off the discovered remains of civilised life.

How would we know for sure that it was our imperative to continue the human race – or let it die out, finally and perhaps for good? How could we be certain there weren't people who had survived on other continents?

"We could travel the world on boats," he said with the kind of boyish glee that makes my heart melt in affection. I thought how much I'd love to seed the world with his babies, but I was skeptical as to whether humans could be trusted: after all, they ruined it again, after Noah's ark. Maybe we've been given enough second chances.

"But this time", he said excitedly, "there would be a new race of humans, ones who are enlightened and can re-make the world from that place of knowing who we truly are."

"Spoken like a true Utopian," I said, the obsessive reader of multiple Dystopian novels – The Handmaid's Tale, Bone Clocks, Cloud Atlas, Station Eleven, The Road. When I listened to him, though, I could almost believe.

We walked around the corner and basked in the purple heather and bleating sheep. There was still not a single soul around, as there hadn't been for days. I saw the white of the van gleaming in the sun. A last ceremonial pee, outside on the asphalt, and I smelled my own strong animal scent – a scent I was unacquainted with. I liked it. I knew I was being shown something.

HURT

Tonight, we have a tantra session scheduled. We've both sensed a break in our connection that we want to work on together. Thor has been doing his usual practice of connecting with his inner child, which he calls 'my vulnerability', and I've been doing some womb meditation work. I hope that we're both well-resourced enough to be able to gently reconnect.

We were both looking forward to this time together, but as the day moves into evening, I start to feel like it isn't going to happen. Thor is sitting on the bed with his head out of the skylight, looking at the water. I sit with him for a while but the throat tickle I've been plagued by for a few days is getting annoyingly loud and I don't want to draw attention to the van from the locals.

I go to the sofa and he stays on the bed. With the long silence, an insecurity creeps up in me, inexorable as the tide that's moving closer and closer to the van. Eventually, I swallow my fear and go back up to him. "I was waiting for you to finish reading," I offer, in an attempt to be open and vulnerable, but the angry teenager in me has already uncoiled her rejected fangs and is waiting to strike.

As we move into the session, I find myself trapped in an energy that I can only describe as 'daughter' to his 'father', so strong that I feel unable to move into a more reciprocal, adult to adult space. When I tell him what's going on with me, he says, "I can tell you're very 'small' at the moment. I can meet you there."

This is a comfortable, familiar place for him, one he's also initiated me into, so I allow myself to go fully into my 'little me', giving expression to the child who's scared and vulnerable. At one point I surrender to full on crying.

But as memories of childhood pain — scenes of playground torture in particular — come up, the anger flares again. I want someone to know, to see what happened to me. Even as the judgment at my own self-pity comes hot on the heels of that thought, it's too late: I am in the grip of an inner teen who wants nothing more than revenge.

We move into wildness, animals burrowing into each other, wrestling, play-fighting, playful yet vulnerable at the same time. And from there, into making love. At that point, something strange happens to me. I become like an inert deer, completely devoid of feeling and desire to move. With this tantric practice, although the movements need only be minimal, the energy does need to be circulating. I know with a dull certainty that there is no energy moving between us – I am blocking it at every turn, my hatred and anger condensed into numbness.

I wait for us to break through, like we usually do. To find the connection that I know is there, under the surface. But it never happens; it only gets more and more dead and painful. A few times, I look into his eyes, but it's not in a tantric loving way; I'm just staring him out, quietly furious. Eventually, we stop and lie next to each other like beached wales in despair. But my teen is stronger: she is satisfied. She has made him hurt as much as she did.

He soon goes for a walk to clear his head. *Shit. The fallout is going to be massive. Probably days long.* But he's soon back, willing to talk and for us to hold each other. It emerges that he was triggered into remembering a past relationship – his second girlfriend, who, due to trauma in her past, had been totally non-responsive during sex, which had, of course, been very challenging for him.

At his words, the memories come back to me: lying passive in the arms of my first boyfriend for four years, ashamed of feeling nothing; being so drunk I couldn't move while my best friend's brother took advantage of me after her birthday party, trying to push him off but finding myself utterly paralysed; having to be told by friends that I had had sex with a guy I just met the night before when I was comatose on the beach. The shame.

We make love again, and this time it works. We get outside naked and put our feet in the water of Chichester Harbour, which has – at one a.m. – come right up to the van.

In the morning, everything is OK again. Flotillas of ducks float close to our little home, looking curious.

IMPOSTER

As I wait at the gates of Jay's new school, I find myself in tears nearly visible to the parents around me, all strangers. It's freezing, early December, and my toes are already starting to hurt in my thin socks. I'm camouflaged as just another mum but I'm painfully aware that this is only the second time I've seen this building – the first being the school tour.

On that nerve-wracking day, Luke formally introduced me to the secretary – "This is Jay's mother" – but she barely glanced at me as we entered the school, perfectly signifying my relegation to the periphery of my son's life. It used to be him – Luke – trailing behind me, disinterested as we engaged with teachers, refusing to talk to other parents. It was he who avoided coming to school tours and parent-teacher meetings, who kept his head down and texted constantly at the Halloween school do, leaving me all the hard graft of integrating into these communities.

Now, he strode forward with a confident handshake as I scrabbled for airtime, and it was he who was handed the relevant forms. A few weeks later, I was to hear that he'd invited a new school friend of Jay's for a playdate, and that it actually happened.

Still, as the school tour continued, I was the one to ask the most questions. I knew what to ask, because I had been intimately involved for ten years while he was the alternate weekend dad, the fun parent. I knew to ask about homework and lunch times. I knew what to be concerned about. Soon, I was the one the head teacher made the most eye contact with, the one who walked first through each door as we navigated the huge building.

Yes. Don't you forget it. Don't you forget I'm The Mother.

In the car, Jay shrugged and avoided eye contact as I talked to him. His answers to most things were "Yes, it's fine." Trying to acknowledge the complexity of the situation, I made some kind of ridiculous statement about mixed feelings being alright and normal, and he said "OK" as if I were talking about the dinner menu, eyes flicked resolutely forward to the road ahead.

And here I am with these fully-fledged mothers, the swan among the ducks again. When I check with another mum that I'm in the right part of the massive, confusing grounds, we flow into a conversation. I feel pleased with the ease of it – I can still do this – until she inevitably starts asking me questions I can't answer: "Are you coming to the Christmas fair?" (When is it? I can't admit I don't know). "I'm not local," I reply. "Um … so his dad tends to do those things." (Lie: he'd rather stick pins in his eyes).

At the gate, his face lights up but he doesn't run into my arms and hug me as he used to do, and still does in my fantasy of this occasion. Instead, as soon as we're in the van, he leans into my body, grips my hand, then holds it for a long time, admitting he'd not wanted to do this outside the school gates. "I haven't seen you for six weeks."

It was only three, I point out, but I realise with a sinking feeling that time is relative. I soak up the precious moments of the three of us being together for as long as it takes to drive to the station. Jay is happy to see Thor but mostly focused on me.

Everything has changed: only a few hours ago, I was feeling nervous about the approaching three nights away from Thor, wondering how I would find my anchorage without my man, with whom I've merged so strongly, so deeply, more than with anyone before. Now, my focus is back on this being who was part of my very body for three quarters of a year and remained as close as a limb for the next two.

We're off to London for the weekend to stay with Marion and her son Zeb, while Thor goes to see his own kids, taking my home with him. Every time this happens, my true state of homelessness lands as a reality every time, even though we've formally agreed that the van belongs to both of us now.

In the seats in front of us on the train, a clearly 'weekend' dad is asking his son what his favourite subject today was, carefully revealing interest as well as inside knowledge with comments like "Mom says your French has been going well."

I wrestle with self-consciousness, feeling that my own conversation with Jay is on display. Surely it must reveal that I am the 'other', non-residential parent. I dart surreptitious glances at the woman behind me, in case she's listening and assessing the situation, but she's young and staring at her phone.

Jay has shifted out of his school gate self-protective mode and no longer seems worried about observers. He openly leans into me, snuggling up. "Your coat smells like the van."

"What does the van smell like?" I ask, remembering that it used to have a certain, impossible-to-describe smell to me too, before I lived in it.

"Like Thor."

To any listeners, this remark would clearly signal me as an odd kind of being – but my sense of shock is about much more than that. As Marion astutely points out when I tell her the story later, "It's primal. You smell like someone else now."

*

For the first twenty-four hours, I grate against the ugliness and busyness of London. Amidst my excitement to see Jay, I've also been feeling the jangled nerves of the approaching trip, which, after the simplicity of vanlife, seems suddenly highly complicated. Navigating between once familiar places on the London transport system feels like a strain requiring far too much brain power.

And indeed, these fears are not entirely unjustified. My debit card – my only source of money since I cancelled my credit cards – is swallowed by a card machine outside Sainsbury's Local. It happens as I'm standing there, hating London and everything it stands for, wanting desperately to return to what I thought I might need a break from soon. I borrow money from Marion to get me through the rest of the weekend, but it makes me feel horribly vulnerable.

But maybe it is still important to keep in contact with the grimy underbelly of life that the Big Smoke offers. The slurring woman with lipstick smeared all over her face, calling out "Merry Christmas! Have a great time!" as she staggers resolutely down the litter-strewn street; the grinning homeless guy at the entrance to the subway with his beer cans either side of him, one empty, one full, giving a thumbs up to Jay and nodding along to the Christmas tunes of the accordion player next to him, who gives me a wry smile.

I'd also forgotten how much the cultural life of the city could fill my well with inspiration: the soaring psychedelic pop sounds of a new band, Manuela, in the Union Chapel at a Daylight Music event, the antics of musician and spoken word improvisation artist Alabaster de Plume who says to the audience: "You're doing very well, people; it's not easy being, and you're all precious. We're all precious."

Yes. This is all good, too. If I can just let it in without flinching.

I'm worried about how thin-skinned I seem to have become. It makes me wonder: in our vanlife, are we just burrowing away in an easy life, like hermits in a comfort bubble? Copping out of reality?

It's strange to think of it that way, since most people who live in houses regard vanlife as the tough option. But this urban life seems harder – so much more gritty, brutal and unforgiving. In the van, we can largely avoid Other People and all the challenges they bring. We are cushioned by the softness of nature and the freedom we have to just keep moving.

When I share my ambivalence about these trips with Marion, she suggests I have a discussion with Jay about our contact arrangements about what we both want and what could work. So, I summon my courage and say to Jay: "I want to see you as much as possible, and sometimes it will only be every three weeks if I am too far away." His downturned mouth tugs at my heart. "But," I go on, "I will try to do two weeks whenever I can. And when I do see you less often, we can be together for longer." He brightens a little, but I still feel awful.

What I can't say is, "I want to see you as much as possible, but I can't deal with towns, sorry." I can't say that because he's supposed to be the most important thing to me – more important than my need to feel comfortable or safe. And he is, but how can I serve him best, and myself and everyone else, when I'm on a deficit?

When I'm reading his new Tom Gates book to him in Marion's bed, which she's kindly loaned to us, he says, "Oh this is nice, but it's not the same as being in our own house, in our own bed."

And in the next moment, it's all different again. We're on one of the brown sofas at Marion's and Jay is nestling into me. It feels amazing and I suddenly want to rearrange reality. It's so exquisite being with him right now that I want to have him always with me.

It's good to catch up with Marion: as always, her relaxed, laid-back demeanour sets me at ease and her excellent listening skills allow me to drop into spaciousness. I notice an interesting change: I no longer feel that I need to share loads of stuff about myself. I used to feel like I had to run everything by my friends, to make sure that they knew what was going on with me. It was as if my experiences weren't real unless they were witnessed and reflected back by these people whom I'd given some kind of interpretive power in my life.

Now, I feel more confident that what I'm doing is valid, without that affirmation from outside. Maybe my new detachment comes from the fact that I've so clearly stepped outside of the norm with my lifestyle choice. But it's more than that. I'm living with someone who doesn't habitually validate me, who is unflinchingly honest and doesn't try to please me at the expense of his own truth. For the first time in my life, I know that any feedback I get is genuine rather than coming from obligation.

When we leave, Marion hands me her house keys. "Just let yourself in, anytime," she says, her soft, warm brown eyes telling me she means it. My tears fill with her kindness. Having been without a fixed abode for some months herself, she really gets what it is to not have a home.

On the train with Jay on the way back to Sussex, the tears come as I suddenly realise I only have two hours left with my boy till I don't see him for another eighteen days. And that if I changed the rhythm to monthly, as would be likely if we settle somewhere further away like Devon, I'd see him only twelve times a year. I imagine how much he would change in each month.

Jay has said to me a few times over the weekend, "The van's where you live now really isn't it? It's where you live most of the time," like he's still computing it in his head. I'm surprised by this, because he knows I moved out of the Lewes house shortly after he moved in with his dad, but I realise now that he's not really thought about it, from his egocentric child way of thinking. I guess it's also confusing because when we see each other we're staying in other people's houses rather than in my 'new home'.

When Thor brings the van to pick me up and we take Jay inside to show him around, it seems to help him to see it concretely, that this is where I live now. He exclaims excitedly, "Oh, you've got Christmas lights!" but they're only the normal lights we use every day to navigate around the cupboards.

It's not that I lack curiosity about what he'll get up to on the trip, which involves a lot of outdoor adventure activities that would have filled me with horror as the bookworm child I was, but which he is excited about. I know I'll be a little frustrated at the monosyllabic answers he'll provide on his return. But the sense of panic and bewilderment at being excluded from his lived experiences, so prickly when he started nursery school, is now absent. What IS present is excitement and pride, which feels good.

After the drop-off, another mum at the school, who I'm mildly friendly with, gives me a lift home. She tells me that she's been watching Jay walking home each day as she drives past. He's recently started doing the walk alone, something he's been wanting for a while but I didn't allow him to do until I was confident about his road safety.

"I can see him so deep in thought, the cogs turning. There's loads of wisdom waiting to burst out from his boy-self into manhood," she says, her blue eyes lighting up with excitement. "The other day, I had this conversation with my son Michael about what his grandchildren might be like. I mean, the future generations will be born hard-wired for community. It will all be completely different."

I don't know if I fully believe that, but to think that Jay could be on the spearhead of that shift fills me with awe. The unknowability of the world his descendants (and mine) will inherit is exciting. I love the fact that he's going beyond where I can go, even if it does also make me tearful.

MY OTHER HALF

I remember my single mother friend Rebecca, in love with a new partner, telling me: "It's amazing what having a man who adores you can do", and thinking, *When will it be my turn?*

Now, Thor is poking the woodburner and I'm sitting cosily wrapped up under the duvet. I'm supposed to be saying something profound into the Dictaphone, for my book-to-be, but I'm feeling a bit self-conscious. He might be listening to me over there, crouched over the woodburner like a Neanderthal man, a very hot Neanderthal man. Looking at his ribs gives me a surge of energy in my lower abdomen.

It feels so bizarre that only three hours ago I was in the craziness of a big city and here I am, looking at the stars through the top of the van. *Yes, this is what it's about.* In this space – not just the physical space, but the space we create between us – I can feel myself as love, bliss and expansion. I suddenly know with complete certainty that it's perfectly okay to spend a lot of my time simply embodying this state. It seems to me that there's nothing else I should be doing.

And, I realise, I can do this in other situations, too. I can be in touch with this way of being when I'm with Jay; and this last weekend with him, I did feel a lot of love for him. In the past, anxiety often blocked this love: worrying about his needs and feeling stress with the effort of meeting them. This is softening now that we're not together all the time. It's still there – the roles are definitely still in place – but it feels as if there are more gaps for experimentation.

After Thor has stirred the fire into full life, we sit next to each other on the sofa, breathing in time with 'Om Satyanandana' by Deva Premal. In the corner next to his knee, I can see the rainbow strap of his guitar, draped over the drum he only brings out at festivals; there's the surrounding debris of crushed, flattened empty plastic water bottles, a pile of cardboard, half a bag of coal, a teapot, and some kefir ripening in a jar. The floor around the Indian rug badly needs a sweep and I smile, remembering Thor's assertion that he finds it relaxing to live with me because I don't notice mess.

My belly feels full. My heart is satisfied, too, because I have a companion. *My other half*, the words unfold inside me. Because after spending nearly three days apart, I'm astounded at how much I missed him and how much relief I felt to be with him again. "You're my lover, my best friend, and my beloved," he says, and I cannot believe my happiness and good fortune. This man, who, every morning, wakes me with kisses on my neck, making me think, *surely this can't last*.

But after six months together, we still behave as if we have just met. In fact, I've been wondering how I can continue to just get more and more attracted to someone, more and more into them, rather than less so, over time.

At the weekend, Marion observed that I seemed different: more confident and comfortable in my own skin. Is that all the lovemaking or the new lifestyle? Is it being loved so fully for the first time? Or is it being untethered from all my former life stresses?

So many things are coming together for me here, in this adventure: my long-held desire to make space for my writing and time in nature, my yearning to share an adventure with someone, to have a companion in life, to experience deep joy, ecstasy and communion in connection with another, to connect deeply with my womb.

Instead of holding the masculine polarity as I had to do for so many years as a single mother of a boy, I am now experiencing being held by the masculine. And it's illuminating to find out just what I can accomplish with that support: shedding layers of anxiety, dropping deeper into my writing, feeling permission to simply *be*.

THE VAN VORTEX

January 2018, Barcombe Mills

Mrs Lewis took an ambivalent attitude to obvious power. This is the road to civilisation, sure enough, but its cost was a loss of diversity, of the quiet kind of flourishing that goes on where things are not being built and goals driven towards. ~ Rachel Cusk, 'Aftermath'.

I have started to call it 'The Van Vortex': the phenomenon where I think to myself, "Let's go out and have a nice walk" and two hours later I'm still there, making tea, chatting to Thor.

If I were following my astrologer's advice to have fun as a karmic duty, I would be doing very well indeed. Most days I'm not out of bed before ten, often twelve. My hours consist of walks in nature, making love, singing and playing music, writing, reading and, perhaps the least 'fun' in the conventional sense, but also a deeply satisfying part of being on a healing journey, processing what comes up for us as a couple.

It's like permanent Dance Camp – falling into the arc of a day, letting go of the time you think you should have eaten lunch by, accepting you'll be up later than you sensibly should, following the little nudges and impulses towards magic and connection that come your way.

But having a companion who's almost always available for interaction makes it really hard to do anything else. I thought I'd feel claustrophobic within days of moving in, but I don't want to be separate the way I used to. It's started to scare me, and I've been giving myself a hard time for wanting to be near him almost constantly.

I've always needed a lot of alone time, since I was a child. My mom has often described how I would get up early in the morning, before everyone else, and play happily on my own with my doll house for hours. I'd ask to be taken home before the end of birthday parties, overwhelmed by the noise and stimulation, and return with relief to my own space.

When I lived with Jay, crowbarring solitude into the hours after he went to bed, I often felt compressed and hard done by. On some level, my inner dialogue was: "Oh, what is it now? What do you want? Why can't you just let me read and be in peace?" While on the surface I continued to try to love and serve him in every way; until he, ultimately, chose to leave.

But in the van, the cloying irritation I usually feel with others' continual presence has no space to be.

Thor has become such a fixture of my environment that I don't feel his presence as an intrusion in any way. I can be alone *and* together – just what I always wanted. And he seems to feel similarly, telling me "You're just part of the furniture now".

And yet, the vulnerability teeters on the edge of pain. By entering into such whole-hearted togetherness, I'm facing up to the perpetual question of my life: will I be good enough like this? Or like that? Is my love enough to make up for my delicate sensibilities, my fuck-ups, for the fact that I'm fragile as glass? For the days when I cry for no reason and feel inexplicably scared? For my clumsiness and misunderstandings?

I'm facing up to years of conditioning: seeing the painful dependence of my mother on my father, knowing there were probably generations of my ancestors in this patriarchal condition. My belief is: *You must prove you can be on your own. If you can't, you're a weakling who deserves to be alone.* It's like a prison sentence.

*

And then, just like that, the Pusher is back.

When I finally get out of the van at near lunchtime, sheets of ice cover whole sections of the car park. Coffee cups and other debris are strewn around, despite the sign warning people to "take your rubbish home as other people do".

The leaves are frosty too, covered in a thin coating of white dust. The river has swollen its banks but not enough to make us worried, although last night when Thor went for his walk at about ten p.m., he said there was a lot of water energy around: "The bridge felt like it might fall, it was shaking a bit." He did some healing on my sacral chakra afterwards, telling me, "I brought back the water energy from the river for you," he told me. The water, he's often explained, is the element of the sacral chakra, the energy centre where our emotions, creativity, and sexuality flow. All I knew was that it felt good.

As I walk, I encounter a barrage of intrusive thoughts about wasting my time. The idea that I'm 'not doing anything' is so persistent – I'm coming up big style against my concepts of what it is to be a person of value. But then I stop and look at the detailed lichen on a tree and it's absolutely something I'd never have had time to do; before. I notice the bits that look like dried paint and the other bits that look and feel like algae. I take in the frothy foam that's collected under the waterfall. I notice a guy fishing nearby.

I have to be repeatedly reminded: I forget what it's all about. My inner Pusher rebels every now and then, trying to claw back my former sense of identity, which from school age on was based on achieving things.

The perpetual question seems to be: do I spend a lot of my time doing tasks that move me towards an imagined future – writing, creating a new website – or do I spend more of my time living, which of course will feed into my work, but can make me feel like I'm getting nowhere?

I wonder whether the way forward is to hone my shapeshifting skills, so I can move fluidly and without resistance between the different modes – doing and being. But I usually don't want to let go of one to move into the other – at least, not a moment before I am truly ready. When I'm in work mode, deep into my writing or other projects, I feel resentful having to stop and cook to take care of my basic needs while my mind is moving a million miles an hour. When I'm lying in bed reading for hours or making love, the last thing I want to do is power up any kind of achievement-driven motor. The clash of my conditioning and the call of the present moment creates a near-constant tension in me.

Later, that afternoon, I tell Thor that I'm having a 'purposeless' day. When he responds, "I feel like that sometimes," I'm surprised. I usually perceive him as being so deeply in the moment, so naturally content without the need to do anything.

"What do you do when you feel that way?" I ask him.

"I just get into the attitude that it's all just happening and it gets better. But," he adds, smiling at me and circling his hand around my neck, "that won't work for the feminine. Because the feminine needs to feel herself as love and to do things that allow her to feel that."

We decide to do an exercise from spiritual teacher David Deida's work where we take turns telling the other about our 'purpose', staying connected to our heart as we speak. The other lifts a hand if they feel we are going below a seven out of ten for being in our heart. The intention is to fine-tune the connection between us and see what really feels true for us.

As Thor explains the exercise, I feel nervous. I have no idea what my purpose is anymore. In fact, I've been feeling some pain from this sense of loss; being a full-time mother gave such direction and shape to my days, even though I often wanted to break out from under that shape, like the clothes I used to put on my paper dolls.

Now, I'm nervous about this topic of purpose, and it seems ludicrous that a few years ago I co-facilitated a series of workshops called Passion, Power & Purpose. I feel like a total newbie.

But maybe beginner's mind is helpful in this case: the exercise turns out to be beautiful. I find myself talking about my purpose as being in nature and carrying that vibration; being in my heart and helping others to be in theirs in my presence; having fun and feeling joy; going deep below the surface and then expressing that experience. As I speak, I become aware that I can express these purposes every day. And it's easier to do so in my new environment than it's ever been.

THE HOUSE SIT

"I just feel like a mess," I confided as my friend Jean manoeuvred her Renault down the narrow roads towards the venue of the workshop we were co-facilitating in Kemptown, the hub of Brighton's LGBT community. It was a movement, discussion and writing group for mothers for a charity I'd been involved with for some time, and the two of us had recently begun to forge a friendship beyond our work.

It was the week after my Stonehenge Equinox freak-out, and my head was going around and around the same question: *how can it work for us to share the van?*

"The only two options I can see are to live in the van or get a full-time job just to be able to rent a small room in Sussex," I explain. "I feel exhausted just thinking about working full-time. I haven't done it for a decade, and I'm scared my chronic fatigue will come back. And also, the 'buckle down and be sensible' option feels like moving backwards rather than forwards … we have all these dreams of living off-grid together. I'd just end up feeling stuck in a town, he'd only be able to visit occasionally, and I'd probably go into survival mode and abandon my writing and other projects altogether." I knew Jean, as a fellow writer, would understand this.

I sighed and added, "But it just doesn't seem to work for us to be in the van together – I need space."

Jean had listened in sympathetic silence throughout, without giving advice or judging. Then suddenly she announced, "We're going to Australia for three weeks. You're very welcome to stay in our house while we're away. There's room for the van, and you can just use both spaces as you need."

"Really?" I was dumbfounded. Jean and I didn't know each other that well; it seemed like a very trusting thing, to offer up one's home.

"Yes. I'd be really happy for someone to be using it."

Relief and gratitude washed over me. I felt exultant: *the universe does, indeed, look after me.* I knew that a temporary reprieve could be really helpful as I assessed what to do next.

When I enthusiastically told Thor later, though, he was noncommittal as to how much time he'd actually spend in the house. "We can use it as a temporary second base," was all he would say, and I was reminded again with a sinking feeling that the van was still his domain, even though I'd been invited into it.

*

About an hour after we arrive, in mid-December, at the rural, homely three-storey family house in Barcombe, he changes his tune: "I want to live in a house. Why can't we live in a house?".

"We're too lazy to work enough hours to rent or buy one, remember?" I joke.

It's called Besley Farm Cottage and it used to be two cottages, so the staircase curves around in a peculiar way. We roam around the unnervingly enormous space: so much complicated furniture to put stuff on, while in the van your teacup goes either on your lap or on the windowsill shelf. And, as we soon discover, numerous places to forget you've put stuff and many trips up and down the stairs to find them.

Although I'm excited about entering this experiment of sharing space while also doing our own thing, the desperation that created this situation feels like it's flown the nest. I'm in a completely different space from when I accepted Jean's kind offer: I'm so much in love, so open that I feel vulnerable. The thought of being separate from Thor actually scares me.

We do four loads of laundry, avail ourselves fully of the kitted-out kitchen, and enjoy romping around in a bed where you don't have to worry about hitting your head on the low ceiling. I'm surprised by how, after only a couple of weeks of my offgrid lifestyle, the use of resources in a house already baffles me. There's a profusion of light switches to locate and remember to turn off, and it's odd to drop the water supply worry and use several van days' worth in one load of washing up (with *hot* water!).

While we're soaking in an ecstatically hot bath together, Thor says, "We'd get tired of living in a house after a while. Probably in a week."

"Yeah, and all the housework!" I agree. Domestic maintenance in the van basically consists of washing up two plates and bowls as we go along and occasionally shaking out the rug. I dwell briefly with vicarious horror on how much hoovering this house would involve.

And it seems that I'm a complete failure at cleaning house: the unpleasantness of the outside world has recently intruded on our bubble in the form of a check-out report from my rental agency. Despite my herculean efforts, they claim I did only a 'basic clean', leaving 'cobwebs in nearly all the rooms' and failing to clean the insides of the windows (even though I spent four hours on that task alone).

Here, I feel pleasantly grounded to be in one place, and grateful to be somewhere we have a right to be, for now – where we can't be moved on. The sense of precariousness that makes things both more alive and a bit more frightening is gone. I can see, though, how its continued absence would lull me into a bit of a stupor; how after a while, I might even start to take the beautiful countryside views for granted.

*

And then something odd happens: I change my independence orientation completely. I find myself wanting to go into another room, away from Thor, and gorge myself on books Since Jean shares my taste in psychotherapy, feminism, and fantasy books, it's like being an addict in a crack den. Every time I walk past the bookshelves, I see another one that entices me.

I choose to go on a walk on my own when usually I would be just as happy for Thor to come along with me. I dance around the kitchen while cooking, enjoying the fact that he's in the next room working. I expand into the space available.

I wonder if what I thought was a honeymoon joined-at-the-hip phase was simply a function of the fact that it's impossible to be truly separate in an environment where every tiny action you take affects the other person. The only way to cope with this is to become a symbiotic unit, or, as my vandweller veteran friend Rose put it, 'very interdependent', like little animals holing up together.

I also wonder if this being a neutral environment makes a difference to our dance of autonomy and union. Do I feel I have the right to do my own thing more here than I do in the van, which has been Thor's home for the past seven years, which he has set up to suit him? I haven't fully acknowledged, until now, that I have come into that already established space, rather than co-creating a new home with him from the beginning. Have I had to merge to make that manageable, in a way that I don't have to here?

In the house, there's no need to consciously state that you need space, to declare that you're about to take it by going up to the bed area and drawing the curtains. Here, we can just bimble about, doing our own thing, and space happens naturally.

By the third day, I'm bubbling over with ideas from all the books I'm reading and from my own work. I have a desire to share that, to bounce thoughts off another mind. But Thor is in the deep, silent meditative space that he often goes into, witnessing his thoughts rather than bringing them out into the light of day. From that place, he'll listen impartially to my thoughts but doesn't pick any of them up to develop into a discussion. I find myself feeling frustrated and disconnected.

In the van, all I wanted was simple companionship, lots of cuddles, and to sing and enjoy meals together. Now, when he can't fulfil my need to have my mind met and my expression heard, I feel silenced.

We try to talk about it, as we always do. Thor says that he sees it as a classic feminine/masculine split. "The feminine wants to dance with all of creation," he says. "To express, to play, to be in the many facets fully and deeply and connect them all as she weaves between the different modes. The masculine wants to hold it all, be the open, empty space that witnesses."

Well, maybe we are in this. The question is, how do we connect from that place? And is it even possible?

I realise that I'm still learning how to keep a connection with myself when I'm in the kind of 'merging' zone that vanlife involves. It's like every now and then, I reach a limit where I need to define my parameters again, to get clear on where I end and where the other begins. And that's where I'm at now.

After some tussling with myself, I can accept that I must meet my current needs with other people – a realisation I'm sure I've had a thousand times before in other relationships. I try to think of a friend I can call up, someone to have an intellectual discussion with. But the idea leaves me flat. It's connection I want, and connection with him, specifically.

Yes, we could merge in the wordless space of lovemaking, which usually works for us, but it feels like the river of separation has now grown into a sea, and I can't imagine setting sail to attempt a crossing. After only a couple of days without intimate touch, our bodies have become unfamiliar, separate vessels, and I wonder how couples who spend months or years in physical disconnection manage to ever find each other again.

I wonder if it's more complex than a simple binary of masculine/feminine, as Thor so often frames things. Unlike me, Thor has not walked a path in which his expression was consistently shut down and suppressed, even laughed at. One where it feels imperative to express, to bring out your thoughts and have demonstrable proof that they are heard, valued, and taken seriously. As well as the particulars of our family and schooling history, he was also born a man in a culture that values male expression more than female.

And then, when I'm on my daily nature walk, feeling the stillness and contentment of sitting under an oak tree, my mental struggle feels meaningless. Why try to describe and delineate an inner world? Why not just sit in the void and feel it? Maybe Thor is right, in his lack of interest in the life of the mind, in achieving anything in the outer world: what *is* the point of it all?

Although nature still connects me in to the current of life, the sense of presence I felt so strongly in the van appears to have vanished. I can't seem to stay with my meditation for more than a few seconds and I wonder if reading so much really does take me out of the moment. "You're not being with yourself," Thor tells me sometimes, to my annoyance.

But the steely truth is that I have been fantasising about staying in the house, reading and writing to my heart's content while he goes to Stonehenge for winter solstice, our next planned trip. Both my reading and my writing have been refuges from an unhappy childhood; I've hidden in books, away from the abrasiveness of other people's voices, demands and expectations on me to be someone other than who I am.

Although I'm on the autonomy end of the continuum right now, there's still a sinking feeling in my stomach when Thor says, "Being in a house has made me realise that it would be better for us to live where we could have this amount of space. Ideally, we'd have two structures like a yurt and a van. It would be better for me, and I think for you too."

"Yes. I'd love us to manifest that, too," I agree, but I don't speak for the very young part of me, who never wants to let go, who wants to immerse in togetherness all the time.

That part resists being on her own path and doing her own work. She *wants* to get distracted from it, because she's terrified of taking responsibility for her own wellbeing. She doesn't trust that she can do it.

Until the inevitable backlash, which has played out over and over in my relationships. It's what happens when I overdose on coupledom, lose my sense of my own energy, and become frustrated and resentful, which is unfair on everyone. I try to explain this inner dynamic to him, but he says I'm contradicting myself. *What about the Walt Whitman quote?* I fume inwardly. *"Do I contradict myself? Very well, I contradict myself. I am large. I contain multitudes."*

*

The house, with its out-in-the-sticks location and creaky sounds, soon starts to spook me. My heart clenches as I go up the stairs each night: I suddenly realise that I am going into the darkest time of the year. Every year, it's scary; every year, as it approaches, I forget how full on it is.

As the gap between us widens, Thor's announcement that he might go to Stonehenge without me lands as panic. *It's going to be a repeat of those years when I did Christmas on my own.* Even last year, although I was invited to a friend's family Christmas, I still felt lonely, a tag-on, missing Jay and feeling the impact of not being with my family, who despite everything had always had good Christmas celebrations. Now, I feel rudderless at the thought of a Christmas spent totally alone. It makes it worse that my closest friends seem unavailable, either too busy to talk or too self-occupied to really engage. I mostly talk to my Dictaphone, recording notes for my book.

Maybe my feeling of being unanchored is something to do with staying in the house of someone who has a very stable situation: Jean is married to her partner of ten years, is a mother of three, and seems financially secure. I feel the contrast with my own life, and what only a week ago felt wild and free now feels painful and empty. Although I know Jean often feels stifled by her life, hers is a stronger legacy than mine – I only have one boy who doesn't even belong to me anymore.

The contrast seems to highlight my own need for security, which up until now was made dormant by the novelty and excitement of being a hippy traveller. But as life has shown me recently, any certainty I might have is an illusion. With my long-term rental lease that had been secure for four years, I thought I had a place to live indefinitely – and with our close relationship, I thought Jay would want to live with me at least until his late teens.

My thoughts circle back to what Marion said at the beginning of my whole process months ago, when I was trying to decide where to live and what to do: *Just don't get attached to it all landing any particular way.* Even now, my mind wants to make a story and attach to it – to go, "OK, so living in the van doesn't work, I need my autonomy. So, I have to look for my own place. And this relationship doesn't work either." But when I can zoom out from this perspective, I see that living in the van has been working very well on the whole, and it was only when we began the house-sit that things started to go weird.

*

"I'm bored of this now. I'm wasting my time."

He throws these words at me across the kitchen, and they hit me between the ribs.

It's clear he's become like a domesticated animal in this house. Slouching around, purposeless: a tame animal isn't so sexy. But now, with his blazing eyes and voice full of authority, he's suddenly compellingly attractive to me again.

But I'm stunned and shamed when I remember that this is exactly the kind of phrase my father would utter. "Why would I want to be here?" he'd shout at my mother before storming out of the house, leaving her pleas behind him to escape to a bar or back to his fast-food outlet, the one that was slowly destroying our family, eating all his time and energy. As far as I could see, my mom was a boring drag and a doormat to him.

I see suddenly that I've dragged Thor into this. It's my old pattern of creating constriction until I subconsciously manifest a rupture in connection. Subconsciously trying to be both my clinging on mother and my escaping father at the same time, unable to create healthy boundaries, I wait until the other person wants out, handing the responsibility to them.

I face him, crumpled in posture, defeated and churning inside. I feel like a damaged, complicated, helpless girl. Our conversation started with him expressing vulnerability about us not connecting much lately. But the tide turned when I said I was unsure about going to Stonehenge with him. "It's not that I'm opposed to this ancestor path that you're on, but I just want to see if it's my journey and I'm not just tagging onto yours."

That's when he becomes fierce. "Well, if that's how you feel about the ancestors, maybe you shouldn't come to Stonehenge," and he storms off.

A few minutes later, he is back, his warrior mode slightly softened. "You know what working with the ancestors is about … this is both of our journeys, potentially. They were much more in touch with the earth than we are these days, and that's what's making us sick. So, we connect with them just to bridge that wisdom they had into our present time. And it's also about connecting the ancestors of different lands, often those with very difficult relationships, like Africa and Europe and Britain. The only reason you resist the ancestor stuff is because you're jealous of Lila and you think I had big experiences with it through her. But it wasn't even her, it was Jemima, my ex after her. I've had enough of it."

He sees my face fall and says, more gently, "I believe you're on the same path, you just maybe don't use the same words for it." This feels true: I am a total pagan and all he is talking about is earth connection, really.

All of this feels so unfair, because going to Stonehenge for solstice and Christmas was something I'd deliberately chosen. It emerged out of the weirdness of a family estrangement: my younger sister Robyn had stopped talking to me a month ago when I told her I could only come to one of her two wedding ceremonies – one handfasting, one registry office – due to my long-nurtured plan to volunteer at Buddhafield Festival with Thor for three weeks.

The split between us – not the first time she's stopped talking to me – feels set to continue for some time, throwing my plans to take Jay to hers for Christmas into disarray. Jay then chose to stay with his father for Christmas, wanting the bells-and-whistles 'family Christmas', with the compromise that he'd come to me for a few days afterwards. I did what I usually do – make the most of a loss and change direction, by going to Stonehenge.

Now, this bold sentence from Thor, "Maybe you shouldn't come," triggers me into such a place of abandonment, even as I recognise my resistance to going, the anxiety that I might lose control in the power of this sacred place. As soon as I'm told I may not be able to go, I feel devastated, thrust aside from this shared experience of nature communion and magic.

I can see now that hidden just beneath the surface of my longing to immerse in books is fear: what if I go crazy on my own here? There's a terror in me of going that deep into myself and into my work. And on a simple human needs level, ten days is just a long time to be without any company, while all my friends are immersed in family Christmas celebrations.

"Is there something you don't know that you want to learn from me? Something in my nature connection?" his voice pulls me back to the discussion. I don't know. Maybe I have been putting him on a pedestal and I already possess this knowing myself. Maybe I have access to my own feminine divine mysteries and am simply failing to trust that.

There's no doubt that I have been stepping into these realms more and more lately – but I've lost it now, I've descended into a premenstrual chasm which takes me out of my body and has only got worse since I've been in a house with lots of books to read.

"Maybe you could stay here for another three days then come up to Stonehenge," he suggests, and I burst into tears. I'm nowhere near a train station and it all feels too much. I feel stuck and powerless whichever way I move. If I stay here, I'm trapped; if I go to Stonehenge and things go awry, I'm stuck there, too. And that's my life at the moment. I'm stuck being where other people allow me to go or are willing to take me.

Victim, I chastise myself. I feel as vulnerable and raw-skinned as the strange, sinister fluffy chicks on that photo on the wall, the ones that Thor says look like genetically modified sheep. I am like that – I need taking care of, and if the person who's taking care of me and providing a home for me disappears, what then? What a heavy burden for any relationship to bear.

In that moment, it all becomes very real: my itinerant situation, my essential homelessness.

But as we keep talking, I come to a new insight. In my white South African upbringing in the 80's, the word 'ancestor' was associated with 'backwards' superstition. Because of colonialism and the subsequent apartheid regime, I grew up in a cultural context where anything that the indigenous black population did was viewed with derision and contempt. The power and reverence that the 'witchdoctors' (or what Thor calls 'African shamans') gave to their ancestors fell into this category.

My mother would remark disparagingly on the 'witchdoctor' practice of giving their clients – people like our housekeeper – something called 'muti'. In her opinion, and that of most other white South Africans, this medicine made from animals and plants didn't really work and prevented people from getting the proper medical treatment they needed to stay alive. Rumours appeared in the newspapers that witchdoctors advised AIDS-afflicted people to cure themselves by having sex with infants. Naturally, I dumped the belief in ancestors in the 'rubbish basket' along with all the other practices of a culture that I didn't understand.

My primary association with my own ancestors is the last few generations, who I feel have nothing of value to share with me. I imagine them as fucked up, repressed colonialists, anything but wise and knowing. But now, Thor points out, "One hundred, two hundred, three hundred years ago, people were already lost. They had no wisdom, no connection with the earth. They were also in the space that I am trying to fix. The problems I am trying to fix in the world …"

And this is where I glaze over slightly, because I've heard him say many times that there's nothing to fix 'out there', it's all 'in here': that we shift our world by shifting our state of being. Why do I expect him to make sense? He's no more consistent than me. With a sigh of relief, I again take him off his pedestal and face him as a human.

I remember a quote from feminist Rebeca Solnit's book, 'Men Explain Things to Me', from the title essay: "Having the right to show and speak are vital to survival, to dignity and to liberty. I'm grateful that after an early life of being silenced, sometimes violently, I grew up to have a voice, circumstances that will always bind me to the rights of the voiceless." Maybe the ancestors are the voiceless too?

"The thing is, you're very close to this ancestor thing, because you're from that land, Africa," he says. "You're a bridge to those ancestors, and you're also linked to what destroyed and damaged it, through your white ancestors. You could potentially be someone who creates a lot of healing there."

Finally, after twenty-four hours of wrangling, Thor insists that I need space and leaves to park up somewhere locally for a day, announcing he will return to pick me up for our Stonehenge trip but that I can also choose not to go with him.

To my surprise, after he's left and I finally stop crying, I exhale in enormous relief.

At last, I have the space and autonomy that I was so afraid to give myself, afraid because I believed, underneath, that he would not come back. And now that I have the space, a day doesn't feel like enough. Because I know I will go to Stonehenge with him. Even though I'm nervous about going back in the van now and I dread being bored. I just know, somehow, that going to the stones will be the right thing.

MOTHERLOAD

One morning, I wake to a sadness I can only describe as my mother-with-empty-arms grief. Although it's painful, I'm reluctant to let it go, like a skein of wool I've earmarked for some bigger project, though it's been sitting unused for ages.

I've been feeling so relieved at being let off the hook of school run 'hurry-up's, PTA and homework; the pressure to always be organised and know what I'm doing. I could easily discard that ill-fitting outfit and move on without a backward glance. But now, all I can feel is how much I miss the day-to-day mothering that used to oppress me.

I miss walking down the street hand in hand with this being I partly made, who clearly is my offspring because he looks like me (more and more as he's got older) ... who loves me and whom I've successfully raised to the age of ten. With so many other things I've tried to achieve in my life, that led to dead ends, this feels like one I can hold my head high about.

'Mothering' used to be always having my finger on the pulse: being embedded in the day-to-day of Jay's activities and needs. Now that that place has been taken by Jay's father and grandparents, I'm trying really hard to stay in touch with my role, but I'm grasping at straws.

In a desire to show Jay what I have to offer him when he comes to stay after Christmas, I send him videos of Besley Cottage and the rope swing nearby. I waste time on a Facebook group called 'Motherload', replying to people's requests for advice as to where in their house they might have left their keys, commiserating with their motherhood woes, feeling a once-foreign sense of kinship to these women who share nothing else with me apart from a child-producing womb. As a full-time mother, I never bothered with this sort of thing.

I notice a post in the group about weekends being the hardest thing to deal with as a single parent. I respond that for me it was too, when I was in that boat. I realise my 'story' has become, "I *was* a single parent for eight years". I once thought the ending to that story would be that I find a new partner and we all make a new family together, with perhaps another child joining. This wasn't the ending I expected.

I notice that the 'word cloud' Facebook so usefully provides as a summary of my past year, assembled from the words most often used in my status updates, is comprised mainly of 'motherhood' and 'mother' in large letters, with words like 'dancing' and 'writing' in small letters, just like the year before. I wonder what the cloud will look like at the end of this year.

Perhaps it's okay – in fact, more than okay, normal, but just not normal in our society – to give birth to someone, raise him to an age where he's basically his own person, and then let him go, even from your mental space. The truth is, I no longer frequently wonder what he's doing and how he is, which sounds callous and distant, but maybe it's just not co-dependent. Maybe what more children need is to be allowed their personhood separate from their parents, to receive loving presence from them when they're around but to otherwise get on with their lives. To send them love but not get into their business.

UNKNOTTING

At the most important of the pagan sabbats, winter solstice, the road closest to the sacred site of Stonehenge – the Drove – becomes an odd cross between a festival, a community camp, and something else that cannot be defined.

After we park up in the line of vans, we head out for a walk to gather kindling for our own fire together. On the way back, we visit the special beech tree that we spent time with when we were last here, three months ago at Equinox. It's a tree being Thor has had an on-going relationship with for several years and which has also found a place in my heart. As we walk on, Thor encourages me to look at the brightness of the green moss on the ground. I remember what he told me about the inner 'Magical Child'. When you're in touch with this part of yourself, colours are more alive and everything looks more visceral, exciting and new. There is something about that beech tree that draws me into this world.

By the time we come out with our firewood findings – me vaguely proud of myself for having sawn wood for the first time and being trusted to do so – the sun is setting. I watch it carefully for its potent moment of disappearance. We pinpoint a different exactness for this transition, with me watching the last glowing ember right until it's vanished and Thor seeing that as only a reflection on the clouds – "It's already gone."

The next day, although I'm feeling shy and anxious about being a useless fifth wheel with my lack of practical skills, Thor persuades me to join him and a few others on a firewood-gathering expedition, via one of the burial mounds. Before climbing over the barbed wire gate and into the woods, we ask for permission from the spirits, which Thor says may be hiding out there in the woods to avoid the tourists. I tend to humour this way of thinking, as although I am a total tree-hugger, I don't sense the reality of human spirits myself.

In the woods, it suddenly occurs to me that what I've waited so long for, what used to feel like a holiday I had to work hard to deserve, *is now my normal life*. Climbing over a fence to commune with trees at a sacred site is now a totally everyday occurrence in my life; there is nowhere else I am expected to be or anything I am committed to do.

*

In *Big Magic*, one of the books I devoured at Besley Cottage, author Elizabeth Gilbert revealed an exciting concept, which I enthusiastically shared with Thor on our drive to Stonehenge: that ideas are actual entities or things that exist alongside people, animals, plants and the rest of the world. They want to be brought into being, so they approach individual human beings to see if they'll enter into a creative partnership with them, to give them birth.

If you aren't willing or able to hear an idea communicating with you, or you give up on the idea half-way through this contract, it will move on to another person and find another outlet – the same idea, channelled through someone else. Gilbert explains how, when she was unable to complete a novel due to personal crisis, the plot outline and character travelled from her brain into another writer friend's, despite the fact that they had never discussed it.

After a philosophical detour ("It can't be the truth of how things are, because it's an idea in itself"), Thor took the concept and ran with it. Soon after arriving at Stonehenge, we bump into a woman he knows, Sally, who's now pregnant with a child she will raise alone. I make a point of mentioning to Sally that "I have a boy". I like my motherhood being seen, I realise: for this story to be validated. Now, and especially here, it's invisible – people don't see me, in my current lifestyle, as someone who is likely to be a mom, and they don't see the evidence. I don't look old enough to have a child who's grown up and left the nest.

Sally and her partner, it turns out, split up right at the start of the pregnancy, when he became involved with someone else, in what Thor joked was an episode of Stonehenge-Enders.

"That was what I was planning to do with my last girlfriend," Thor explains. "We agreed I'd give her a baby and she'd have it on her own as we knew our relationship had a shelf life. The idea must have moved on to them."

Then, "I wonder how long the idea of us being in love will last. Maybe it will last forever!"

I keep silent. Of course, I hope for forever.

But then, the idea full-time motherhood, once something I was passionate about, wasn't a forever one for me. I was given ten years before it moved on.

With his usual astuteness, Thor has picked up that I'm in some sort of funk. "Is it because of no babies to love?" he asks. "Is it broody time again?" His tone is patient and caring; this happens almost every month around my ovulation time. But that's not it – I've only just finished bleeding, yet I'm mourning both my grown-up baby and the babies I never had and never will have.

*

Later, Taliesin, a druid who holds ceremonies here eight times a year, pops into the van to say hello and give us hugs, but ultimately to deliver "MDMA made by a mate's lad" to another van-dweller. Taliesin was one of the candidates for the handfasting ceremony we were planning for Equinox, although Thor chose Phil in the end, a less outwardly intellectual, more heart-felt kind of man.

In the van, Taliesin doesn't sit down, but shows us graphs of when the sun rises and sets so we can figure out when the daylight will become more substantial again. Thor estimates that it will be mid-February before things really start to lighten and we have enough solar energy to power the van more efficiently.

The discussion gradually gets more esoteric, and I remember Thor telling me that Taliesin always has a daily lesson to impart to others. I can see that others have little choice in this process: Taliesin hauls out diagrams depicting interlocking different theoretical time zones or frames that we can be in. Apparently, we can step into these spaces at any time with meditation and using 'the word'. Thor enlightens me later that this is the Druid version of 'Om', pronounced E-R-O-M.

"The first time zone is from birth to childhood. This is when time seems to go really slowly," Taliesin explains. I can easily believe this: I remember the way six weeks of summer holidays, and even a single school day, would seem interminable to me as a child, while these days I barely seem to have got dressed before it's time to make dinner and dark is encroaching. "N-time – Now time – is the goal, the place we want to be inhabiting most," he goes on.

Maybe this is the clue to getting rid of my time-scarcity mentality. Even though I now live without a young school-going child, the obligation to work a certain number of hours a week, and an entire house to maintain, I still find I don't seem to have quite enough time to do everything I want to. Not even close. It's hard to fit in the two hours of writing a day that I'm aiming for – where did the extra time go? Have I slowed down and chilled out to the point where productivity is a thing of the past? Or is it really as Taliesin is saying, that the time thing is a portal becoming more and more constricted as we get older, so that we have to enlarge and expand it with the will of our minds, the intention to be free again?

After Taliesin leaves, Thor explains what he thinks the druid was talking about. "Each human being," he says, "has to unknot themselves so that they can experience themselves as everything at the same time. We are all just strings of vibrations which are knotted together through the localisation of our perceptions and the bundle of vibrations that we are. Our path is to unknot that so we can become all of it."

The last part sounds so appealingly simple, but I know it's not easy. Most of the time I'm so identified with my bundle of complexes and neuroses that to break out and connect takes something truly mind-altering: a deep dance experience, nature speaking to me clearly in some way. But this liberation is feeling more accessible now that I've stripped my life back to its bare bones, and the experiences we're having in nature together offer little glimpses of what's possible.

After tea, we walk up and down the Drove, which is now extremely muddy, spattering my green velvet skirt despite my best efforts to keep it out of the way. Most of the women I've seen here so far are wearing practical trousers and wellies, but I now spot a few new arrivals with the characteristic hippy rainbow skirts and braids. I try to catch their eyes –"I'm one of you" – as they walk past, but mostly they're involved in their conversations or their children, the hippy children I never had, with their dirty faces and long hair.

I'm reminded that I don't truly belong here: I'm a newbie to this traveller world. Part of it is that the other women seem tougher than me – and it's not just their superior practical skills. I feel so sensitive and open, vulnerable in contrast to their competent outer shells.

There's an excitement in the air. I can feel the energy building towards the solstice celebration in the morning. We pass Taliesin, who's just returned from holding a sunset ritual. He chats to us while slowly removing his ceremonial garb: elaborate belts, amulets, and decorative ropes. I can now accept him as magical much more easily than when I first met him, wearing a checked shirt and looking like an ordinary man in his sixties, announcing he was about to have a spliff. In fact, both druids – Taliesin and Phil – are at first glance people I wouldn't expect to be in this role, or even to be 'serious spiritual people' of any kind, in my old preconceptions of the world. Phil has a strong London accent, a heavily lined face and tobacco-stained teeth and fingers. His down-to-earth warmth and straight-talking insight soon grow on me.

Hanging his druid gear from hooks on his van, but keeping his white druid robe on, Taliesin says, "You can have a lot of partying tonight if you like partying because there's 17 hours of night and only 7 and a half hours of daylight. So ... a long party," he chortles. A few years ago, that prospect would have filled me with excitement; now my response is an internal "ugh" as I worry about feeling shitty and sleep-deprived tomorrow.

A drunk-looking guy passes by, looks Taliesin over and says "Different levels" in an amused way. I guess he's referring to the contrast between those like him, who are celebrating in their own way by getting off their heads, and the deeper worship of people like the druid.

I remember that when we came here for Equinox, I was still deciding whether to move into the van. Watching the revelling around the fires, the drunken drumming, and the unpredictable behaviour of sozzled, stoned men staggering around and shouting, I'd recoiled when Thor said to me, "These are your people now". He was only half joking – despite being an experienced vanomad, as a teetotal drug-free person he didn't identify with most of these people. Still, I felt my middle class, entitled roots threaten to throttle me. I had a university education, and I could live in a house if I wanted. But I just wasn't prepared to sacrifice all my time to do so. These folks ... I saw them as having different paths, led to this place by harder, less choice-full circumstances.

This time, nearly a month into living as a van dweller myself, I'm a lot humbler. When Sally told me earlier that day with visible embarrassment that she was waiting to get housed by the council because of her pregnancy, I was anxious to show that I had no judgment. After all, there was now only a hair's breadth separating her from me. After all, I'm here because I was essentially evicted from my house.

As is his traditional practice, Thor walks with his rattle up and down the Drove several times with me at his side, rattling to clear the energy and, he says, "the chaotic spirits that come at this time". As usual when he makes shamanic statements about other realities, I only half believe this is happening, but I try anyway to support his intention as he requests of me, by focusing on the sound of the rattle, even though I'm a bit hyper and distracted by all the people.

Every time I take my hand away to have a drink of water or adjust my hair, he beckons it back, "Don't break the circuit". I feel both proud of walking beside him, holding his non-rattling hand, and a bit self-conscious. I don't want people to judge me as someone who thinks they're something great, one half of an important shamanic couple.

I'm still debating with myself about whether to join the Shakti Sings choir with my old choir leader, Sophia, in the stones at sunrise. I got the email yesterday, inviting all the members of her other choirs to join in, and I've been practicing the songs just in case. I'm strongly drawn to it but feel hesitant to fully commit. I want to be free to be part of ceremonies or spontaneous gatherings, to walk around, tune into the stones, and be with Thor.

But is that just me abandoning my post and my path, of which singing is so much a part? Do I really show up and sing in the centre of the stones for the whole hour – which could give me a powerful sense of purpose, joy and belonging? Even if it means risking less connection to Thor and missing out on spontaneity? I resolve to see how I feel in the morning.

At my insistence, we venture out – I'm feeling more sociable - during what we think is solstice eve, but we later find out isn't: we got the date wrong, despite all our conversations with Taliesin about sunrise and sunset charts. We should have known: there's only one fire and no music blaring. We hover by the fire but one of the drummers being cringingly out of time puts Thor off and we walk on. We return when there's nothing but darkness at the end of the Drove. I found out it's called the Drove when Phil the druid's husky, Dog – one blue eye, own brown – jumped up on my white jumper and I had to change into a brown one, pronounced 'better Drove clothes' by Sally.

Thor suggests we can get the drummers in time with our rattling, so we pull out our rattles – mine is feminine-shaped with a round end and his has several beads stacked under each other – but I find it hard to relax. There's a cynical-looking guy in his deckchair opposite, smoking and putting a hard stare around, and drunk guys shouting outside a van nearby. A young dreadlocked man nods over a beer and gurns against the fence, and the brief exchange of words between him and an older guy makes it clear they've been trying out Taliesin's MDMA. I feel like a judgmental snob, but I can't help wanting to be in a proper sacred atmosphere, with people who respect being conscious.

When Thor joins in with the drumming and moves away from my side, I feel the emissions of the drunk and drugged people more. It makes me feel jumpy and vulnerable. So, I nudge him to tell him I'm going back to the van, and he returns only a few minutes after I've nestled back into the safety and familiarity of our home. 'There's only so much sitting around a fire you can do with drunk people.'

But at the sunrise ceremony, the seeming division between me and the other Stonehenge van-visitors dissolves. I sing with the choir in the centre of the stones: odes to the earth and to the return of the light, and almost cry when the others crowded around join in, feeling the swell of unity. Afterwards, I dance to the drummers for a long time. I see Obi, the notoriously perpetually off-his-head guy, carousing and grinning his face off, and feel nothing but affection. I'm full of the excitement of the turn of the wheel: winter moving into spring, inexorably.

We all trundle back to our vans when the security guards escort us off and I'm high, in my own way. Who knows, I might even have unknotted.

WILD GEESE

You do not have to be good.
You do not have to walk on your knees
For a hundred miles through the desert, repenting.
You only have to let the soft animal of your body
love what it loves.

Tell me about your despair, yours, and I will tell you mine.
Meanwhile the world goes on.
Meanwhile the sun and the clear pebbles of the rain
are moving across the landscapes,
over the prairies and the deep trees,
the mountains and the rivers.

Meanwhile the wild geese, high in the clean blue air,
are heading home again.

Whoever you are, no matter how lonely,
the world offers itself to your imagination,
calls to you like the wild geese, harsh and exciting —
over and over announcing your place
in the family of things.

~ Mary Oliver, Wild Geese

Hard benches, gum on the floors, dead-looking food behind plastic, people who seem thickened up, like they're wearing puffy suits protecting their tender bits, the bits I've spent the last weeks excavating.

It's strange – even though I've been back in towns a couple of times since moving into the van, this time I feel much more vulnerable. It reminds me of when I used to come out of retreats, in the days when I could still afford such things: the time I did a week of intensive Kundalini Yoga in the French Alps and found being in the airport afterwards so traumatic – the sights and sounds so overwhelming that I was overcome with terror. I couldn't stop crying and my friends had to support me.

This isn't as high on the scale of altered states – or maybe I've just got more accustomed to inhabiting them – but I feel myself just as thin-skinned and unready. I can sense my hyper-alertness, along with darting eyes and unsmiling face. There's suddenly so much space around me but it's not the supportive, gentle kind of space that nature is. Why have we built such ugliness?

"The trick is to stay where you are even when you go out into the real world", Thor said as we drove into Salisbury. But this is the downside of the extreme adaptability that allows me to accept all the vicissitudes of living in a tiny space with another human being – compost loos, un-private pooing, and no showers for weeks. I know I won't be able to hold onto it. I will let this abrasive, concrete, corporate world in. I will merge with it into another robot – even if only temporarily.

I stare at myself in the bathroom mirror at the rail station. I notice that my scalp is dry and flaking and it's clearly visible to anyone. I have the unfamiliar feeling that I am 'passing', and that my current appearance might blow my cover. Passing for what, though?

I look deeper: my eyes look as innocent as a child's. Something has changed. Lately, when I read the Facebook posts of my friends, it's struck me how caught up they are in the loops of their own thinking, their repetitive dramas. I feel so far from that now. It's become harder to connect with friends when I talk to them, because they seem to be so in their heads, always talking about their problems and analysing them.

Once I'm actually on the train, I start to settle. The near-constant sounds of beeping phones around me start to feel normal, although I know my nervous system dislikes it. I remember with relief that I have earphones and can tune out some of the stimulation, although I still feel a bit apologetic for my existence when I have to sit next to an elderly woman who's chatting away to her husband opposite.

*

With time to fill before going to a Brighton friend's house, Jay and I walk through the Royal Pavilion Green, known locally as Pavilion Park, a beautiful garden which surrounds a dramatic Regency style palace. Jay immediately remembers it, lighting up with a commentary about how he used to walk there. It triggers my memories too, the hours of watching him run after pigeons and seagulls, the busking musicians who created an oasis of culture in a long day of being alone with a child.

As we make our way to the bus stop on North Street, Jay's flood of memories continues. "In our Brighton house, where we lived with Daddy, I remember watching this program on TV, and I used to go, vrroom vrroom while I watched it." I smile. He was twenty-two months when I moved out of there; I'm often astounded by what he remembers. When certain mantra tracks come on from his early toddler years, he has clear recall of which house we lived in and what we usually did at the time when that song was the soundtrack. Snatam Kaur's 'Ong Namo' is forever associated with 'The Bear Road House', where he remembers pushing around a wooden trolley full of blocks.

Now that my nervous system has adapted somewhat, there's a strange comfort in stepping into this old life: the noisy bus routes, the big park where I once whiled away many hours, Jay travelling in a sling close to my body. It's all just as it was. Now, Jay's impatient for the bus to arrive. He exclaims excitedly as the 'due' appears on the digital sign, and a woman breastfeeding her baby in a sling, both wrapped up in multiple layers, shares a conspiratorial smile with me.

I want to tell her I remember breastfeeding in the dead of winter. Jay was an October baby, and it was often brutal, having to stop on a pavement in the cold and feed him because his wailing pierced through me so much I couldn't wait until we reached a bench.

As the weekend progresses, I become aware of an uncomfortable stretching. The demands of my living situation with Thor can be intense – but they've already become familiar, and our life is a simple one. Here in the city, with its complexity, things seem to so easily tip over into unmanageability. I suddenly find myself severely mentally challenged by things like working out whether taking the train or bus to a given destination is more economical.

I start chastising myself for becoming so insular and infantile – but a kinder inner voice soon comes in. Maybe you've had enough stretching. Maybe being effectively homeless, living on the road, and having had no work for months is enough of a leap out of your comfort zone. And I relax again.

*

My idealisation of the past with Jay is thoroughly deflated by the time we finally end up, after midnight on Saturday night, at Kristen and Graham's house in Ringmer, after a marathon of a fiftieth birthday party. I'd turned up to the party already exhausted and stressed, with a moaning Jay. He'd kept up the litany of complaints throughout our thirty-minute walk through Lewes, burdened as we were with luggage, and I was reminded that these kinds of tedious moments had been frequent when we still lived together.

Although it was a child friendly party, with several children there that he knew, he wasn't in the mood to socialise. Eventually, taking pity on him in his boredom – and wanting an easy life – I let go and allowed him to go on his tablet. After years of restricting device use, I've let go of the responsibility now that he has a TV in his bedroom. Something I was not, of course, consulted about.

A large part of the evening consisted of music, poetry and other performances, since Graham is a singer-songwriter and all of their daughters love to dance. I originally met Graham and Kristen at a community camp where Graham was usually seen with guitar in tow. I performed a song accompanied by my ukulele, a Laura Marling and Johnny Flynn cover, which was a real edge for me – the first time I'd performed in front of so many people and a nerve-wracking experience. I basked in the effusive praise I received afterwards – the best one being that I was a modern-day Joni Mitchell and didn't even need the ukulele. I felt grateful for the support Thor has given my music, for the boost to my confidence I've gained through playing so much together.

Now, Kristen and Graham's house feels as safe and comforting as ever. I've spent many hours here, getting stoned together, listening to music, having family dinners. I glance at the mantelpiece, decorated with descriptions in childish handwriting of glitter and special outfits for 'Mummy and Leora'. I reflect, admiringly and with a dash of pain, on what a well-oiled machine Kristen's blended family is. They spend their weekends together doing violin and dance recitals, going on nature walks, making films and other wholesome co-ordinated things. They also struggle with step-sibling fights, frequent whinging and an insomniac eldest child – but they are undoubtedly a family.

I should be enjoying this. All the space around me, not having to navigate around someone else in what is effectively one room all the time. But I'm not. It's been a long, exhausting day and I realise that I'm merely enduring it all. The pain of living separate from my child is something I can forget most of the time in my all-consuming vanlife bubble, but it's right on the surface when I'm with Jay. And the strange thing is that although I now have his company, my overwhelm means that I long to go back to my life in the peace of the countryside, flowing with my days, free.

In our shared bed, Jay clings tightly to me. I could have taken the sofa, but I felt his need to be closer. I soak up this feeling, and in the morning, I wake and remember the sadness that feels like it'll never go.

The sense of enduring through the weekend to get to the end vies with a longing to capture every moment with Jay: his fuzzy sticking out hair in the morning, his huge grins, how much he enjoys Leora and Tina's little pet rats crawling up into his jumper hood, his long monologues about his latest Lego Playstation game. I feel guilty for my joy at the thought of returning to Thor and the van tomorrow. Less than two months ago, this town life was my real life. Now, it's hard to admit to myself that this has changed, because that reality excludes Jay.

On the way back from Graham's party, we got a lift with a friend, along with a twenty-something band member who asked me politely where I lived. "Nowhere, I'm living on the road at the moment. I'm staying at Kristen and Graham's tonight and Jay's staying with me." And Jay calmly and pragmatically pointed out, "I live with my dad".

I felt ashamed and awkward. What am I? I can't really call myself a single mom anymore, now, can I? The only references to 'part-time mother' that I see on Instagram are mothers being slagged off for failing to be there for their kids. Mothers who neglect to attend their children's football games and ballet recitals, leaving others to pick up the slack.

At the end of the full-on weekend, on Sunday night after I've returned Jay to his dad, I stay at Wendy and Thomas's house, a street away from where Jay and I used to live. By now, I've surrendered to the chaos and found a sense of basic OK-ness, which is how I'm able to deal with Wendy's five-year-old son Damian screaming inconsolably in the background at being put to bed.

When that ordeal is over, Wendy listens attentively with her kind eyes to my stories of what's unfolding in my vanlife. She tells me that perhaps I'm regressing, in a good way, in the safety of the healing space I find myself in. That I'm allowing myself to feel the feelings of the child of years ago, to let her play and be.

A few minutes before, Damian showed me his toy dragon and enlisted my opinion on which bit of the dragon the rider should sit on. I found myself genuinely engaged, even excited, and I remember that I was powerfully drawn to the pink winged soft unicorn belonging to Jenny, a little girl at Graham's party, the night before. Maybe I am regressing.

*

When I return, Thor holds me as I cry and confess how much I wish we could all three of us be together as we thought it would be. Later, we talk about the mobile home lodge that his parents have recently given him and how, if we find a good place to put it, then Jay would have the option of living with us.

"The thing is, if we live in a house, my reason for not being able to live with my kids no longer stands," he says wistfully. "I'd feel bad if I had someone else's child living with me, because why can't my kids be with me then? Maybe Elrik could …" he trails off, and I still my reaction: Jay needs me more than Elrik needs you.

I don't even know if this is true. But it is true that fourteen-year-old Elrik is a lot more used to doing without Thor; it's been eight years since he left the family home. And that Thor is his father and never had the visceral physical connection and closeness his mother would have had with him.

But maybe Jay will get used to being without me too.

THE CROSSROADS

May 2017

Dare I write a poem for you? I know the first line already.
Everything has a beginning and an end.

~ Journal entry

When I met Thor, I knew that here was the deep connection I had been seeking for so many years. But our love was to go through several intense tests before we were able to commit to each other and create a safe container for our relationship.

As I travelled back from Into the Wild Festival in Kristen and Graham's van, all of us still on a festival high, Kristen's two young girls were chanting, "We like Thor, we like Thor". Graham put his two cents in: "Call Dylan now. Do it now, before you change your mind. Thor's far more right for you."

My circuits had been completely rewired by the 24 hours I'd spent with Thor, and I knew Graham was right. Though breaking up with Dylan seemed the completely obvious route to take, it was also scary, of course. I rehearsed it in my mind: "I've met someone, I'm sorry."

But as soon as I saw Dylan the next day, I knew I couldn't go through with it. As he walked through the door, I was taken off course by the amount of love I felt for him. When he immediately launched into everything he was worried about, I found myself holding him and stroking his hair.

In its own way, that relationship had a karma to fulfil. I remember looking at him on the banks of the River Ouse in Lewes one freakishly hot April day only weeks before, when the very clear message arose in my mind: "You have to love this man," like an assignation. And I followed it.

So now, on my sofa, I laid the words like poisonous jewels on his lap: "I've met someone I feel a strong connection to, and I want to explore this further," but I didn't say that it was over. I held my breath and waited for the fallout.

But he only looked at me steadily with his brown eyes. "OK, so you want to be open?" Polyamory (consensually open relationships, sometimes called 'conscious non-monogamy') is fairly common in our friendship circles, and many relationships go through at least a phase of it. We'd had a casual conversation about this possibility shortly before heading our separate ways to different festivals – his suggestion, as there were other women he felt drawn to – but he'd soon retracted, saying he'd not be able to handle the jealousy on his side.

"Yes," I replied, the relief coursing through my veins, replacing the truth serum I'd thought I was going to deliver. Now that he'd said we could be open, I felt I couldn't tell him it was over and that I wanted this new person to be my partner instead. Partly this was because I felt so loving towards him. My heart opening with Thor seemed to have the unexpected side effect of deepening my connection to Dylan. But it was also because he was in such a vulnerable place in his life: struggling to find work and a proper place to live, in early recovery from a weed addiction. Maybe it was cowardly, but I couldn't do it to him: I just couldn't cut him loose.

And that was that.

He didn't ask me what I'd done, physically, with Thor: to my dual guilt and relief, he seemed to trust me to stick to our arrangement that only non-sexual cuddles were permissible with others. And again, I couldn't bring myself to tell him the truth: that while Thor and I had not had sex, things had got pretty intimate over the course of the day we spent together. That I'd had the most powerful sexual experience of my life with him – without even touching.

After our visit to the yew tree, Thor had invited me back to his van for a hot chocolate. This was possibly the best hot chocolate anyone had made me, containing Green & Black's cacao powder and almond milk. We sat on opposite ends of his maroon-striped sofa – the very one I'm now writing on – while staring into each other's eyes. We'd virtually not stopped doing that since we first connected. Kristen joked later that when I'd introduced the two of them at the evening's entertainment, the beautiful folk-singer Martha Tilston, we'd given our attention to Kristen for mere moments before locking back into our mutual gaze. "I was like, hello! I'm here!" she laughed.

Our cups forgotten on the windowsill, we dropped into the tangible feeling of the cords between us, the growing, pulsing, living ribbons of energy that connected us as strongly as wire. I started to feel something rise up from my pelvis, into my belly, moving up my spine. I began to jerk and shake, and he was having the same response outwardly. I knew it was happening for him inside too.

The feelings rose in intensity. It felt as if we were merging, our energetic bodies moving into each other in a mutual penetration. It was an ecstasy that never quite reached a crescendo, just kept building and building. I couldn't believe I was feeling this intimate with someone I'd only just met; but at the same time, I was so in the moment that it was all just happening.

"It was energetic sex," I said in amazement to my friend Carrie the next time I saw her. "That's the only way I can describe it."

Strangely, the actual bodily sexual connection between us was much more clunky and awkward. When I'd finally kissed him on that sofa, as we were lying there cuddling, it was far from an instant click, and later, it took a while for us to find our sexual flow. But the energetic template we experienced on the sofa that day created a foundation that we both knew would eventually manifest in reality: and, with patience, it did.

But I'm getting ahead of myself. At this point in the story, I was still in a weird triangular situation. The poly arrangement with Dylan lasted only 48 hours before he got too jealous and declared that he wanted me all to himself. Feeling guilt-ridden and not wanting to put him through pain, I stuck to the loyal path and agreed to just be friends with Thor.

I felt I needed to see it through with Dylan, even though he was slipping up on his sobriety and his ex-girlfriend was causing more and more problems. Meanwhile, it had turned out that Dylan and Thor knew each other from crewing at festivals and had even met up to play music together, which felt weird.

I was both disappointed and relieved at the end of my polyamory experiment: disappointed because I'd been curious about being in a poly relationship for years, and relieved because, in truth, my nervous system couldn't handle it all. I felt ungrounded and frazzled after seeing the two of them over the space of two days and kept getting distracted by thoughts of whichever one I wasn't currently with. Perhaps I was, as Thor said when he first visited me, really a one-man woman. Not that I'd given it enough time to really know for sure.

Either way, Thor said that on that first visit, two days after Into the Wild, he'd felt the energy of Dylan palpably in my bedroom: "I kept wanting to say, your partner's put some voodoo in this room."

Then, while Dylan was away on a Buddhist meditation retreat, Thor, who I'd stayed in occasional contact with, invited me to come to a Rainbow Gathering for a day: a drop-in, month-long hippy camp he'd been staying at for weeks. When I told Dylan, his already wavering commitment to the retreat morphed into complete abandonment and he announced he was going to come too. "I miss you." Me telling him I was still drawn to Thor didn't help the situation; of course, he wasn't going to let me go alone. And so, the stage was set for an episode of "Hippy Eastenders".

In retrospect, it was bound to be a drama and allowing the two of them to be in the same space was a stupid idea. But at the time, I must have been in a mixture of denial and poor boundaries: I wanted to see Thor and I felt it wasn't my place to tell Dylan not to come to Rainbow. It's as if I was letting the chips fall where they may because I couldn't take full responsibility for the situation.

Arriving at the clump of tents in a green valley just outside Brighton, I was feeling a little adrenalised: I'd come with Jay, Kristen and Graham, and their girls, and there was a lot going on, especially when two members of the community camp shouted at me for breaking the no-phones rule – of which I wasn't aware – by taking a phone call from Dylan to give him directions.

I was grateful for the time to connect with Thor before Dylan's arrival. Seeing him after the long gap, I was a little taken aback at first: he didn't seem as attractive as I remembered. His nose was sun-burned and he was wearing what I then thought of as a funny hat. But as soon as we sat together and I leaned back into his arms, I felt 'home' again.

Since Dylan still hadn't got to grips with the directions, Thor offered to meet him at the gate to guide him down to the site. I felt this was probably a bad idea, but again, didn't say anything, convincing myself I was just trusting in life – but really, it was more a case of not listening to myself.

I found out later that Dylan responded to Thor's Rainbow-style greeting of "Welcome, brother" with "Don't you come with that hippy bullshit. I know what you're doing. You stay away from her. You let her come to you, okay?" and that all the way along the path, he'd continued to verbally attack him.

But at the time, I had no idea how hostile Dylan was being towards Thor. I was just happy to see Dylan after our week apart. We embraced and sat together, staring into each other's eyes for a long time. As he started to play the guitar he'd brought along, I glanced down at the fire and saw Thor sitting there with some of the others. He was staring at us, and I looked away quickly. But in a couple of minutes, I saw to my alarm that he was getting up and coming towards the top of the rise where we were sitting.

He sat down next to me, fastening his gaze on mine. Dylan continued to pluck at his guitar, but I felt his presence acutely on my other side. I couldn't maintain eye contact with Thor for very long; his unwavering stare was too intense. I broke away and lay down on my back, feeling very uncomfortable but trying to ground my energy. "Are you okay?" Dylan asked. "Yes," I said automatically, but he didn't buy it.

"What are you doing?" he said, turning to Thor. "You're making her uncomfortable. I told you, stay away from us."

Uh-oh. My gut twisted.

My memory of what happened from that point on is hazy, but I know it got very ugly, very quickly. Dylan was hurling accusations at Thor and Thor was listening patiently and not responding in kind. In fact, he barely said anything, which only infuriated Dylan further. His rage seemed to rise in direct proportion to how calm Thor was. Karuna, an older woman we all knew, tried to mediate, but Dylan practically shouted at her, "He's trying to hit on my girlfriend!" Meanwhile, I could see the worried frowns of Kristen and Graham, who were sitting on the other side of Thor, a little distance away but able to witness the whole scene.

I was called away by the needs of the kids and left with relief, looking back over my shoulder to see Dylan gesticulating wildly. I'd only once seem him so angry before, when he and his now-ex, while still together, had a huge argument in front of everyone at a kirtan gathering. He'd lost control at one point and begun to shout, and I remember feeling quite alarmed, though not frightened. But this time, I was directly involved, something Karuna, the would-be mediator, was quick to point out. "I think this has something to do with you," she said disapprovingly as I galloped past to the children's fire where Jay and the girls were playing. A stab of guilt and shame.

The argument went on interminably: eventually, I saw Dylan get up with his guitar and stride over to me. I stepped away from the happily playing kids. "I'm sorry," he said, shaken. "I know I'm freaking out. But I told him to stay away from you. He's crazy. Coming up and staring at you like that ... what was he thinking?"

He explained what had happened between him and Thor at the gate. "The thing is, I realised on the retreat that I've really fallen in love with you. I'm sorry to tell you this way, but I love you."

Despite everything – how much of a tosser he was being, my own feelings for Thor, the whole mixed-up mess – in that moment I felt a wave of love and compassion for him. "I love you too," I said, and we hugged for a long time.

But only a moment later, he went back into his battle. "I mean, did you feel uncomfortable with him staring at you like that?"

"Yes."

"Will you tell him that? Because he doesn't believe me."

"Okay," I said reluctantly. Somehow, I found myself walking with Dylan, back to where Thor was. But once we were there, I was mute, stunned by the awkwardness of it all.

Finally, Dylan said, "She has something to say to you."

Thor looked at me expectantly.

"I did feel uncomfortable when you were looking at me," I mumbled, feeling like a child forced to apologise. It was beyond awkward.

But it was Thor who said, "I'm sorry."

Before I knew what was happening, the argument had started up again. "You see? You've made her uncomfortable," Dylan insisted. And so it went on.

People sitting around the fire were starting to look over at us, and I could sense the discomfort radiating from Kristen and Graham. "You're upsetting people," Thor said, still in a calm tone. "Let's go and have this discussion privately."

Eventually, Dylan agreed, and I sighed in relief as they walked an inaudible distance away and sat down together. At one point, it even looked as if they might be getting somewhere, talking softly together. But then I saw Dylan lose it again, exploding into shouts and gesticulations.

"He's a dangerous man, Morgan," Kristen said fervently. "He's not safe. He's behaved so badly ... and Thor's been amazing. He's just been amazing."

Graham agreed, and they both expressed their concern for me. "I think you should ask him to go home," Kristen urged. "Shouting that way – if he can act like that, it's only a matter of time before he does the same with you."

I knew she had her own history with frightening, violent behaviour from men, which was probably slanting her view. I couldn't imagine Dylan shouting at me; we hadn't had one argument. But I felt pressured, and also ashamed of Dylan's behaviour. "Okay," I relented. "I'll send him home."

At that moment, Dylan returned from his discussion with Thor, throwing his hands up in the air and saying, "He's crazy, I can't get through to him."

I swallowed. "I want you to leave."

He looked at me for a moment, then said in a measured tone, "OK," and started to pack his stuff up.

"OK, if that's what you really want. Is it what you really want?" He stopped packing and looked intently at me.

"No," I said, feeling like a fool.

I looked down at the communal fire and saw Thor's back. The powerful pull I felt towards him was coloured by an odd mixture of sadness and fear: I knew I was at a crossroads moment. I could easily say goodbye to Dylan and stay the night there, with Jay, in Kristen and Graham's spare tent, give myself time to feel more into this connection with Thor. But I just knew, deep in my bones, that he was going to turn everything in my life upside down. And I was scared.

I went home with Dylan, after giving Thor an awkward hug goodbye in which I could feel his enormous sadness. "He's heartbroken," Dylan commented on the way to his car, able to be sympathetic now that he 'had' me again. "And I understand why. After all, I'm in love with you too."

A day later, Thor and I had a 'closure' chat on the phone. He felt he had been out of integrity getting involved with me when I was in a relationship and he gently asked me if I thought I had been in integrity, to which I answered, no, I had not. He told me he had found the whole Rainbow episode incredibly painful and traumatic but had received some healing and listening afterwards from an empathetic community member, which helped him integrate the experience. We agreed to "let things go for now", but at the time, I thought that was just a euphemism for the end of our story.

My relationship with Dylan, briefly invigorated by his newfound 'love' for me, fell apart only a couple of weeks later when his ex-girlfriend Sharon threw one too many spanners in the works by throwing him out of the Colourfest volunteer team because he and I intended to go together. In the end, he chose her.

Angry and grieving, I spent a lot of time feeling into whether it was the right thing for me to still go to Colourfest when I knew that Dylan would be there rekindling with his ex. I also knew Thor would be there – he had told me he would be on the crew – and that this was a chance to reconnect with him, but I wasn't sure I could take the pain of seeing Dylan and Sharon together.

I had been attached to him, after all, and I felt jilted and hurt. But Marion was going, and our kids played well together. I had been looking forward to Colourfest's nourishing mix of devotional singing, dance, good bands and time in the woods and I didn't want to give it all up just because of Dylan.

I tested the waters by texting Thor, figuring that his response would be my deciding factor. Perhaps this wasn't very 'empowered woman' of me, but I needed to know. I told him that Dylan and I had split and asked him if he'd like to talk on the phone sometime soon. I also asked if he was at Colourfest. His response, received in the middle of a 5Rhythms dance class where I was trying desperately to get into my body and not think about it but failing to refrain from checking my phone, sent my heart into explosions of butterflies: "Hello beautiful. I'm sorry to hear about the end of your relationship with Dylan. Yes, I'm at Colourfest. Would like to talk. Signal bad here – be better if you came here. It's going to be a good one."

NIGHT LIFE: BELONGING

A dream, November 2017, first days in the van

Jay is driving a car. I am sitting next to him, heavy with anxiety because surely, he cannot reach the pedals. I look down and yes, his feet are too far away. I can somehow keep control over it all by just watching, though. I can see if he is OK. So far, he is, but my God, the anxiety.

A dream, December 2018

Jay and I are in the Barcombe house. I feel unsettled and strange, like the house isn't the right place for me to be and I'm scared to be there alone, just as I was at Christmas. I am failing to organise him being at school and making a mess of getting his sandwiches right – I can't find the mayo. I keep trying to drive somewhere and getting a bit lost and then, suddenly, I remember the view from the top window, the fields, and think clearly, Aah, that's where I want to go.

When I wake, I remember that I threw away his marmite and mayo with sadness when I had to get rid of everything from the Lewes house. I stare at a photo on the altar, of Jay and myself when he was ten months old. He's in a sling, content against my body, in an autumnal moment next to a lake, frozen in time. I look so much younger. His happiness radiates out from his smile and his body language. I look out the van window at the blue sky and think, Yes, this is what it's about, this is why I've chosen this, it's about nature … and something beyond this that I can't even put into words.

A dream, January 2018

My own parents have taken over the care of Jay, ostensibly to give me time to focus on my work. However, they soon move from a supportive role to being 'the parents' and no longer take my input on key decisions about his welfare. I feel like an imposter in my own house, where we all live together, and the guilt at my own selfishness in letting go of my primary caregiver role is crippling.

Another dream, January 2018

I wake up around three-thirty a.m. from a dream in which I'm desperately trying to call my sister to resolve things, but instead reaching my Mom on the phone. She's irritated with me and won't let me through to speak to Robyn. Thoroughly awake at once, I start composing emails to Robyn in my head. By five a.m. I am vividly imagining a scenario where I move in with Marion and Zeb in London while I get on my feet, find a job, go to 5Rhythms classes and have a totally different, thoroughly urban, life.

A dream, February 2018

Luke is drunk and Jay tells me so in a matter-of-fact way, like it happens often. I realise, in the dream, that I've made a terrible mistake letting him live with his father full-time.

A Dream, date unknown

A few nights before visiting Jay, I dream about going to see him. He is living with another family who seem to have unofficially adopted him, and he has a female 'sibling' as a playmate. I feel enormous joy at seeing him so happy and settled, seeing that I can let him go with confidence, knowing he's in the best place possible. But underneath my relief is a sad undercurrent of He's better off there.

A Dream, June 2018

I am sharing the house that Jay lives in with his father and grandparents but am clearly the odd one out. I discover that they have made plans for the weekend to go to a seaside resort without me. I desperately try to fill my empty weekend with a 5Rhythms workshop but when I find one online, it suddenly turns out to be a kids' fairground experience.

POWER AND LOVE

January 2018, Salisbury – Glastonbury

It's the first week of our six-week exploration through the South-West of England. This time, we've started our journey from Salisbury. After so many times setting off from Sussex, it feels like we're finally making progress.

We recently survived a night of frightening storms, the first of its kind since I've lived in the van. I was sure the van was going to tip over, more than once.

Now, everything feels fresh, new, and exciting. I put my phone aside, tired of flicking through Instagram, ready to be available to the now. The jealousy and sense of unfairness I felt just a few moments ago, seeing pictures of my friend Karen's fancy, perfect newly converted van, evaporates instantly as I feel the promise of a new adventure.

After a sunset walk at Old Sarum, the spooky ruins of a hill fort that was the centre of South-West England in the Iron Age, we stop at the base of Silbury Hill. Turning off the engine, Thor says casually, "There's a lot of anger in Silbury Hill. Can you feel it?" I don't give this much weight, but within minutes we get into an argument, for reasons that are typical. Thor is angry with me for making us stop in a noisy place with a lot of passing traffic because I was having a blood sugar crash or a 'food panic', as he sometimes calls it jokingly, and simply couldn't wait a few more minutes to eat. I get fed up and let my anger out physically in front of him for the first time, even throwing an empty water bottle across the room deliberately.

Instead of retaliating, he looks at me with bright, excited eyes. "Finally. Some real anger from you. Come on, have at it. Express it some more." But the moment is already gone for me. As soon as I express anger, it seems to leave me, and I feel self-conscious or start giggling. I learned as a child that anger was scary, that it meant people getting hurt and that I was not allowed to be angry – only my father had that right.

It's too windy for a proper walk up the hill, but we do get out the van and have a little amble around. "Look at this," I call to Thor, and show him a natural heart shape in the bark of a tree. Present moment or not, I snap a picture for Instagram.

The next day, before heading to our next destination of Glastonbury, we stop for a brief firewood-gathering walk in West Woods near Avebury, which I'm happy to return to after our Christmas time retreat there.

As we head into the woods, Thor explains the Native American Indian way of walking so you can track animals without alerting them to your presence. "Press down with the front of your foot first. That way, you sense the ground and don't step on twigs to make a noise. This is how I managed to sight a deer and a hare in the woods around Stonehenge." We try it for a while, but I find it tricky with wellies and high mud levels.

Every now and then, Thor picks up a piece of dead wood and smashes it down on a tree stump or a half-rotted tree, each time releasing a guttural grunt. When we reach another moss-covered tree stump, he hands me a big, heavy piece of wood. "Here. You can let some anger out. Now, it's heavy, but if you use your wild animal nature you won't hurt yourself. You might have to smash it in a few goes. Just feel the wildness all around you and tap into that."

I feel nervous. We've been talking lately about the need to channel my anger more: the dormant rage that's coming up from its hiding-place, as I feel safer to express myself. Now, I'm not sure if I'll be able to tap into this wild energy or have the strength to do it without hurting myself. In an instant, the usual fearful self-conscious thoughts ran through my head: Will I make myself look stupid? Will I fail to do it unselfconsciously and will that be obvious?

It's the same sense of vulnerability I used to get as a school-age child, doing P.E. – having to launch a ball over a net and knowing I had no chance whatsoever of doing it. But this time, the feeling passes. I know that I am loved and that I can't, truly, get this 'wrong'.

So, I stand for a moment and, instead of conjuring up past injuries – although that would've been easy enough to do – I imagine a bear. No, a wolf is better. Like the line in one of the only three songs I've ever written, "I know the wolf inside me will devour everything".

This wolf is ruthless and strong and all at once I feel it in me, animating my muscles and skin. In the moment it fully takes hold, I let go of my mind and swing the piece of wood like an axe. A big piece breaks off against the stump, then another, and then another. Vaguely, I'm aware of making noises, but they are coming out of me without volition. I hear them as if they are coming from someone else and I feel satisfied: I've done it. I was wild.

And then, in that moment of awareness, the spirit of the wolf is gone, and I find myself standing there, arms hurting, looking at what I've done.

Thor comes up to me, holds my arms gently but firmly, asks me to look at him. "Now come back to your rational self," he says. "Feel the animal energy there, and feel them both there, but know that you're in control, your rational self is in control." I feel myself fully returning, while the animal part of me gradually fades in my awareness.

In a couple of minutes, we carry on with our walk, but I realise suddenly that I've left my ash staff behind, the one Thor helped me make when we were last here. I feel a momentary panic and sadness, convinced I've left it under the little beech tree we sat under earlier like two hobbits in love. Unlike all the bare winter trees around it, this one had a golden blanket of leaves on its lower branches, making it look like a magical way-shower. But I don't feel confident that I could find it again in this thick forest.

To my surprise, the staff is lying next to the stump where I released my wolf anger. I pick it up, as relieved as if I've rediscovered an old friend.

We head back the way we were going, and this time a long thorny plant catches my coat and pulls me back insistently. I stop, annoyed, and remove it impatiently. "Let's go back," Thor says in that way that I've learned to trust, to know that he is acting from something important and instinctual.

Back at the stump again, he stops and stands opposite me. "What do you see?"

My brain freezes. I have no idea why I am back here, what I'm supposed to be seeing or doing. But then it comes clear: "It's a heart." I point at the stump, bright green with moss, where I found my inner wild. It's shaped like a heart, just like the Silbury Hill tree heart.

His face lights up. "What do you want to do?" This, too, is as obvious to me as it was unclear a moment before. "Stand on it." I go over to the heart and climb on top of it. All my self-consciousness is gone. I feel like an excited child with joy bubbling up in my heart. I'm holding my staff and all at once I feel like a queen, a bit like a child dressing up as a queen who suddenly finds that she is that.

I beam at Thor as he sits watching me on a tree opposite, and then I look up at the trees with their branches etching the dove-egg blue sky, the clouds drifting by like delicious portents of what is to come.

It's New Moon today, I remember as we walk on a few minutes later, heading back through the mud. A time for new intentions, a new cycle. Thor is excited by what has happened and eager to tell me his theory. "Our subconscious tries to speak to us all the time. And sometimes it comes through thoughts or the words of others, but sometimes it can't get through that way, so it acts through the outside world. So, your subconscious, your magical child, knew there was something else you needed to see back there. First, you left your staff so you'd go back and find it, but you didn't look, so it then needed to get your attention by pulling at you with some thorns."

He asks me to describe my experience in detail, and just as I'm explaining what being the Queen felt like, a branch scratches my cheek so badly that it draws tears – for a moment, I'm convinced it has drawn blood, too. Shame flares up in me – not from the fact that I've started crying, but because I have the thought that if everything in the animate world is reflecting my subconscious, the scratch must be saying I am giving myself airs and being far too arrogant, thinking I could be a Queen.

"Or," Thor suggests when I share this, "The scratch happened at a moment when you were doubting yourself as a Queen, and so nature was showing you that you were going off track there."

"Yes. I can see that. Like it was arresting me to a moment of presence, to see the knot I was getting myself into mentally."

Thor is impressed that I've been able to access the wild animal level of anger so quickly and easily. He describes having done the same process of using wood to let go of anger a while ago, when someone recommended the practice to him. "But I had to sit and meditate a long time to access that wild animal energy, and you seemed to just go straight into it immediately." I wonder if my embodiment work in 5Rhythms has helped me to be able to shapeshift into these spaces more easily. Either way, I feel encouraged that I can feel my anger as power and not be afraid of it.

*

The afternoon is mellowing into that pre-dusk laziness and we decide to go with it and have a nap. After sleeping and then making love, Thor is lying next to me, gently tracing different spots on my skin – the nape of my neck, the edge of my collarbone, an area just next to my left nipple. Each time, he tells me that he's found another very soft bit of skin. He encourages me to touch each area myself, and I do. "The key to touching yourself is to feel both the finger that is touching and the skin that is being touched," he says, and I sense another 'workshop' beginning – knowing how he would respond to me calling it that. "Don't call them workshops," he's said before. "'Cos then you'll get sick of being in a workshop all the time and start wanting to watch TV and be normal. It's just life."

Now he says: "Try it. Go into the finger, feel how lovely it is to feel this gorgeous soft skin ... Then be in your skin, feeling how delicious it is to have this lovely finger touching you."

I try it out, alternating between being the touched one and the one touching. It feels surprisingly pleasurable and real, even though I am doing the touching myself. Some areas even feel ticklish. I don't think I've ever generated a tickled feeling in myself before. Last year, I did a writing and embodiment online course where one of the exercises was to touch your hand with different objects; I'd found it excruciatingly boring and irritating. But this was different – I was actually feeling something.

"Now," he says, "Be both at the same time. Feel the pleasure in your skin from being touched, while you feel the finger touching, and let yourself receive that." After a few minutes, he adds, "This is a really good way to give love to your vulnerability – your inner child. Try it on your heart – stroke your heart and feel yourself receiving the touch and letting it go right into your vulnerability. And your vulnerability really feels that love from you because you just have so much compassion for that part of you and you really love it. Now be both at the same time – and let it all just flow, just surrender to it."

I find this a lot trickier. It's easy enough to feel love and compassion for my little girl, but to hold the focus on giving that while also being the girl receiving it is more difficult. But the workshop is moving on: "Now let's bring our hearts together and give to each other and receive too." We lie so our chests are touching, our hearts against each other. This comes more naturally to me. "Be the love that is expressing itself by giving to me and that is receiving from me, and let your vulnerability receive it too."

And then it comes: the surrender, the dissolving into love. It's real.

*

As we draw near to Glastonbury, I catch an unexpected glimpse of what looks like a young eagle, perched on the top of a gate, beautiful in the late morning light. It looks as if it's simply surveying the view, without any sense of tension or impending missions. I quickly point it out to Thor. "What does the eagle mean, do you think?" he says, turning the corner.

"Turning death into life," I speculate, "so, transformation. And far-seeing, having the bigger perspective. What do you think?" I ask.

"Well, birds of prey hover over a scene for a while and see the bigger picture before they strike. So, maybe it's watching out for danger, observing carefully."

"Hhmm," I respond. It doesn't feel like a warning to me. I've been in a bubby, exultant mood all day – but I'm learning to see that there's a continual expansion and contraction in this life, which was obscured by all the details of daily urban life. Sometimes – like today – when we're on the road, I feel so deeply contented looking out the window at the rolling hills, fields and blue sky that nothing else seems to matter:

Not doing my work, with its necessity and occasional anguish; not the money worries or the fact I don't technically have a home; not the fact that my sister isn't talking to me. All of it pales into nothingness beside the real, raw moment of being alive on this beautiful island. I feel reconnected with the pleasure and excitement I felt when I first moved to England and began to discover it all.

My thoughts drift back to what he's saying. "Glastonbury is the Mirror of Avalon. It shows you whatever is going on inside you at the time, wherever you're at. And you have to go at the right time for the magic it needs to give you. Remember, there were three times we didn't go to Glastonbury that we intended to go. First it was because we had to go back to Sussex for the

Barcombe house sit, then it was you having to go back to see Jay, then it was the storms that meant we had to park up somewhere sheltered."

Hearing his words, I feel a little apprehensive. The Mirror of Avalon. I wonder what will be reflected to me this time. Last time I was here – the only other time I've visited Glastonbury – was September 2015, when I was dating a much older guy called Dom.

We were totally unsuited to each other. We'd gone up for the weekend and done the 'tourist' thing, staying at an over-the-top fairy-themed guesthouse and a wall-to-wall white 'Angel House', all of which struck me as twee and uncomfortable. But I did have an otherworldly experience on top of the Tor. I felt as if I'd stepped into another time and space, one of power and mystery where I belonged and wanted to stay.

As we set off that morning, although I have a strong sense of faith in the synchronicity of the universe, I also know that life has a way of disrupting such trajectories and throwing me into a pool of despair only hours later. I determine to ride the wave, whatever it is, and not judge it or get caught up in it.

The Tor itself swings into view even though we're still some thirty miles away from the actual town, and I see for the first time that Glastonbury is indeed an island. It really is the Isle of Avalon. "The Tor's like a beacon that calls all who need its magic," Thor pronounces.

When we reach the park-up spot Thor usually uses, it's rammed with caravans. We park instead near the bottom of the Tor, only temporarily so Thor can access internet to do his remote programming work for a travel company. My energy has dipped and I'm desperate for a nap. "Don't panic about your tiredness," he says. "It's just how the energy of the place is affecting you." I assure him I'm not panicking but I know that resting will help me integrate into what's here, which I can already sense is intense.

When I wake up, I feel uncomfortable and restless and want to get on with doing some writing. He gets irritated with me for wanting to work while he's working, because the noise of my typing distracts him. "I've been driving and I haven't eaten and you just checked out and had a nap instead of thinking about what was needed," he complains.

There's a kerfuffle as he tries to find earphones to block out my typing noise.

Apparently, the sound of me drinking water from my bottle is now a disturbance too, so he tries to convince me to drink out of a mug instead. I refuse. I feel adamant that I am going to work now, because I want to, and I'm not going to be guilt-tripped out of it. After all, we agreed that our work has equal priority. But he seems to have forgotten this.

A bit later, I accidentally knock the curtain rail off from the bedroom. I anticipate a storm, but Thor is humorous about it and fixes it easily. I find myself joking, playing with him, rather than going into my usual apologetic, childlike demeanour when I make a mistake.

At one point, he says he wants to talk to me, and I say I am still working. It feels unusual – and satisfying. He starts joking about me being 'Miss Empowered Bum' and asks how he can serve me while I work: perhaps I would like my pussy licked. It's true: I do feel different since releasing my anger in the woods.

*

The next morning, we're going to go into Glastonbury town centre. This is our first excursion for some time into proper 'civilisation', apart from petrol stations and Tesco's, so I have my first go at washing my hair in the van. I've avoided the need to do this, so far, by washing it at friends' houses when I visit Jay, but it's reached that distractingly itchy point now.

We pour water into the washing up basin and Thor shows me his complete, precisely timed method. Just as you finish lathering up, you have to pour in a second batch of newly boiled water from the cooker for rinsing.

As I bend over the basin, I feel strangely comforted by the sensations of his fingers on my scalp: no-one has done this for me since my mom used to wash my hair in the bath. There's the familiar feeing of scrunching up my eyes to stop water getting into them – Thor intuitively passes me a towel – and being at the gentle mercy of someone's care for me. Maybe Wendy is right. Maybe this is a time in my life when I can regress a little, let myself be the child I didn't fully get to be because I was scared and troubled and sad so much of the time.

Before the slight bumpiness around my assertiveness yesterday, we had spent several days in a loved-up, close zone, our usual state when I return from a weekend away. We've been sharing so much togetherness that the worry about being 'myself' around him, that I faced so starkly only a week ago, seems like a distant memory. I feel safe. I'm off guard and don't foresee the fallout when I say, "Are you going to change those trousers?"

The multiply-stained tracksuit bottoms Thor has been wearing for days, if not weeks, on end, don't bother me on trips to Tesco while we're on the road, but somehow, I had expected him to wear 'proper' clothes when we went into the town itself.

"Why should I? You were perfectly happy with me wearing them before." Even then, with defensiveness creeping into his tone, I don't see how touchy this subject really is.

"Well, look at them, they're full of stains. You could wear your white trousers maybe?"

He retrieves those from the cupboard, only to find they're covered in mould from the damp that we recently discovered creeping into the van: the result of the extra condensation of two bodies breathing.

He gets out his red trousers instead, muttering with annoyance. "They're too tight around the ankles." I sympathise, but in my head I'm adamant: the tracky bottoms are just not suitable for outside the van. In a town like this, a gathering place for hippies, spiritual seekers and artists, I'm more than likely to bump into people I know, and even if I don't, I have standards.

The truth is, I'm afraid it will reflect on me. And Thor is someone I'm proud to be seen with. He's beautiful, and if he wears those trampy trousers no one will know it. Yes, it's image bullshit, but it's been so long since I was in a happy, loved-up, secure relationship couple with someone I'm also proud to be seen with. Can't I enjoy it a little?

While he's finishing getting ready, I grab my own scruffy Doc Martens, spattered from numerous muddy walks, to give them a quick wipe down. "What are you doing?" Thor says fiercely, marching over to me at the sink. "You can't clean those in the sink. That's disgusting." And again: "What are you doing?"

Only, I don't remember him saying those words – he has to tell me later, because I go into a total freeze response and am conscious only of his anger, not of the content of our exchange.

"What?" I say vaguely, not looking up from my task. "I need to clean them ... don't worry, I'll clean the sink after."

"You can't get mud in there, that's unhygienic! And dog shit! For fuck's sake!" He's shouting now. He takes the boot from my hand and throws it across the room. It's not aimed at me, and it doesn't land near me, but now I am really scared.

"This is how you clean them. Come outside now." I follow meekly, still in a state of freeze. He shows me how to clean my boots in a relatively clean puddle, using an old sponge. It's humiliating. I feel like a publicly told-off child; I glance around to make sure no one is watching. It reminds me of playing Putt-Putt with my grandfather, when he was determined to show me how to tee off properly, taking my hands and making me do it. I didn't want to do it; I don't want to do this now.

Back in the van, he takes my shoulders. "Let's clear this before we go into town."

"We can do it on the way," I reply, looking down at the ground, not wanting to talk to him face to face. But he insists: "Just vent, just say to me whatever you need to. You go first," he says.

I express my upset, but it's robotic, distant; there's no real emotion in it. I've closed down out of self-protection. He is quick to own that his reaction to me cleaning my boots was an over the top one triggered by my perceived criticism of his clothes. He shares that a previous girlfriend was happy for him to be scruffy when they were in a field, but the minute they were in a town she changed her tune and wanted him to dress differently.

We go back and forth a couple of times and it feels civil enough for us to continue our mission. I feel little residue as we walk into town, holding his hand without effort. The moment of the boot flying across the room, and the sound of his raised voice, has been tucked away in the place where scary things go.

Our first stop is the Goddess Temple. Last time I visited Glasto, it wasn't open, and I was disappointed, but now I feel a little nervous as we look up at its purple door, preparing to go in. Despite my long acquaintance with ritual and religion, having grown up Christian and visited many Spanish cathedrals on the Camino, I still find such spaces intimidating. I sense that there's a proper way to behave, a reaction I'm supposed to be having, and I'm unsure of both, which often conspires to make me knock things over, say the wrong thing, or need to blow my nose at an inappropriate moment.

Sometimes, I simply feel awkward, like I don't belong, and find myself devoid of any kind of spiritual connection while others seem to be having rapturous experiences.

Thor takes hold of my upper arms, looking a bit intense. "Now just remember, when you go in there, it's made with good intention. There is some ego personality stuff going on there, but it was created with a good intention. Try to stay open." This hardly helps my apprehension, but I nod and resolve to be as open as I can.

From the moment we step in, the atmosphere is overwhelming to me. I read disapproval on the face of the intimidating-looking older man who guards the entrance to the space as I take, as usual, ages to remove my boots and winter paraphernalia.

Thor and I split off in different directions. At first, I sit at the altar with the amethyst theme, but I feel too exposed there, with the other meditators able to watch my back. I feel frustrated with the resurgence of my tendency to see everyone as a potential threat, even in a meditation space. But I remind myself that this is just because I'm in a new, unknown place, not yet registered to my nervous system as safe. I approach a circle of standing straw goddesses, which feels a bit more inviting with its beautifully designed cushions spread around, and sit down to meditate there.

Usually, it takes me a while to still my thoughts enough to access a meditative state. Here, in the goddess temple, the energy is thick with a presence that takes me and drops me deep into this space with an immediacy that's almost shocking. I stay there for some time, but I notice that I am still uneasy on a visceral, physical level and can't quite settle there.

Every now and then, I open my eyes to check on the others: Thor sitting on the floor in the front of the main circle, a middle-aged woman in purple sitting on a straight-backed chair, the old man near the door, who I find out later is the space-holder and isn't just opening his eyes periodically to judge everyone. A young couple enters and the woman, pretty with curly red hair and a gentle demeanour, sits opposite me. We smile a bit awkwardly at each other, then close our eyes dutifully again.

I feel deeper into what this presence is. It speaks to me as raw, mighty power, as an ancient goddess in the temple demanding a high price: nothing less than absolute obedience. I search for the comforting, nurturing, mother side of the goddess that I'm so familiar with from Red Tents and other women's spaces. But there's nothing but this heavy power, dragging on me like an undertow. A power that offers no refuge.

Maybe, I reason to myself, I don't need that mother presence because I've been cultivating her so much inside me; I mother myself on a daily basis, often several times a day, drop into my pelvic bowl and bless it, hold myself when I am scared or feel vulnerable, say comforting words to my inner child and hug her to me.

But after a few minutes, it's clear to me that I don't need or want to be in this place any longer; that there's nothing for me here. I do not belong. I get up and make my way to the door, glance over at Thor, and slip out after the interminable re-assembling of my winter weather shields. As I do this ritual, I read the posters on the wall: feminist meetings to discuss cultural appropriation and inclusion; moon rituals; something going on that very night, a meditation led by a High Priestess to 'meet the goddess'.

I remember a time when all of this was highly appealing to me: I felt drawn like a bee to nectar by the mystery and glamour of long silver and purple cloaks, incantations and cauldrons; I used to collect sets of tarot cards and crystals as if my life depended on them. Now, I feel nothing but a mild curiosity and a slight repulsion.

When Thor eventually joins me outside, he says, "I thought you might be resistant." My heart droops at his disapproval, but I say nothing.

We peruse the crystal shop, where I buy him a heart-shaped necklace made of preselite, the grey-green-blue stone from the inner circle of Stonehenge, while he goes to retrieve his forgotten hat from the temple. After a bit more browsing in town, including the African shop where Thor buys another shamanic rattle, our last stop is the White Spring opposite the Chalice Well Gardens.

I expect it to be a pumped water source on an outside wall, like the Red Spring we went to the night before, but it's a full-on experience. A dark, candle-lit chamber with the continuous sound of running water and shrines in each corner of the room in honour of mainly female water deities, with the exception of the Cernunnos figure representing the male in the far right corner. As we walk in and go straight to the feminine shrine in the left corner, where it feels peaceful and beautiful, I feel a sense of wonder and magic.

After a little while, Thor leads me to the Green Man corner. It's here that the sounds and the darkness start to combine to create a feeling of disturbance in me. There's a naked man roaring in one of the bathing areas and suddenly the noise of the continually running water seems sinister.

Feeling vaguely panicky, I decline Thor's offer to take my shoes off with him and walk up to the fountain, getting my feet in the water. I wait respectfully while he does this ritual, then decide to return to the first feminine shrine, where I felt so safe. But there's a woman standing in front of it, completely blocking my access. She stays there, unmoving, and I wonder what this means, that my only place of safety in a space that is feeling scary to me is inaccessible. Something snaps, and I decide to leave.

A few minutes later, Thor follows me out and asks me about my experience. When I tell him I liked it at first but then found elements of it scary, he responds, "You really react to these places, don't you? I forget how I used to feel when I first started going to places like this."

Even though his tone is kind, I feel patronised, and remember his comment when we went to the Goddess Temple, that I was 'in resistance'. But I keep silent, not knowing how to verbalise what I'm feeling.

It's time for us to say goodbye – it's twenty minutes until I meet up with my online friend, Neil, at a local café, and Thor returns to the van. "What's wrong? You seem like you don't want to be close," he says as he draws me to him for a goodbye kiss. "Nothing's wrong," I say, but the moment I walk off down the street alone I feel a humming sense of relief and freedom. This is the first time I've gone off on an individual social engagement since I moved in with him.

I've only met Neil once before in the flesh, briefly at a festival, but we've been chatting online for a while. More recently, I joined his self-love online group, where we got to know each other a bit more, even sending each other some voice clips to share our processes. I turn up a few minutes early and get myself a decaf almond latte. My relief at being off the heavily-vibed high street turns into unease at the surrounding patrons, an odd paranoia that I don't fit in with my beanie hat and long corduroy brown coat.

When Neil, a man of medium height with round cheeks, knowing brown eyes and a neat beard, arrives, I'm nervously chattery, asking too many questions and feeling out of practice at socialising with anyone but Thor.

He raises an eyebrow when I tell him that I've been to both the Temple and the Spring today. "It's quite intense," I acknowledge, suddenly desperate to have someone validate my experience of it all being a bit too much. "It is," he says, and when I go on to explain my experience of the energy in the temple, that it's all about power, he says, "That's exactly what it's all about, there. A lot of my clients have been involved in the Temple, and that's been their experience."

And then I do the thing I often do, that I'm not proud of: I share a bit too much about my intimate relationship with someone I don't know very well. "My partner thought I was being resistant, because I didn't enjoy the Temple much."

"Or," Neil responded, "You were bang on with your sense of what the energy is there, and you moved away out of a sense of what's right for you."

Just under an hour later, he invites me to get some food at the café but, already feeling talked out, I feel the pull back to the van to make some dinner so Thor and I can have the option of going to the ashram for some chanting. The ashram, and the Chalice Gardens are the only places in Glastonbury town that I feel really good in. I wrap it up and leave, feeling relieved.

When I get close to the van, I get a text from Thor saying "Have you seen the moon?" just as the crescent sickle swings into view. I smile and let myself in.

But immediately I know something is wrong. His usual warmth is absent and he seems jumpy. He asks me what my meet up was like, what we talked about, and then says testily, "I thought you were meeting to talk about 5Rhythms. Or Ayahuasca." I'd been considering doing an Ayahuasca – plant medicine – ceremony for some time, and had told him Neil knew about these.

"Well, we did talk about Aya a bit, but you know how conversations are – you end up talking about what you talk about," I say lamely.

"I don't know anything about this guy. Why were you meeting up with him? Who is he? You say you met him online. But I don't know anything about this."

"I told you. I mentioned meeting with him a few times." I'm genuinely puzzled.

Then we get to the core: "My heart started hurting from the time you were meeting him and carried on until the time you must have left." His eyes look pained and distant. "Why would that be? Why would my heart be hurting?"

Even though I'm 100% positive that I have zero sexual or romantic interest in Neil and that he sees me only as a friend, I swing immediately into defensive mode. And, again, say perhaps too much. "Maybe that's because we were talking a bit about the different experiences you and I had in the Goddess Temple. He felt that I was right about the power stuff. So maybe you felt uncomfortable with me sharing that."

He says nothing, and it all starts coming out. "Sometimes I feel like you frame my experience of things within your own way of looking at them, as if yours is the template of how it 'should' be. What you said about my reactions to the Goddess temple and the White Spring makes me think that you judge my experience as wrong and less evolved somehow. It's like you're telling me that I should be able to face and be in all these energies no matter how uncomfortable they feel to my sensitive field."

And so begin hours of intense processing, continuing into the next day. What I intend as a reassurance that I am not about to start cheating on him, backfires badly. He feels blamed, convinced that I think he's doing loads of stuff wrong.

Maybe becoming 'part of the furniture' to each other isn't always good.

The patterns we've learned from our childhood breathe in this familiarity: they love it, and they love to destroy everything.

"There's a distorted feminine power energy in Glastonbury and I think you've got hooked into it and just run with it," he says at one point. "Women find their power here and then they express it in a masculine way." My feminist hackles rise, but it's true – I have felt more empowered since we got here, doing more of my own thing within the van without consulting him, not swinging into a deferential manner when he's in a grumpy mood. And it feels good – but it's obviously shaking things up in our relationship.

He finally admits he was jealous of Neil, and I admit I was still upset by his angry explosion with the boots yesterday. We realise that we've been on a journey of exploring anger since I broke the piece of wood in West Woods and even before that, when we faced each other at Silbury Hill a couple of days ago.

"I want you to express your anger differently because I know our communication can be better than that, and I had re-traumatisation symptoms after the boot-throwing episode," I say.

"I've actually done a lot of work with my anger, and I would never hurt you," he responds. "I'm a safe person to explore this stuff with."

Maybe he's right. Maybe our journey together is partly to work out this anger stuff consciously; for me to face the fear of male anger and the original trauma and react differently this time, to resolve it in my body and mind. But I know it's not going to be an easy road. I'm so scared of ending up in an abusive relationship again, in a slippery slope of justification and denial.

When I share this with my friend Marion later, she says: "The power dynamics between men and women have been encoded in this way for generations and are never completely absent from male-female relationships: this sense that they can hurt us in ways we can't hurt them." This lands heavily with me, but I don't know what to do with it, so I put it to the side.

BEING THE GIRL

I unravel the texture of my aloneness and watch it catch the light, wonder why I no longer appreciate it in quite the same way as I did when I first gained free spaces of time. Why I want to devour more and more and more of it, drink alone-time like lemonade, spilling over and running down my cheeks all fizzy and full of sweetness.

A few mornings after the storm that was Glastonbury has passed and we've been recovering in a couple of watery nature reserves, I awaken with what feels like several inner children clamouring in my head. I take the time to give them the attention they didn't get when I was woken by an alarm, screeched into wakefulness each morning, and then dealing with Jay's resistance to every phase of getting ready for school.

There's the six-year-old me who used to sit on a rock in a forest with her Murdock-from-the-A-Team cap on, tapping into a mystery and magic she didn't know the name of. All she knew was that she preferred the feeling there, on that rock, to being with the family she was supposed to belong to.

On one of my previous Jay visits, when I stayed with my friend Carrie and her partner Tom, I was touched to hear Tom share about his experience with nature as a young child. "I realised that the seeds for my later exploration of nature, plant medicine and indigenous culture were sown by my childhood experiences of being in nature, in my garden. This feeling of immense peace. I didn't even know what it was, at the time. I couldn't have explained it to anyone, and I didn't try to. This experience of everything being one thing – it wasn't something that was happening to me as an individual, it just *was*."

When Tom said those words, something in me sounded a resounding YES, and I sensed strongly that this had been my experience too. I used to make up imaginary worlds in the back garden: flower fairies who visited the nasturtiums, a family of friendly moles that I convinced my friends actually lived there, and a place called Gloryville where the Morning Glories wove in and out of a patchy brick wall overlooking our neighbour's garden.

And now, I'm reconnecting with this magic, and it's no longer restricted to vanlife – it's seeping into my visits with Jay. Walking back from the local public swimming pool one weekend with Kristen, her girls, and Jay, my eye was drawn to a willow tree with a beautiful, perfectly shaped hollow near the top of it. I felt the tree's energy, and later I walked back to it on my own and spent some time receiving it. I knew there was something there for me – there always is. I can't put my finger on what it is, but it is there, and it feels special.

Today, there's another 'little me' present, an older one. She's a 15-year-old with zits and chubby cheeks and a Nirvana T-shirt who lies on her bed for hours listening to Smashing Pumpkins, feeding the emotional frenzy inside with lyrics like "I fear that I am ordinary, just like everyone, to lie here and die among the sorrows, drift among the days". She has no idea she'll be loved, one day; no idea that people will listen to her ideas.

I hold these younger versions of me and feel such love for them. They survived so much. I feel their experience as threads I don't want to follow home, but need to hold tight, anyway.

NIGHT LIFE: GUILT

Jay has gone off on his own to the shops. My instructions were for him to come straight back again so when he has been gone for a long time, I become anxious. I try to trace his steps, take a few wrong turns, and realise that the route is more complex than I realised. Now I'm starting to really worry about him, but to my relief, he returns. I feel guilty. I expected more of him than was right at his age.

When I wake up, I think about how bad I feel to be extending the two-week gaps between seeing each other to three weeks. It's a pragmatic decision: I simply don't have the funds to travel fortnightly – I've had no significant work for three months now – and the time it takes, and the organisation and strain involved in staying with different people and keeping Jay fed and occupied on those weekends without my own home base is taking its toll already. I know my limits.

My guilt is rooted in the fact that when he made his decision to live with his dad, he'd said to me, "I'm just going to be living with Dad in the week. I can see you every second weekend and Dad said he'll bring me to you in the week whenever I want."

I remember the moment clearly: he was standing in the kitchen looking at me hopefully and my heart was like lead from his very recent announcement that he had chosen to live with his Dad. It felt as if he was trying to reassure me.

What is happening now is so far from his expectations. Will he feel I've let him down?

Will he resent Thor and feel that he's taken me away, or that I've chosen Thor over him?

Will he feel he's made a mistake in his decision? Will he later, when he understands the financial implications of his decision – the fact that him moving out meant I lost all my government support and could no longer afford to rent a house – feel bad at what he's inadvertently set into motion with his choice?

Occasionally, when I've had to tell the story of my new domestic arrangement to another mother in my social circles, I would hear, "But how could you let him go?" And, so far, I always answered, "How could I not?" But now I wonder: am I letting him go further than his maturity is able to withstand? And what will be the fallout?

BOOKENDS

I am in the middle of my cycle, full of creative energy and desiring to fill pages and build my new website. But now is not the time, because we're travelling and there's lots to explore. We've been gathering geographical honey as we go along – Wiltshire Honey, Somerset Honey.

"Bookends" by Simon and Garfunkel comes on the random music shuffle. From the sofa, I see a Marauder caravan parked in front of a spindly but proud tree and next to it, a Black Pearl Kitchens & Bathrooms van, which we know belongs to a Stonehenge acquaintance of Thor's. A bank of cloud advances over the houses of locals whose opinion I wonder at but don't truly worry about, since we are one of several vans parked up on this road.

The sunlight glitters on the rain-created lake that's formed on the field opposite. I wonder if, like Simon & Garfunkel, I'll remember this as "a time of innocence", "a time of confidences".

*

Driving from West Hay Moor National Park to Bridgwater Bay Nature Reserve, Thor has the excitement of a little boy at the fact that we are finally exploring new territory. Up to now, we've either visited favourite spots of his that he wanted to show me, or gone together to places we both know a little – largely the former. But this is a spot he's unearthed from Google Maps and doesn't know at all. This is a place barren of past associations and memories of past lovers. Many times, my jealousy and insecurity has been triggered when I'd realise he'd had beautiful moments with other women in a particular stand of woods.

At Bridgwater, I go for a walk at sunset on the mudflats. Birds are flying like silver waves in their special formations, so beautiful it takes my breath away. The wind has passed over and everything is so still and peaceful. Suddenly, the strip of mudflat at the tide's edge turns into a golden stripe with the silver birds flying above it, a stunningly mystical scene, with the hulking blue-purple shapes of the island and the hills in the distance. I can't figure out why it's turned golden – it looks almost like sand dunes, like I'm in a desert. The array of stones on the shingle banks strikes me as beautiful candy in a candy box, the posh kind I used to get as a kid from my rich grandmother, pink and blue, purple and friendly.

Little pools of water glimmer between the rocks, bunches of seaweed sitting with eternal patience. It's a moment of sanctuary away from the near constant cosiness and closeness that Thor offers.

However, the presence of human civilisation and its attendant ugliness is impossible to fully escape. When we arrived here, at what we thought would be a seaside haven, the first thing we saw was a huge fuck-off tractor taking up most of the car park. Humans driving off the threat of nature with monsters of machinery. Here, banks of shingle have been erected to stop the land being taken over during floods. Thousands of pounds are spent on this endeavour of keeping the sea at bay, of stopping nature from having her way. This morning, when we were still in bed, the tractor came right up to the van and made an earthquake happen. But what initially appeared as an irritation ended up being an effective barrier to the strong winds that night.

On the way to our next destination, we have just a few miles to find washing water – and there are no garages en route. Luckily, we have something else to fall back on – churchyards, which sometimes have a water source to keep the graveside flowers going.

I'm assigned to search the next graveyard for taps while Thor looks in the churchyard itself. I'm triumphant as I immediately find watering cans and a hose. "You mustn't tell people about finding water in churchyards, though," he urges, "or loads of people will start living in vans because the main problem that puts them off is finding water."

This is often a concern for him and is the reason I'm forbidden to give away our park up spots. I've had to say no to friends with holiday vans, keen to pick my brains on good park ups.

Great Wood, where we'd hoped to make our home for the night to find shelter from the strong winds predicted, repels us with a pay and display car park. "Shit. It's locked in an hour's time," Thor grunts. We drive on, disappointed that our because our first foray into the unknown, off Thor's charted map of established park ups, has led to such a dead end. The encroaching dark brings a slight sense of urgency – it's after five p.m. by now – but I trust Thor and the winding road absolutely. There's a sense of security in the simple knowledge that we have our home on our backs, like tortoises. If worst comes to worst, we always have shelter and food, so I don't panic.

On the way, Thor tries to school me in finding likely park ups. "Expect to be told no a hundred times," he says, convinced I will find this difficult. But I know I will be so useless at it that I won't take it personally. And sure enough, another woodsy spot reveals itself further on. A bunch of cars are there already, with men in headtorches going out for a night walk. Thor does a wind direction check to decide which way to position the van, using his compass as another teaching point.

I start making videos for Jay. In this one, I show him the mudflats at

Bridgwater Bay and how very necessary my new pink wellies are as they sink into the swampy ground. I know my video can't possibly convey how beautiful the light is. But I need to do it. I need to stay connected, to let him know I am here and thinking of him. Somehow, we never seem to get a chance to talk about my travels during our chats.

The last video call we had was our second attempt in a few days – the signal wasn't good enough on the previous occasion. We soon ran out of words and Jay ended up making funny faces at me, me doing the same in return. Thor is much better at asking questions that inspire Jay to give answers – no matter how often he advises me not to ask questions that have a simple yes, no, or 'OK' answer, I always forget and run through the same things:

"How was school?"

"Did you have a nice weekend?"

FAERY RING

Our next stop is the Quantock Hills on the border of Exmoor. I'm fascinated by the red, clay-like soil and the cute little periwinkle-like green shoots that appear in clumps. On one of our walks together, Thor collects quartz stones along the way, sometimes wading through the river to get to them. He invites me to touch my staff into the water to draw the water energy, and I also follow my own little impulses, putting my staff in the confluence of two streams where a mini waterfall has formed.

We come to an oak tree and, feeling drawn to it, I suggest we sit there. Then that thing happens: I feel the tree move. We both do.

"Here you go," Thor hands me the stones he's been collecting, wet from the river.

"Connect the tree to the stones and connect the tree to the water," he suggests, and I go inside and do it. Dimly, I hear his voice: "Now swim with the water."

I feel myself float in the water, allowing myself to be carried along as if I'm actually in the river. It's so pleasant and peaceful; I could stay there forever. Then I feel the tree put its arms around me and hold me. The two energies of Earth and Water merge as one and it feels deeply right.

As Thor places the stones around me in a little fairy ring, I immediately feel a jolt of energy, strong but pleasant. Suddenly, he goes into the water, rolling his trousers up. He yelps with the cold and becomes, in an instant, feral and growling. I turn away, worried he'll want me to meet him in this energy, as he often does, but he soon calms down and leaves me in the peace of my faery ring.

Later, on the way back to the van, he shows me a bloodstone he's found in the river. "Maybe that's why I drew the ring around you, for protection from the energy I was in. This bloodstone reminds me of the dark energy of the Nazis". He recently shared with me about his fascination with the occult history of the Nazis, and the period where he delved deeply into accepting the 'Nazi part of himself'. As ever, his fascination with the shadow.

DISASTROUS DAYS

From the comments on my Instagram and Facebook posts, it seems that everyone is gleaning I'm leading a carefree lifestyle full of natural beauty and harmony. The truth is, sometimes it's just shit.

Even when it starts off well. One morning, while Thor's still asleep, I go for a beautiful solitary walk in the Quantock Hills. After communing with a circle of oaks, I come back and dip into the magical world of Deverry in my fantasy book while eating breakfast. We flow into a deeply connected and loving time together, then set off for Exmoor to do some errands.

Thor is pleased with me for locating, via Google search, an outdoor self-service launderette at a service station. But then it all goes wrong. We miss the 18kg washing machine by literally seconds when a guy in a 4x4 pulls up and starts putting his washing in just as we're gathering ours together. Thor goes into a mood, convinced that this means there's no room for his laundry (scant in comparison to my multiple skirts and pants – I've not yet adopted his van strategy of wearing the same clothes for a week). "Now I have to wear dirty clothes for another three weeks," he glowers.

Then we both need the toilet at the same time, but of course the service station has no public loo. The van's compost toilet is full up after I've gone, so he has to perform complex manoeuvres to shift its contents enough to make room.

The entire time I'm on the toilet, he's arguing with me about having too much laundry, and I vehemently point out the fact that he discouraged me from taking my own washing to my friend's house in London last month. Suddenly, annoyance turns to comedy and we both break into laughter.

We relocate to an appropriately named launderette called Bubbles in the town centre itself, and it turns out to have much more efficient dryers than the service station one, which failed to dry the 4x4 guy's copious amounts of bedding. Later, after the two-grocery-shop, I offer to treat us to fish and chips as it's getting too late to feasibly cook dinner and my blood sugar is plummeting.

The takeaway I locate with my superior Google Map skills is run by a vast Englishman with heavily tattooed arms. We laugh at the illustrated, off-colour jokes he has plastered all over his walls, especially, "I think I want to get back with my ex. Just kidding – I'd rather shit in my hands and clap".

"Do you like my sense of humour?" he says proudly. And when he asks us if we are local or passing through, Thor tells him enthusiastically, "It feels nice in here". I feel both touched and slightly embarrassed by his childlike openness, his lack of the self-censoring I rely on in my everyday communications. I hang back shyly, avoiding conversation.

We eat our fish and chips shivering on a bench in the square nearby, opposite a church and a cosy-looking pub we debate entering to have a lime & lemonade, since neither of us drinks alcohol. I feel its inviting warmth, its sense of 'normal people', then remember how my friend Ariane posted recently on Facebook about witnessing travellers being forcibly evicted from McDonalds simply because of the way they looked and dressed.

In the end, we decide not to go in, but agree that it's good to know we can.

On another disastrous day that ends well, we are travelling from our park-up just above Minehead to Exmoor. The problem we face is finding a sheltered spot when we know there's more strong winds ahead. The wind was so intense the night before that it rocked the van to the point where my heartrate increased every time a gust blew our way, convinced that we would be knocked over. Thor eventually invited me over to his end of the bed – we're now sleeping top to toe, to disturb each other less at night – for comfort and cuddles, but it still took me hours to fall back asleep again. Every time I started to drop off, another gust would gather strength. I started to feel angry at the wind after a while.

I seldom feel good on lack of sleep. In the morning, Thor wants to snuggle endlessly in bed, but he does sense my restlessness after a while and tells me to "go and beat up your laptop keys". Feeling resistant to writing, I say no, but a few minutes later change my mind and do just that. I write quite well, despite feeling like shit. But then I get a message from Luke alerting me to the fact that my tax return code has still not arrived. Shit. I'm going to be late with my return. So, without thinking, I immediately get on the phone to HMRC and multitask being on hold for ages while continuing to write.

It's a bad move. After 45 minutes of being on hold, I'm cut off halfway through security checks when the phone signal goes. Thor is hurt because I sprang out of bed, leaving him, and he sees it as me having cut off and gone into my weird productive mode. He tells me we are moving now and that we won't have signal, but he suggests that when we go into town to get some provisions, I can use the reliable reception there to accomplish my HMRC business. I reluctantly accept this compromise, resentful of our reliance on man-made inventions despite our attempts to be one with nature.

In town, he offers to do the shopping so I can carry on with my admin. I'm starving and we stop at a town carpark to have some food. All this time, Thor is being tolerant and patient. He even buys a pair of green stereo headphones for me, like the black ones he bought a few days ago. Later, he plugs my jack into his and shares his music with me, and I remember a film

I saw years ago where a new couple skips happily along the road plugged into the same music source – I thought it was very romantic.

It takes us hours of driving to find a suitable park-up. The moors are too open, and we'd be obliterated by weather there, while the more protected area near the river is too built up. We try a few spots by the forest, but they are either too muddy, risking us getting stuck, or it's impossible to get the van flat. Finally, we find a spot between stands of trees where it feels lovely. But as soon as we're in the van, it all comes out. "I've been doing everything today," he begins. "All the navigating, all the planning, the driving, the shopping, and you've just done your own thing. I feel like I'm just doing this all on my own."

My stomach plummets. Uh-oh. Here we go.

"You said it was ok for me to do my admin. You actively encouraged me to do it. And to do my writing. Then you react to it."

My mind races. What was I thinking with this crazy, fucked up experiment in the middle of winter? I am so ready to pack it in. The conflict between my needs as an individual and this whole notion of us being a couple on a mission together feels too bloody hard. Living with this impossible human being and realising all the ways in which I, myself, am impossible.

We try to talk it out, but it doesn't work. He walks out to get some air while I'm making chicken curry and when he returns, he frantically removes all the bedding and cleans the slats underneath with bleach. Tea tree oil has turned out to be ineffective with the mildew that's produced by two bodies breathing there. It's been causing us both to sneeze profusely at night, another source of sleep disturbance.

After dinner, we lie next to each other on the bed, exhausted, looking out the skylight at the moon, who keeps going in and out of the clouds. Every time she disappears, I feel the darkness and sadness come into my heart, and every time she comes out, my heart lifts. It seems to me like our love: when we're in the patterns and the triggers and the conflict, we can't see it.

PROPERLY TOGETHER

I get up just after sunrise and take in the slanting sun coming through the tall trees, sending shafts of light upwards. A puddle reflects the moving trees and the orange of the sun. I take the path through the trees to where the land opens out, into a vista of hills, green fields, and sea – and a rainbow spanning the sky, falling from the trees into the hills opposite, their brown and green merging with the rainbow colours. I stand taking it in for a long moment, feeling the hope and excitement that only those seven colours can evoke.

The relentless gusts and driving rain of the past few days have faded into a gentle hum of a breeze in the trees. The landscape reminds me of Cape Town, and it feels right, and worth it, after all the shit we went through yesterday. I feel happy that I've got up early and gone out.

I have this idea that if I go for walks alone, I'm more connected. But often, the run-on monologue in my head is more talkative than an external companion – certainly more than Thor, who is usually silent. My thoughts keep drifting to "Oh, we've been together nearly eight months, and in May we will be at the place we met, Beltane Into the Wild Festival, celebrating a year of our relationship." *For God's sake, this moment, only this moment is guaranteed, let's just stay with this, be with this.* After years of meditation practice, it's still such a challenge for me to do that.

As I walk on, another thought takes hold: I have chosen this adventure, something not possible within the constraints of my former life, and yet I've started to imprison myself again. The 'Pusher' inside me has snuck her way back into the front seat and constantly tortures me with expectations of doing hours of writing each day, on top of paid work, my relationship with Thor, and all the tasks of living in the van.

I'm struggling with the erratic phone signal, frustrated by being unable to take care of business, and it's really hitting me how impossible it'd be to work properly in this lifestyle. How would I even hope to get new clients, to expand beyond my 'hippy' market, and be accountable and professional?

When the Pusher takes over, I lose my flow: my mind becomes rigid, I see everyone and everything that stops me from working as an obstruction. I lose my compassion and connection. I stop listening to signals both from my environment and from within. I miss the magic – and that's the whole point of this, isn't it?

It's so humbling to realise that I carry these conditions with me wherever

I go – this is my inner landscape that I superimpose on what's outside of me. I was annoyed with Thor yesterday for lecturing me about something he read in an astrology book: Pisceans are either swimming upstream, which is going against the flow, or swimming downstream, going with the flow. He said I run into trouble when I go against the flow.

But he has a point. Trying to sort out my tax return issues when we were just about to move the van was guaranteed to cause me problems. It definitely wasn't surrendering to flow.

What about actually *living* this experience, spending time in nature, enjoying the freedom I had so longed for?

Looking down at the hills, I see purple spindly trees, little patches of holly clinging to the banks and tall ivy-covered trees with moss-covered branches extending outwards. I descend down the valley into deeper forest, what feels like a lonely path, and the thought comes: How can forests be witness to atrocities? I find myself thinking about how many murders and rapes have taken place in forests, remembering how I was often afraid to walk there alone in South Africa where the crime rate was so high (but sometimes did it anyway).

How strange that the trees, these beloved allies of humanity, stand by when the unspeakable happens – but what else can they do? They're just helpless witnesses. I think to myself that if I was going to die anywhere, I'd like it to be in a forest – and peacefully.

*

That night, Thor sits down on the sofa and says to me, without warning, "I think you should start researching other places to live."

My heart sinks down into my belly and immediately starts to compost a pure pain mixture.

"It seems like you just can't do what you really want to do, living in the van. You told me you would do your own thing here most of the day, if there were no consequences to our relationship. And I would rather be properly alone and just see each other when we can both fully focus on being together. I don't want to sit here in the van while you're tapping away on the laptop for hours. If we were in a house, it'd be OK, but not in a small space like this. We need to be properly together here, or not at all."

It seems to me that in a relationship you repeatedly lose yourself and then find yourself again. Both experiences are part of the process; there's nothing wrong with either of them. I guess we're in the 'finding our individual selves' part of this process now.

The difficult truth is, ever since Glastonbury, I've had regular thoughts of leaving. I'm so terrified of being caught up in a control drama again, like so many relationships I've been in. And I feel controlled about lots of things.

I'm not tiptoeing around like I used to, but still, I feel that my time and my focus are not under my control. I can't follow my own flow. It makes me want to jump out of my skin.

Still, it feels awful to hear him actually suggest I leave. It's painful to have the decision taken out of my hands, to be rejected because of my needs for autonomy and space. *I always knew I'd be pushed away if I tried to claim my space. This is why I've been scared of taking space in all my relationships. Because this is what happens.*

"But ... I thought you said it was OK for me to do my work," I begin. "That I should just take the space I need and not consult you about everything. And the last few days, it's been fine – we've each been doing our own thing every day and then coming together at other times. I thought it was working."

"Some of the time, it has," he counters. "But that's only because I've gone into separation mode."

It's true. He's been walking around with his new stereo headphones, tuning me and my typing out. "That's not what I'm in relationship for. I chose to go into this relationship to explore who I am through love. And you've told me that your time for your writing and other stuff is taken up by making love and processing. Those are the main practices for exploring the depth of love, so how does that work?"

I cringe. I knew I'd end up regretting saying that particular sentence. My sense of doom grows: this is so painfully familiar from past relationships. The minute I start speaking my truth, asserting some needs and trying to carve out some autonomy, there's a backlash and some form of rejection or abandonment. He goes on to clarify that he's not talking about splitting up at all, just about living separately, that he could even end up living with me again if I found somewhere nice in the countryside to live. But I'm not truly listening anymore: all that's running through my head is *I don't have an income to rent anything with. I'm fucked.*

We talk and talk until some kind of compromise is reached: three hours maximum of working time for me per day, and one hour on days we're moving from one place to another. It feels reasonable, possible. But although Thor has softened his stance, saying he only asked me to consider moving out because he feels that to love me is to not stop me from fulfilling my purpose, my heart feels hollow and the trust that this was a relationship I could feel safe in has been eroded.

I try to persuade myself that it doesn't have to be easy and happy and perfect all the time in order to be right. We always knew that living in the van together was going to be a challenge. Waiting for a mythical perfect situation is a waste of time because I know from experience that every living and work situation I'm in turns out to be frustrating or limiting in some way. I need to find my inner peace with it.

But the truce is temporary. The next day, another bomb drops. Two, in fact. We've had a nice enough morning, me doing my new yoga, meditation and writing routine while Thor sleeps, then connecting with each other, then getting ready to move to a spot with reliable signal so I can do my tax return. He's a bit grumbly about this break of flow but it feels OK. When we're in the nearest village and I'm waiting for the HMRC website to load up, I check my email. Shit. An email from my sister, entitled "The Truth". I glance at it, my stomach already churning. I see the sentence "I just can't ignore this uncomfortable feeling I have whenever I think about you," and that she's addressed me by the birth name that I've not used in thirteen years. The insult is heavily meant, I know.

My body is already going into a trauma response from a mere glance at the email, so I ask Thor to read it and tell me if there's anything I absolutely must know. After he's read it, he tells me that nothing in it sounds like the person he knows, that either I've changed a lot since the times she is talking about or the whole email is a load of projection – probably a bit of both.

When he offers to immediately delete the email, I say no and he archives it instead, so I'm not tempted to open it every time I go into my inbox. I sit hugging my arms and shivering, the turbulence in my stomach only increasing. "Just take some time to calm down," he urges, "Before you do your tax return." I do some breathing and somatic trauma recovery exercises. My nervous system starts to calm down, but my thoughts keep kicking it back into action.

The tax return is, of course, not straightforward and there are problems with internet connection going in and out. Thor steps in to help me and when he makes a suggestion, I distractedly say "Obviously", with a slight tinge of irritation. He reacts with an angry, "Don't talk to me like that, I'm just trying to help." It's so exactly the kind of thing my parents used to say, and I'm triggered yet again. Where do all the years of meditation practice go?

"Hang on," I exclaim, fed up, "All I said was 'obviously'. You've been telling me to shut up regularly lately. And I don't want to be spoken to like that."

"You're being rude, you were being rude saying that."

"And 'shut up' isn't?" I burst into tears and storm out of the van. The sun is almost blinding. There's an outside world here – we're in a village called Allerton, which I only realise now, looking at the sign, and the children have just come out of school, a sight that always brings sadness, now that I'm no longer part of Jay's school day.

The hills in the background are stunning and the blue sky is irreproachable, but my heart is breaking. I cry despite the children, stumbling around in search of a toilet, but the only likely one, the village hall, is shut due to storm damage.

Finally, I give up and return to the van, where Thor's first words are "I'm sorry I said shut up. I was feeling frustrated because I know a lot more than you do about technology – I do this for a living – so when I make a suggestion, I need you to trust that I know what I'm talking about." I take in the apology but switch off at the justification, especially when he begins to explain how my 'Obviously' was just as rude as 'shut up'.

I burst into tears all over again and collapse into his arms. "I don't feel safe," I cry into his chest. "I don't feel safe, and I have nowhere to go. My only option is to go live in London, and I don't want to do that." I'm so in child mode that I don't care that I'm telling him, in effect, that he feels unsafe to me.

He holds me and feels unconditionally loving for a while. Then he says calmly, "You were triggered by the email from your sister, and then you were stressed by your tax return. In fact, I think you should read the email because there's a lot about what you're saying right now that rings bells from that."

So, I brave it. It's full of hostility, accusations, and a complete re-writing of my family history as I see it. My memory of our childhood interactions is that we would be close friends for a period of weeks, only to fall out when Robyn seemed to turn 360 degrees against me. I'd resolve never to trust her again but because I had no other allies in that home and lacked friends at school too, I'd let her in again. I remember writing angry, upset journal entries saying "That's it. Never again. I'm not letting her in again – ever."

I remember her behaviour as vicious and humiliating to me on several occasions, and the cherry on the top was her cold distance and unhelpfulness when she came to stay with me for some time on first moving to England.

I was so disappointed because I'd thought that finally I had some family to help and support me in my lonely situation living with Luke and Jay – but she slept till noon and failed to do the dishes, then got angry with me for asking for rent money after a time. In the email, she dredges all this up again, casts aspersions on my parenting, claims I was horrible to her throughout our childhood, and accuses me of making everyone tiptoe around me lest they offend me. I am furious at the projection. This is how I've experienced her all my life – as someone who would jump down my throat if I ever tried to raise an issue.

The difficulty with Thor is forgotten as I grapple with the hurt in my body and my heart, and he's supportive and loving as I process it through the rest of the day.

FOREVER FEELING

I wake up around three-thirty a.m. from a dream in which I'm desperately trying to call my sister on the phone and resolve things, but I just get Mom on the line, and she's irritated with me so won't let me through. Thoroughly awake at once, I start composing emails to my sister in in my head – just as I knew I would. After half an hour of trying to get back to sleep, I get my phone and catch up on the voice notes Marion left for me earlier that day.

I listen to her slow and measured voice telling me about her recent meeting with her new love interest, and how they both are completely open that they have the 'forever feeling' about each other. I'm happy for her, but the aching thought comes: *I used to feel we were a forever possibility. Now it seems he no longer feels that way. If he ever did.*

And that's it – I've gone from worrying about my family drama to anxiety about the relationship, vividly imagining a scenario where I move in with Marion and Zeb temporarily while I get on my feet, start a job in London, get involved with the dance community there, and have a totally different life – one where I can't see Thor fitting in at all, since he hates cities.

Another aborted attempt at sleep later, Thor wakes up just as I'm giving up and getting my E-reader out to escape into the fantasy world of Deverry. I know he senses I'm not OK, because he says, "Come and have a snuggle," in that tender way. I join him on his side of the bed and he asks me what's wrong. I tell him about the dream and that I've been worrying about "Us". He listens with his usual attentive quiet and I feel so much love and need for him.

I know I've swung the other way, just like I do in all my relationships – from desperately wanting my independence and fighting for it, seeing my partner as an impediment, to being terrified they'll leave me, and I'll be alone, just like I always end up. The same tragic scenario re-enacted and having to be embarrassingly reported back to my family who wonder what's wrong with me for never making a relationship stick. Especially since my sister, despite sharing my fucked-up family life, has ended up with a lovely fiancé and a planned pregnancy.

"What've you been worrying about? Is it us?" he asks calmly, stroking my arm.

I tell him about my London scenario, that I've given myself that option so that I know I am freely choosing to live in the van, despite all its difficulties. I tell him that I feel I need a safe container of commitment around our relationship in order for me to keep exploring it. That despite his reasoning around suggesting I move out of the van, it felt to me like a lessening of commitment to a shared future. And finally, I take a big risk and I tell him about the Forever Feeling. That I have it, have always had it about him, and that I'm afraid he doesn't have it.

"I think you know I've had that Forever Feeling. But the way you've treated me in the past ten days, since Glastonbury, has been really difficult. And I've experienced this in relationship before." I know who he's talking about – Lila. The mention of her no longer stings me, though. I'm beginning to see how much we resemble each other. How I'm a bit like a second go for him, at being with this shape-changing, beautiful but damaged creative Piscean woman who would pull him close then push him away.

And sure enough: "It destroyed the relationship – after a certain amount of time, she just started to attack the relationship and find fault with me. And I don't want to be in that again." He pauses, then goes on: "As for commitment, I've offered you a commitment twice – the handfasting at Stonehenge, which you decided not to do, and living in the lodge my parents have given me, which you said you weren't sure about."

I suddenly see it: I go to the precipice, I'm about to push off, I'm trusting more and more, then I pull back. Just in time to save my sense of myself, which I'm so terrified of losing. Destroying the trust in a relationship in the process.

"I know I unleashed something when I invited you to express your anger in West Woods that time," he says. "Ever since then, you've been in something. The thing is, you have the full force of what your dad did behind you."

*

The next morning, we go for a walk down a highly treacherous, slippery path to the river, past the heart-shaped pool where we had a crazy lower body dip the day before. Zero temperatures and our feet numb within seconds, but surprisingly OK on our private parts. Now, I have to concentrate hard, using my staff and digging my heel in to get a grip on the sliding, damp soil covered with wet leaves, often needing a hand from Thor.

There's a moment where we're sitting on a rock and it feels like he's holding space for me, and suddenly, I feel everything around me so deeply, the sense of something bigger than all of this, and I open into love, such profound love, not just for him, but for everything, just *being* love.

When we get back to the van, we listen to a David Deida talk about purpose and this sparks off a conversation about the purpose of our relationship as we see it. We find a commonality: I feel the purpose is love, and for him it's finding who he is through love. So, the question is, how do we organise our lives around this purpose, as Deida advises?

Things feel effortlessly good between us again, and I feel so relieved. It's one of those new beginnings and I hope the horrible phase we've been in since Glastonbury is over.

*

We're parked up in a fairly busy city council car park just outside Exeter, far closer to the now unfamiliar urban built-up-ness than we want to be. But one corner of it does have a beautiful view and it's easy to get the van flat.

When I get my laptop out to do some admin, Thor immediately gets stressed from the atmosphere that creates. This is now a familiar pattern. "I think it's because your masculine is very strong," he explains to me. "You are often in your feminine, but your masculine is very strong – it's had to be, for you to survive, get things done, and be a single mom. But you're not a single mother anymore. You have a partner, and you can rest and relax in your feminine, do your dance, and be held by the masculine."

But what about when we're not together? I think. *What about when I go for those weekends to see Jay and like last time, I feel rudderless because I've not got my usual coping methods – call them 'masculine' if you like? When I can't figure out whether to get the train or the bus ...*

"The thing is," he goes on, "When we're both in our masculine, we end up competing with each other. And your masculine will not win over mine." I remember what Marion said to me: that he could learn to be in a brotherly relationship to other men and to my masculine, that this could be good practice for him.

Thor asks me when the lunar eclipse was exact, and I tell him it was an hour and a half ago. He calls me from up in the bed, "Come and look at the moon." So, I do. It's hanging just behind an oak tree opposite the van. "I'm going to bring the moon energy into me and into you," he says, and we make love. Afterwards, we look at the moon again. She has fully risen now, through the holding branches of the masculine oak, and into the sky where she is free.

SNOW

Finally, we're on Dartmoor in Devon, a huge national park with stark and stunning moors, enormous stone tors, and cute wild ponies. I've been looking forward to this adventure for some time. On previous visits to the area, I've been compelled by its magic – the way the fog will settle and obscure the landscape, only to clear and reveal a vista of mystery.

On our first day, we're going for a walk not long before dusk when a storm of frozen rain begins, hitting us as hard as hailstones. It really hurts. We seek shelter in the ruins of WWII outposts, but there's no roof so it's not much good. I have to put my scarf over my face as we walk back, and I take Thor's invitation to hold onto him. It feels frightening, but I also feel a sense of satisfaction at what an adventure it is.

When we get back to our park-up, we realise it's a bit of a dangerous spot – we've parked just after a bend in the road where people could easily slam into it if they lose control on the icy, snowy roads.

Sure enough, within minutes of the roads becoming slick with the frozen rain balls, a couple of young guys are doing tricks with their cars. We're both getting worried; plus, we could really get stuck there if the road ices over and we can't make our way back down the hill in the next couple of days to get provisions. Drinking water, milk and food supplies are already low in the van and I wonder what's gone wrong with our up-to-now pretty-faultless planning.

After a long debate, we decide to move down to another town, to a spot Thor knows. "It's not a nice spot but at least it's safe in terms of snow." We've just parked up there – it is indeed shitty, right on the road – when an old guy drives almost straight into us, despite the fact we have our lights on. I see his widening, shocked eyes and annoyed expression as he gets closer. It feels like a warning sign, so we decide not to stay there.

But the only other park-up we can find is also on Dartmoor, lower this time, by the river. When we get there, there's a big sign warning us of by-laws: *No parking overnight anywhere in Dartmoor*. This particular carpark has CCTV so, although we were unaware of this rule in our previous nights in Dartmoor, it seems we can't get away with it here. The pattern seems to be, we have a few lovely, peaceful days and then there's a kind of comedown as we're reminded: *You're not allowed to be here*. The reminders are regular and relentless that we're not really allowed to live the way we are living.

Meanwhile, it's well past tea-time and we've had to stop and make food. We did this at the last park-up but didn't have time to eat it before moving on because Thor was worried about the snow. I'm starting to feel really annoyed about always having to do things on someone else's time. I'm perpetually feeling that I don't have enough time to eat or go to the toilet – earlier today, I had to rush my toileting because we were in a carpark to offload recycling and look for water. It's reminding me of early parenthood, being at the mercy of my son's needs and my own going by the wayside.

But by early February, after three months in the van, my inner Pusher has retreated from battle, and I've reached a new acceptance of what this journey is all about. I tap into a trust that I will find the time over the course of my day to do what I need to, without trying to control it. I've come to a new partnership with my creative process, based on knowing that my muse *wants* me to engage with it and will be there.

LIFE CYCLE

We're walking by the river just on the edge of Dartmoor, where you can still see houses. There's a huge, long section of tree jutting out into the water. Thor takes hold of it for a while, then passes it to me, its roots still in the ground. "The tree is moving with the water. You can take in the water energy, into your sacral chakra, if you hold the stick right there below your belly button. You can also use it to let go of energy in your own system."

Immediately, I know what energy he means. I am so furious at my sister, so sad and hurt and angry, and I send it all out into the water, feel the power and force of the river pulsing under me, making the stick move against my belly. I try another stick, which is easier to manoeuvre, and I let this one go down the stream. It gets stuck a couple of times and I will it to let go and go downstream. I want to release this boulder in my heart.

And when the stick follows the water at last, I feel the relief. Maybe it can be that simple.

*

The sun casts bars of light into the centre of the stone circle, which I later find out is called Fernworthy. I immediately feel a sense of friendly welcome. We stand together at the entrance, holding hands, and I am encircled, embraced, by the same energy I felt at other stone circles – that unmistakeable feeling of sacred place.

I ask the stones what we are here for and what we can offer. And after a few moments of silence, receiving sun on my face, I get an answer: *Forgiving our ancestors.*

So, I open my heart to my ancestors, forgiving them for all the mistakes they may have made or feel they have made. I immediately open out into relief and lightness. I thank them for bringing me here, for being part of what's made me who I am now and the path that's led me to this point.

After a few minutes, we wordlessly separate. Just before I start walking, the word 'widdershins' drops into my mind, and I follow it – Thor goes clockwise and I go the opposite way, widdershins direction, around the inside of the circle. We both know what to do; there is no need for a solemn ritual script or a consultation. As I walk, I feel a sense of blessing; we have been welcomed, we belong here. My pink wellies squelch in the deep swampy moss.

After I've walked all the way round, we meet at the front of the circle again. By mutual agreement we walk into the centre, again without words, just moments after I receive an inner instruction to do so. We hold each other and Thor says, "I love you", and the sense of unity between us is strong and beautiful. I feel loved.

Then we walk to the outside of the circle separately again and position ourselves on opposite ends. We're facing each other but I'm aware we're in our own processes. I sit down on a stone and go deep inside.

Eventually, feeling lighter, I go and join him, and he shows me pools of frogspawn in the puddles of rainwater. It's incredible to think of all these little frogs springing up there in a little while. Thor wonders aloud how many will survive, and I marvel at how the mothers leave them there to fend for themselves, to go through the life cycle from tadpole to frog without any holding. It feels fitting, in light of what the ancestors asked for: the signs of a life cycle happening right there.

I know that Thor has been struggling a bit with us going to Dartmoor because there's so many reminders of his time with Lila. He's also found it very healing to go to the same places he's been with her and to face the energy there. "We've gone to these places and made beautiful love and it's been very healing," he told me. In this same circle, he tells me later, he had a very 'convoluted' and 'uncomfortable' experience with Lila and our experience today was such a contrast. As we walk out into the sunshine, it feels as if something important has been completed.

SNIBBLES

I celebrate my thirty-eighth birthday while we are still parked up on Dartmoor. But before we even get to this day, Thor gives me my present: a new travelling companion called Princess Snibbles who he was too excited to keep hidden in the wardrobe anymore. She is a unicorn with big, cute, purple sparkly eyes who's really more of a My Little Pony – but with a mermaid-style tail, wings and of course a horn. A hybrid of magical creatures who feels like a cat's nose to the touch.

Thor once told me that he used to carry a little soft toy raccoon called Andrew around inside his jumpers, against his heart. "It helped me connect with my inner child," he explained. He'd done that until he felt "Andrew" was integrated and no longer needed to be worked with as an external object.

Thor chose the unicorn because I had told him about wanting the unicorn belonging to Millie, Rachel's daughter, and because I was inexplicably attracted to all the unicorn-themed products we encountered during our family Christmas-shopping trip.

The idea is that she represents my Magical Inner Child, the part of me that sees the beauty, wonder and possibility in life, who spontaneously plays and enjoys. This is a part that, like many people, was systematically squashed in my childhood, often not deliberately, with the result that the Wounded Child becomes more prominent. By incorporating her into my life, the hope is that it will help me get in touch with my Magical Child, and that taking care of Snibbles will help me with some aspect of my healing.

Officially, according to her label, Snibbles is called Princess Twilight Sparkles, but we soon start calling her Princess Snibbles, sometimes shortening to Snibbles. Snibbles is a name Thor uses to refer to "little me", when my more vulnerable, snuggly, "needy" aspects come to the surface. I carry her around inside my jumper where she can peek out of my coat, and I can stroke her regularly. I am surprised how powerful it is: how much easier it is to give my love to a creature, even if she's imaginary, than to an internal Inner Child, something I've been doing on and off for years, more consistently since I met Thor. I stroke her when I'm feeling vulnerable or anxious and it immediately "works": I feel a sense of relief.

My adult journey with unicorns began when, nearly a year ago, I attended a workshop with a prolific creative called Jamie Catto. I had been going through a singularly unmotivated, uninspired and even depressed phase, feeling purpose-less and hopeless.

At the workshop, I got "how to train a unicorn" in an exercise where we had to speak to a group for three minutes on a topic we knew nothing about. I was amazed to discover that I had a lot to say about unicorns, waxing lyrical about the difference between stripy and plain unicorns – one being prone to biting and needing more careful care than the other. My group was rapt with attention and laughter, feeding back that I was really convincing. My depression lifted after that workshop, and events in my life accelerated as I started to open to romance as well as creativity, after a long grieving period from an intense six-month relationship.

I discover that bringing my Magical Child into my experience makes a huge difference to how the world seems to me. When we were driving onto Dartmoor after my last Lewes and London trip, I felt strangely indifferent to the dramatic views, knowing they were stunning but not truly *feeling* the nature. But after receiving my unicorn and including her regularly for only twenty-four hours, everything was lit from the inside again and I felt as if life was one delight after another. I saw endless possibilities opening out from each gate in every field we passed.

Snibbles dances to music; she jumps up and down in excitement when we see tors or snow – or "polystyrene attacks" as Thor calls them – a regular event in our time on Dartmoor. When I forget her and get wrapped up in worry about the future or work too hard, she makes herself known. I am playful and relaxed for days in a way I usually can't maintain for more than a few hours.

*

One of the places I take Princess Snibbles is the Fernworthy Reservoir on Dartmoor, which ends up being one of my favourite spots in our West Country roadtrip. On the third day, I express the desire for an adventure, and we decide to walk as far around the lake as we can.

Never one to obey padlocks or signs (this one reads 'Danger of Death'), Thor climbs over the locked gate onto the bridge where the water thunders past, an unstoppable torrent evoked by the combined powers of water and air. I follow him and eventually we're standing at the bottom, looking up at the water cascading down, the wind whipping it into waves. The water smashes against the granite, creating horizontal waves that become vertical as they fall down the wall, splashing up into our faces. It feels as if we'd get whipped down and taken away if we got any closer. The waves explode into mist as they reach the bottom, and I breathe in this fine spray as it comes up into my face.

"Take in this power of the water and air," Thor says. "Take it into your body." I close my eyes and concentrate, imagining I could channel it into our dream of finding a beautiful place in nature to live.

"You could really shout here, let all your yells out," I say above the near-deafening roar. Immediately Thor does just that, projecting his voice across the water. But I feel shy, blocked – a familiar feeling. Eventually I manage to yell a bit, drawing on my feelings about my sister. By the end, my throat is hoarse.

As we come up onto the main path again, there's a little baby-size brown shoe on top of a rock. We're both touched by it and, as I've learned to do, I wonder into what the symbol means.

Just a short distance from that section of the reservoir, Thor notices a dolmen. We sit against one of the stones and at first, I can't feel it moving the way I usually do. But then it happens twice: that clearly perceptible movement, that mysterious re-location. A blonde Labrador comes up to us, eagerly bestowing its licks.

After it's gone, Thor sits in silence for a long time, his eyelids flickering, and I imagine he must be listening to what the ancestors or spirits are saying. Eventually, he says, "There's something under the water ... Another sacred site, buried under there. Way, way before this reservoir was built – it was only built during WWII. Why ... why that expenditure of resources at that time? The Nazis were rooted in the occult – so maybe ..." he trails off, and we both wonder for a few minutes, with no conclusion, before heading off into the growing drizzle. We pass a jolly family of four on the way and get cheerfully lost; wash our boots in the water, get muddy.

Thor laughs, "Well, you said you wanted to go for an adventure."

I smile at him. "You always seem to create these kinds of experiences."

"The thing is, the way to have an adventure is to choose the right moment to go. And to follow your intuition in the moment it comes."

*

We're watching the second 'Hobbit' film on the sofa in the van when Thor suddenly says, "I want to try and see the owl." We turn off the movie at once. Moments later, we're up on the bed, peering out of the window above our heads, listening intently to an owl in the tree outside calling to another owl several trees away. Every now and then, a mysterious unknown bird call interjects. We get out the binoculars to look at a star cluster and talk about Jupiter.

Later, after finishing my recently re-established morning yoga routine, I suddenly hear what sounds like hooves approaching the van. I quickly go to the window.

To my astonishment, a herd of about ten ponies, brown, black and white, are galloping steadily towards us, the light gilding their coats. They look like mystical beings gracing us with their strength and elegance. Then I see that they're playing, following a leader among them. I feel as excited as a child and

I don't squash it down the way I might have before.

"Thor! You've got to see this!" I exclaim. He's still in bed but as it's after ten, I reckon it's OK to wake him up.

"I was sleeping," he finally responds, disgruntled, but then he gets into it, sticking his head out the roof to have a look. "They're having their morning exercise. Did Princess Snibbles see them? Snibbles, that's what ponies do." The ponies circle the van three times, coming perilously close, then as if by divine orchestration they disappear in a long, mysteriously unified stream back to the woods a little way up the hill.

Opening the door a few minutes later, Thor calls me over. "Can you see how close they came? Those are skid marks. Do you think they were showing off or playing?" I peer at the hoofprints with an awe that stays with me for the rest of the day.

These kinds of moments happen so often with Thor. In the spontaneity and lack of fixation on goals that arises in the field between us, I come back into connection with the wonder I used to have as a child and still have glimpses of now. It's as if, together, we multiply the magic that we each possess as singular beings.

HOLDING ON

A few nights before my next visit to Jay, I have a dream where I find him living with another family who have informally adopted him, complete with a female 'sibling' playmate. I feel such joy at seeing him happy and settled; a relief that I can let him go with confidence, knowing he's in the best place possible. Or, if I were going to judge myself with it, *he's better off there*.

In the aftermath of my last visit with Jay, I notice I'm worrying about him in a way I didn't when we lived under the same roof. Without the ability to check his daily 'temperature' of mood and wellbeing, I suddenly have compelling visions of him going astray as a teen and getting into drugs and alcohol early because he doesn't engage in any extracurricular activities that might channel his energy.

I daydream about sending him to a Boys Rite of Passage Camp that my friend Laura is involved in, when he's thirteen. I know he'd probably rather stick pins in his eyes, but I still plot how I could get him there – I just *know* he needs that kind of thing.

It doesn't help that he seems to be wanting to connect less since my last visit; he hasn't initiated one WhatsApp conversation and takes days to reply to those I initiate. I went to a lot of effort to send him videos and photos of the ponies who visited our van, in the one erratic tiny patch of signal under a particular tree in the woods, only to receive no response back. I'm suddenly remembering that he seemed to find me embarrassing at times during my last visit, when we stayed with his similar-aged friend and her mother.

I know this is an inevitable, not-to-be-taken-personally aspect of adolescence, and he's always been precocious with his stages, talking at the level of a two-and-a-half-year-old when he was just twenty months, reading two years ahead of his age. But I can't help feeling a bit hurt and pushed away by it. Is this revealing some core truth, that I've always wanted my own needs to be met by mothering? Is being a mother, in the sense of an active duty and vocation, over for me? This is both freeing and very sad.

*

I have an odd tendency to burst the bubble. Just as Thor and I are getting on and everything is harmonious and tender and beautiful, I bring up a subject that turns it all sour. This time, a couple of days after I return from

Sussex and London, we are in true loved-up mode, and I decide that now is the time to talk about summer plans. Specifically, the two community camps I go to every year, and whether he would like to come to them with me.

It turns out that even though he had previously been open to the idea on principle, enough to get my hopes up, now that we get to the nitty-gritty, neither of the camps is an option for Thor. One of them, High Sun Solstice Camp, doesn't work for him because he's determined to go to Avebury stone circle as he does every year at summer solstice, holding to his path of working with the ancestors. And the other, Dance Camp, clashes with his annual Enlightenment Intensive Retreat.

Once again, I realise with a sinking heart, I will be alone at these camps, without a partner at my side. I wanted to share these communities, so precious to me after nearly a decade in my life, with the person who's closest to me. I wanted to sit around the campfire singing songs with him.

"You're still holding on to something, to this idea of us three together as a family," he says about the family-friendly camp, Dance Camp. "You want him to come to a camp with us so you can show him how nice it is, so he'll want to be in that and want to live with you again," he says, and it hurts, even though I know I hold very little hope of Jay choosing to live with me again – at least not in the near future.

"I know he's chosen the lifestyle his other family offers and that he's happy and settled there. But I do want him to come into *my* life sometimes, to share in it – it's always me coming into his. And you two get on so well … it feels so nice with the three of us."

But I realise later that it's true: I *do* want to connect the people I love the most with each other. I've always liked doing that, and I feel sad that Thor has no relationship with any of my friends. He started developing one with Graham, but it never went anywhere. And then he and Jay got on – better than any of my past boyfriends – but now they don't have any ongoing relationship.

My sadness also stems from the fact that I feel Jay needs other male role models apart from his dad and granddad. I don't want his only idea of how to be a man to come from two gruff, quintessentially British, emotionally shut down and conservative-minded men.

But maybe I should let go of the project. Maybe my role in facilitating Jay's life experiences is over now.

Six weeks after his announcement, Jay leaves for his first residential school trip on a brisk cold October morning.

Although making my way through the never-ending packing list from the school is a little stressful, the two-night separation itself doesn't feel like a big deal. I can see it's huge for many of the other mothers, who stay anxiously close to their children right up until the moment the coach leaves. Jay, accustomed to alternate weekends at his other home and to regular sleepovers with friends, is happy for me to go, and I feel both superfluous and relieved to be released so easily.

THE END OF THE ADVENTURE

"This is the end of the adventure," Thor announces on our third day in Cornwall. My heart drops. What is the van life about, if not adventure, travelling from unknown place to unknown place?

"I'd usually just stay in one place in the winter, like Stonehenge," he goes on. "This is the most I've ever travelled around in the winter. It's easier in the summer to be in the van because by the time it gets dark and you settle in for the night, everyone's cosied up in their own houses. So, they're less likely to see your lit windows and report you for camping overnight."

"Why do people have such a problem with vandwellers?"

"They see us as benefit scroungers who don't pay Council tax and don't contribute. Actually, you couldn't afford to run a van on what you'd get on benefits."

"Yes, and if you were on Jobseekers' Allowance, you'd have to be living in one place, reporting to the Job Centre weekly, anyway."

"Yes."

On our drive to Cornwall, we'd discussed finding ways to finance our van lifestyle without having to work a lot of hours: turning the lodge into a summer rent out while we travel, perhaps buying a better, bigger van. I felt excited as we passed the sign welcoming us to Cornwall and Thor happily pointed out the boats filled with colourful flowers on the traffic islands.

I've been here only twice before, and briefly: a week in the summer when I was twenty-six, staying at a backpackers' on a solo exploration when I was recovering from a breakup; and attending a close friend's wedding a couple of years later. But Thor used to come here regularly as a child on family holidays and has fond memories of the area.

We find a park up in Talland Bay near Looe, right against a roadside grassy bank with beaches on either side. I relax further when I see that the sign only forbids parking during summer months. Waking and falling asleep to the sound of waves sighing and crashing evokes my childhood in Bantry Bay, Cape Town, where I grew up with ocean views at the bottom of my garden.

During an outing along the cliff coastal path, I fall in love with the quaint fishing (formerly smuggling) and touristy village of Polperro: little fudge shops, snug tea rooms, the 'Land of Legend' with its miniature model of the fishing village; the shop windows filled with little faery ornaments; yellow-painted cottages with names like Sun Room 1 & Sun Room 2.

Thor treats me to a belated Valentine's day cream tea – extremely crumbly but delicious, heart-shaped scones and Earl Grey tea. I realise it's the first time we've gone out for a coffee in the eight months we've been together. In the end, I'm shamelessly scooping crumbs up with the jam and cream.

I've sat Snibbles on the table and a little girl walking past recognises her, excitedly announcing to her mother, "That's Princess Twilight Sparkles!"

"I wonder what it was like for her to see Princess Snibbles out and about like that, without a child with her, just sitting on the table," Thor muses. "She seemed so pleased to see her."

It feels so reassuringly normal and lovely; the whole day is, we decide, the most normal outing we've had in our time together.

Even in the normal holiday mode, though, there's a bit of nature magic *en route* to the village, where we sit in a shady forest and put our boots in the stream, feeling the flow of the water. I climb an alder tree with a platform on it, placing Princess Snibbles on a branch where she fits perfectly.

On the way back from Polperro, there's a rainstorm and we seek shelter under bushes on the steep winding stairs that travel around the houses of locals. We pick some of the wild garlic growing in profusion everywhere.

I walk on the beach each morning, alone because Thor has developed a bad cold that's keeping him mostly indoors. There are a few dog walkers and a woman who stands silently at the shoreline, seeming to commune with the water. The beach is covered in red stones and the water runs through a tunnel, over the rocks and towards the sea. I carry Snibbles with me in my coat, and though I feel shy, I start to take her out and let her face the waves. I feel the difference: it's as if her spontaneity and joy at being alive is released into me when I no longer hide her.

I start to regain my former hill fitness through the sheer necessity of daily climbing a very steep road to get any signal on my phone – until I discover I can find it intermittently from certain rocks on the beach. I love that the hours I used to spend online have been whittled down to fifteen minutes of focused, efficient time. For the first time in our travels, I truly feel like I'm on holiday, sitting among the tide's deposits of brown seaweed and the occasional pink curly fronds, watching the sun's light generously bless the waves. We too have been blessed: after days of snow and rain, there's this blissful blue sky and it's so warm I can almost strip my coat off.

*

We stop over for a day in Totnes, a small Devon town known for its 'hippiness', but which also has a solid core of conservatism. It's another sunny day, smiling faces on the streets. We walk past an art gallery and I have an intuition to go in. It's holding an exhibition called 'Totnesity' about the spiritual heritage of the town: portraits of Totnes inhabitants accompanied by aural interviews with them.

We spend some time talking to the plump, bubbly Spanish female artist who, it turns out, once lived in a van with her one-year-old daughter. I feel both touched and embarrassed when Thor tells her about our 'baby nest': the space above the toilet which we've made cosy with cushions and unicorn pictures and joke about being where we'd put our baby if we had one.

After we leave, Thor turns to me. "I thought 'Oh no' when you suggested going in there. I used to experience a lot of unpleasant emotions in that gallery – Lila and I went there a lot because of her artwork. But I followed my impulse and trusted it, because I believe in manifestation and I know that the universe gives you little clues as you try to manifest something – in our case, a home." The artist did have some information for us: she talked about Frome, near Somerset, as another likely place to live, with a similar ethos to Totnes.

But although I like Totnes – it feels welcoming and the people at the conscious dance class I attend that night are incredibly friendly – it takes me a good hour to settle with the busyness of the high street. It just feels like there's so much going on at once. I honestly don't know if I could ever live in a town again.

PROXIMITY TO STARS

After Cornwall and Totnes, our last stops on the Great Western Adventure, we settle at Stonehenge, where we're one of about fifteen vans during the winter. This will be our base for many reasons, not least of which is that currently no-one bothers trying to move these travellers on.

Driving back to Stonehenge, we stop off at an Iron Age Hill Fort situated on a hill beside Camelot Castle in Cadbury, Somerset. As legend goes, King Arthur had defences in this spot. Thor wants to show me a special tree he's connected with there before. As we walk the perimeter of the fort, we look down at the empty fields, so unlike the busy city of Salisbury which sits below the Old Sarum hill fort we visited recently. I have a strong feeling that I've done this before, in another life.

It's a long walk to the tree, and when we reach it, I know at once that it's the one. It's huge, with a big hollow that Thor tells me has expanded since the recent storms. We go into the hollow one by one and sit together for a few minutes before Thor gets out, saying, "You stay here," in that definite way that lets me know he has an intuition about it.

My head is busy that day, but I can still feel the energy going down strongly from my lower body into the earth; a few times, I feel the tree moving along my spine. I become aware of a deep fear of things being 'too good', that they will be taken from me. Thor and I have been so close and loving lately. I feel such adoration for him that it scares me. Then a knowing as sure as my physical presence comes to me, and the words: "You're on the right path."

We share our experiences with each other as we walk back. "I felt a transmission from the tree," he says. "The spirits of the tree acknowledged me for bringing you there and then asked me to leave you alone with them."

The confidence in my path is still there the next morning, walking past the burial mounds in the woods of Stonehenge. I was afraid I'd feel bored and static, being here again, but in fact I've felt a welcoming relief since we arrived. I even feel amused by the army folk running past the van, while in my head I'm organising my social life for my next visit to Lewes, arranging teas with friends I seldom see. As I walk back from the woods towards the van again, all that feels comically meaningless. This – the wide, extending sky and the slow, patient stones – this life is real and rich and raw.

Back in the van, I look in the mirror and see eyes as wide and innocent as a child's.

Later that night, sticking my head out of the skylight and looking at the stars after mind-bendingly good, close, wild, passionate love-making, I look at the stars and wrap a soft grey blanket around me.

I'm totally anchored, here, nowhere else to be or where I *should* be.

All those abstract non-dualist ideas about how there's nowhere else to be other than where you are now, that it's all perfect, make sense to me in this moment. My monthly blood is flowing fully now and I'm full of ideas, so much so that I have to go and fetch a notebook right away.

Gazing at the stars, I remember how exciting it felt, my very first night in the van as a 'resident' rather than a guest: looking at the sky above Firle Beacon in the cold and feeling so grateful that this was my home. And how quickly that proximity to stars has become normal. How soon I get sucked back into Facebook and Instagram and forget this simple purity; how easily I forget why I chose to live this way, forget to look outside and look up.

This is what it's all about.

CABIN FEVER

So much for PMT becoming a thing of the past, as I concluded in my first vanlife weeks.

I'm well and truly in the inner Autumn zone now. Since my cycle is irregular, the first sign of this is that my psychological wellbeing feels utterly contingent on the state of the rugs and the floor: filthy with dirt and bits of coal. Suddenly, I can't tolerate the state of them for a single moment more.

I'm not yet dressed and haven't eaten breakfast – having had to stop cooking porridge midway to walk to the 'toilet in the woods', which later today will become impossible because of the temperature dropping to -3 and snow setting in. I was attacked by another vandweller's dogs along the way ("They're harmless," he shouted to me).

But despite my undressed, unfed state, I get Thor to help me shake the rugs outside and get down on my knees for a good half hour, sweeping the floor with a small paintbrush and a tiny broken dustpan with a huge hole in it. It makes me feel better.

In this zone, I again feel I'm hitting a wall with vanlife. I'm tired of feeling scuzzy and unwashed. I've run out of clean knickers as well as clean tops. I'm fed up with all the dirt on the floor, with having to climb over a tall man's sleeping limbs several times a night to go take a pee. I've had enough of the cold keeping me in bed way past when I want to get going; having to take a shit in a semi-paranoid state because I could be spotted any minute by an army helicopter, farmer, jogger or another vandweller.

After our six weeks of travel in the South-West, we are now between active adventures. The uncomfortable in-between-ness of this time reminds me of the liminal phase I experienced when Jay had left and the house was dead to me, but I still had to engage with it on a daily basis in order to get my precious deposit back.

I already feel nostalgic about the new places we discovered in our first months in the van, the excitement of fresh experiences every day, even though, in reality, this period has been hard in so many ways.

It could just be the end of a long winter, like, fuck, enough now. The cabin fever induced by the severe weather conditions doesn't help. I often have resistance to spring, wanting to stay in winter's cocoon, but now I feel so ready for it, willing the weather to get better.

Then, the coldest spell of the winter hits. As the difference between the temperature inside the van, warmed by the woodburner, hits twenty-seven degrees below the outside temperature, the rigours of life outside of the matrix comes home to me. We elect to seek shelter from the high winds and driving snow in West Woods, where we were once blessed with romantic Christmas snow. This time, it becomes a lot less romantic.

Stocked up with food and drinking water for a few days, we stop to get washing water on the way, but the tap we usually get it from, at a garage near Salisbury, is frozen up. The Kennet River at the roadside is also totally frozen over. Eventually, we find another tap just as we're running out of opportunities. There's a hilarious moment as Thor fills up the water container: the water comes out like trickles of iced turd, then suddenly spurts out. It sprays into a neighbour's garden, and he has to run frantically across the forecourt to turn it off.

It's a good thing we kept looking for water, because as we arrive at the woods the weather worsens – we would've been very stuck without that water supply.

As we drive up to the woods, there's icing sugar all the way on the edges of the road and on the grey banks, but within a couple of days this is to become several inches of snow. Parking up, we see two baby robins, and they become the recipients of regular linseed and oat cake crumbs from Thor over our stay. I love watching the child-like joy on his face as he feeds them.

We realise that, although we've been superbly organised at loading up with provisions for five days, we've forgotten to get toilet paper – and after we've been there for a day, the forecast starts predicting snow for longer bringing fears that we may even run out of water and food. Thor checks the weather with an obsessive regularity and worries, while I try to reassure him. I know he struggles with being responsible for me in situations like this.

Energy for running the electrics of the van is also becoming an issue. When Thor gets up on the roof to clear snow from the solar panels so that they can collect more light, snow rains down from his trousers and socks onto the duvet. Within a couple of minutes, he's howling with pain and berating himself for not wearing gloves.

We both feel bored for possibly the first time since we started sharing this space. As well as the fact that, from my perspective, there's no longer an adventure going on, our shared purpose seems to have fallen away, too. Yes, we're still living in a van, I'm still house-less, but there doesn't seem to be any real point to it other than saving money. I can't really work properly because of the small space, and I feel hemmed in and isolated.

I would almost rather be in a house, where I can at least work properly and not evoke the annoyance of Thor with the sound of my 'hamster-on-a-wheel' typing. From Thor's perspective, I'm just sitting on my laptop writing, while he has no work at the moment and wants to interact. But occasionally we break out of our funk.

One day, I'm working when suddenly I hear a thud on the window. I look up to see Thor throwing snowballs, grinning his face off. I come to the door and the next snowball catches me full on the upper body. I explode into giggles and screams.

Even though it's now only half an hour from sunset, at the end of a tricky day of sniping at each other, I decide to break the spell and go out. Immediately his bounding, boy-like demeanour emerges. "Look, there's deer tracks – and rabbit ones," he points them out with glee.

Suddenly full of energy, he climbs to the top of a steep hill and slides down it as if he has a sled. Although I've stopped halfway up, too tired, I feel hopeful: maybe the magic is back.

But it's fleeting. We don't connect again for the rest of the day.

The next day, the weather seems to have broken – no snow overnight, and no more predicted – and we can't take it in the van anymore, so we set off to an as yet undetermined destination.

Eventually, we decide that we want to go to the lodge in Kent, but Thor can't get through to his parents to organise getting a key.

The alternative is parking up in the Lewes area, since we both need to be in Sussex on the weekend to see our children. Thor has suggested I spend some time with Lewes friends. He's reached his limit with my lack of desire or ability to connect fully at this time. "Either we need to find a way to connect or we take space."

"But why can't we just have space in the van, do our own thing for a bit and connect when we both want to?" I protest. I feel like we're back full circle to where we were the time he suggested I find a new home.

I have massive resistance to the idea of leaving the van, even temporarily; I feel rejected and pushed out of my only home, and resent that I am the one who has to scrounge and ask favours to have the space I need, while it's a given for him to stay where he's comfortable and safe. I also feel deeply uncomfortable with letting go of being together when we've not resolved the tension between us.

But when I get a text from Marion offering me the use of her house in London for a week while she's away, I can't mistake the rising excitement, the big YES rising up from my heart. There's also the opportunity to meet some of my extremely frustrated social needs, as I could see her before she leaves, and other friends as well. It's almost spookily perfect timing: we're on the M25, close to London, and we still haven't heard from Thor's parents about the lodge key.

Although we both acknowledge sadness at the idea of the impending separation, we decide to go with this plan. We stop at the nearest station so I can pack, Thor being suddenly helpful. His whole demeanour has shifted, and he bursts into tears as he hugs me goodbye. It's an emotional moment, but as soon as I get to Marion's house and she greets me with a huge hug, telling me I feel so grounded, I know I've done the right thing.

Visiting two of my oldest friends from university days, Rebecca and Tom, I feel as excited as a child to converse freely with them over a long dinner, to sing harmonies with the ukulele together. It's like balm to my heart.

I feel all that I have been missing. London, for some reason, isn't bothering me on an energetic level this time, even though I used to feel so discombobulated when I stepped out of rural vanlife. Maybe I've integrated the changes more; or maybe the van phase is nearing an end. I don't know yet, but I do know that when the others go out it feels wonderful to be able to sit down at my laptop and work uninterruptedly.

It's the first time that I've broken away from the pattern of feeling like we can only fix what's happening between us by being together. I've been able to let go.

And I've finally admitted to myself that however liberating and real vanlife is, sometimes it's time for a breather.

PRECISELY NOTHING

"I'd like to support you to develop your masculine side so it works better for you."

I look up from my cup of Earl Grey tea a little warily. "What do you mean?"

"So that when you need to access the more archetypal masculine qualities – when it's time to execute a task, to plan or to problem-solve – it's coming from a mature and grounded place rather than a panicky one."

We try an improvised exercise: Thor invites me to connect with the space behind my eyes, to identify with that, and to answer questions from that place. This is what he's learned on his Enlightenment Intensives.

I try it, but it feels so foreign, which is strange, because in the summer in Wales while in the van, we dropped into this space effortlessly together. He'd just come from an E.I., though, so it's possible I was picking it up by osmosis. Now, he instructs me to write a list of all the things I think need doing in the near future, to read it out from the masculine place, and to say my intention that "all these things will be done".

These are the kinds of things that squirrel around in my head on a day-to-day basis and it feels good to get them down on paper and at a remove. "Now," he says, after the third time I read the list, "screw the paper up and put it in the fire." It feels satisfying, if a little scary, to do this, trusting that the items will be remembered and done.

"Go into the space behind your eyes. The place where you know that your nose is itching, or you feel hungry, the place that watches all that. And put your identity there. "Now, what is your purpose?"

"I don't know."

"Your purpose is not to know?"

"Yes."

I've been experimenting with a David Deida practice of spending ten minutes a day being in the not knowing, really feeling and dropping into the truth that I don't know anything. Until (or at least this is the idea), I open into freefall ecstasy.

Fortunately, in my current lifestyle I have a lot of unknowing – certainly more than the average person. I reflect on the fact that I don't know where I, or Thor, will be in a month's time; that I don't know how I will make a living this year, or what I'll be doing next year. I don't know who my friends will be in the future; whether my sister and I will make up; what kind of mother she'll be; how Jay will turn out as a teen and an adult. I don't know how long Thor or I will be alive.

I feel fear about the death stuff – will I get cancer? Will I nurse Thor through some horrible disease as we get older? – but the other questions bring an immediate sense of freedom and expansion. Soon, I'm feeling the delicious openness and joy that David Deida points to.

Now, settling into Thor's question to me, I can accept, for the moment, that my purpose is to not know. To live and walk in this way feels like the only thing I can do, and perhaps the most powerful one: to find the portal in each moment, with the certainty of precisely nothing.

HOME MOVIES

It's our third day in the holiday lodge. After months of fitting myself into a tiny box and into others' homes, I'm luxuriating in the novelty of being in a house that feels almost like our own,

It's the perfect size for us, with an open plan kitchen/ diner, living room, and two small bedrooms. There's even a verandah and an ensuite bathroom, and despite the copious amounts of cat ornaments and fake flowers (Thor's mum's choice), because this is such an occasional holiday house, there isn't a sense that we're walking into another family's energy field. I feel at home.

We talk a lot about how we want to go forward with the lodge as a business venture: whether we keep it, and if we do, do we live in it all the time or rent it out part-time and travel the rest of the time? Or maybe we rent it out most of the time while we travel and live elsewhere? In the end, we decide to find somewhere to put it that we really like and to rent it out when we're travelling. That way, we have the money to pay for rental of the land we are staying on, and also potentially to save up towards some land of our own.

It feels a lot more possible now, like something I could actually put some energy behind, whereas when Thor's dad first decided to give him the lodge, during our post-Christmas visit, there was a feeling of the brakes being on. I struggled with the shift from seeing my life as a solo adventurer – with my lover as an adjunct to my personal destiny – to making plans with someone, being able to consider our joint future and vision as much as my own.

In the lodge, it's liberating to get up in the morning without disturbing Thor, to go into the living room and do yoga in front of the electric fire. But the immediate surroundings are bleak: land reclaimed from the sea, a mix of farmland and suburbia, with forbidding 'Private land: do not enter' signs only a few yards down the road, and no pavement to walk on. A walk to the beach is disappointing: in the years since Thor came here for childhood caravan stays, it's been eroded by worm-farming. It's like walking in quicksand.

Back in the lodge, I'm in the kitchen making tea while Thor sets up the TV so we can watch Monty Python's 'Life of Brian' from his computer hard drive. Suddenly I hear music that's weirdly familiar, though at first, I can't place it. Hovering in the living room doorway, I see footage of animals in cages and my mom, thirty-eight years ago, waddling along through the zoo with me in her belly, wearing a big blue dress.

"Oh my god, it's my home movies! How did that happen?"

"Remember I backed up your PC a few months ago, on my hard drive? It must have been on there," Thor explains.

"No," I say immediately, and I hear that the cringe is given full force in my voice. "I don't want to watch this."

But he is intrigued and a part of me is too, so we agree to watch just the twenty minutes of footage that follow me up to age eight. I'm sure this will be frightfully boring for Thor but he seems genuinely interested, stroking me affectionately on my shoulders as we watch my floppy big-eyed baby self grow into a tottering, excited toddler and eventually into a wary-looking school-age child. "There's no sign of your dyspraxia," he comments, watching me learn to crawl, walk and drink from a cup. "And you look like a happy, confident child."

"It comes later," I say, knowing it will soon be evident.

"Is that because your sister was born?"

"Maybe a little – but mostly I think it's because of the stuff with my dad ... that started when I was two." I am matter-of-fact, having long since digested my childhood, in therapy and workshops, over and over again. But new layers continually surface: it was only when I read the book The Body Keeps the Score a few months ago – a painful if illuminating read – that I realised that my dyspraxia could be trauma-related.

Now, at moments of the video, the close ups to my face are so tender as to be excruciating, particularly since I know my father, absent from most of the footage, is the one holding the camera. In one shot, my navy blue eyes are brimming with feeling and no-holds barred depth. "It's Snibbles!" Thor exclaims, using his name for my inner child. My eyes in the present tense begin to overflow too, witnessing how utterly without defence I was as a child: my vulnerability there for all to see.

But as the video goes on, I watch the frowns increase on the face of this little girl, the openness shutting down as her formerly free movement is continuously curtailed. Standing on the garden path surrounded by her friends, six-year-old me scowls, arms at her sides, looking tense and anxious. The only sign of outward expression is her furious, serious dancing in 'Musical Statues' at her birthday party.

Thor comments a few times on the 'poshness' of my apartheid era, colonial-style South African upbringing: the backyard swimming pool; my mom's appearance with her expertly made-up face and well-cut hair; 'the help', brown-skinned of course, hovering in the background. "Was that allowed?" he asks curiously when Milly, the woman who cleaned our house for my entire childhood and still feels like an honorary family member, appears with her son at my birthday party, otherwise exclusively composed of white children and adults.

I'm soon to be returning to this now crazy-seeming set-up, once so taken for granted, when I visit my parents in their big house with its team of staff, who all live in shacks in 'shanty towns' where, just like in the 80's, only black people live. My parents' bed and breakfast business wouldn't work without this extremely cheap pool of labour; really, very little has changed in South Africa, apart from the right to vote being extended and the emergence of a middle-class black elite. Extreme poverty, lack of education, violence, and instability continue, disproportionately affecting the indigenous population.

Whites struggle to find employment in the climate of an 'affirmative action' job market – my dad, after all, left Cape Town because he could no longer get work as a middle-aged white man – but those who already have the resources, the property, and the successful businesses, continue to hold on tenaciously as they profit from their privilege.

By the time the video has finished, I feel like I've been transported to another world. This world contains damage, damage that feels more real to me than it has done for years. But it also contains the source of my ongoing connection to nature and magic.

Watching footage of the big farm where we used to visit family friends, I smile to see the five-year-old me stroking lambs and strolling around with muddy trousers and boots, the mountain soaring in the background over rampant greenery. I'm shown little me walking happily up and down and chattering to myself in my garden, which my imagination used to populate with faeries and moles. I see my mom showering me with tender affection and care and I remember I was a loved baby, despite what came later.

*

The next night, out of nowhere, the contentment I've been holding close to my heart, the feeling of peaceful co-existence Thor and I shared, comes to pieces. I go into the dark that has visited me periodically for my whole remembered life: a spectre of unwelcome self-hatred that flagellates me even as it convinces me that I am totally deserving of such treatment. Nothing is right, nothing can ever be right, and my tears and rage and helplessness cascade like a relentless flood which seems only stoppable by truly ending it all. I know by the fact that the feelings feel unmanageable and never-ending that this is old, old stuff, not a reflection of my current reality.

Thor asks me if I'm sad that I'm going away soon, and on one level this is the root of it all: I don't want to step into my past life, the haunted mansion of my childhood, into the inevitable triggers that sharing psychic space with my parents will unleash. I don't want to leave my life together with Thor, this safe-feeling bubble. I don't want to expose my budding vulnerable self to what wounded her in the first place.

Thor suggests that maybe my inner child seeing herself in the home movies was what triggered me, and this feels true. And because I don't remember reacting this way when watching them on previous occasions, I also wonder if there was a stronger impact from being with someone who was holding and witnessing me, knowing my story.

"I could see the look in your eyes when you were three," he says. "There was so much strong emotion, like you were thinking, how could this person who's holding the camera do this? Why is he hurting you, then filming you?"

The home movie wasn't the only trigger: I'm processing the fact that Jay chose to stay with his dad on the last weekend he was due to be with me, because I was staying with a friend he was less familiar with and therefore didn't want to be there. After sharing my feelings with a friend, I received a well-meaning message from her that touched to the core of the fact that I'm no longer a hands-on mother.

"I wonder if Jay is feeling rejected, just by the fact that you are not there," she said. "Kids can be funny like that, in the same way they might trip up when small and then get cross with us as though we're to blame." I know she was just trying to be supportive, but it feels so painful to think I've failed in the most fundamental motherly task: to make your child feel wanted.

Of course, no amount of awareness and conscious discussions make any difference. I remain in a trauma response, sexually switched-off and frozen. I cannot feel my body, and I can see how much it's worrying Thor.

THE FUTURE

Although Thor suggests we leave the lodge because of weather warnings, I have work to finish off and my body just isn't feeling to leave yet. Even after two tarot readings, we can't make a decision about whether to stay or go.

And what the readings show is that we are on two different paths. Mine (staying at the lodge for longer) is the fiery element of Wands, the path of action: I could work there, building my career. Thor's is the suit of Cups: the path of water, dreaminess, emotions, and nature connection.

I feel sad. Can our paths find a meeting point? Will my need for achievement and self- expression in the world always conflict with his need for empty space and flow – a need I have too, but not as strongly as he does?

Thor has already said he fears getting bored if he stays in the lodge any longer. "The things I like to do don't happen in houses." And now that I'm not connecting with him sexually, however I might try, I know there is even less reason for him to be here.

I wonder if we both have a tendency to 'do geographicals' rather than stay with and explore what's happening for us here and now.

On a practical level, it's a real dilemma: we're both aware it'll be risky to get on the road, as we might be caught in the snow en route, with no guaranteed good park-ups, but staying in the lodge might mean not being able to get out in time to reach Stonehenge for Equinox.

Rather than forcing the issue, I stay with the process, using what I've learned from recent experiments with different ways of making decisions: feeling into them rather than actively 'deciding'. It's a witnessing approach, noticing what I end up doing, where my body takes me, following how I feel.

I suggest that Thor goes to the shops while I shower and see what comes next, if I will find myself packing up or not. He trusts me with this, which I really appreciate, and goes off to Sainsbury's. When he returns to find me unpacked, he says, "I see nothing has changed" with a light humour.

We stay, and in the end, it's just the right timing. We leave when we are both ready to.

We arrive at Stonehenge on Sunday at six p.m. with frozen feet after a flat tyre just miles from our destination, which was speedily resolved by Thor. It felt like we weren't going to make it, but we did it in four hours, including a Tesco's trip and coal and water collections. Our luck has continued beyond the easily resolved flat tyre and smooth traffic: we just missed a band of snow that was an hour behind us, narrowly avoiding being trapped in Kent or stuck en route and missing the Equinox celebrations.

I'm confirmed in my trust of my body's timing.

At Stonehenge, we're greeted by the familiar sight of the burial mounds covered with snow, the black of the birds wheeling above the white. It does feel like home – not just Stonehenge, but being in the van itself, where my trauma 'freeze' state is now able to begin its thawing process, although on a physical level it takes a lot of effort to heat the van up after its week of emptiness.

I wonder if being in a house again activated my 'family stuff', and that that's the reason I ended up feeling so out of sorts. Thor suggests, "Maybe you get so comfortable in a house that you're not tending to your inner child in the same way that you would in the van, where it's quite on the edge, and you have to be more aware."

And it's true – there's a more precarious feeling about being in the van, a constant awareness that things could change at any point. I also realise that my inner child, by making herself so loudly known, was perhaps calling me into presence with her before I go and face my parents. Because if I just rock up in that vipers' nest without being in good, close relationship to my inner child, she could feel very unsafe.

But right now, I'm simply enjoying being more free-floating again, in a way that being in a house doesn't allow. And this freedom goes beyond my joblessness and lack of responsibility. "Being in a house is like squeezing ourselves into a box," Thor declares.

Neither of us knows why we're here or what it is we're really meant to be doing. All we know is that it feels right to continue.

What about the future? There's no denying the feeling of fear that comes up when Thor says, "In a few years, we can sell the lodge and buy some land, but we can't do that right away." Am I really that sure? Can I be in the long haul with somebody like that?

Pre-Jay, I had no problem with this concept. I assumed that as a matter of course I would get married or at least have a lifelong co-habiting relationship. I was engaged to Luke for years, although the intention of actually marrying became thin to the point of transparency by the end of our four years together. But before that, I had two long-term partners for four years each, both relationships I saw continuing indefinitely. Now, why is it so hard to believe that I can have stability and longevity? Have I given up on lasting love?

Between Luke and Thor, I made many attempts to settle down. But all of the men I dated either lacked staying power as the inevitable challenges emerged, or we just didn't have the powerful connection I longed for. Many of them were confronted by the closeness of my relationship with Jay and threatened by the challenge to their masculinity that a boy with strong willpower and free expression represented. They either tried to change my parenting methods (which never went down well), or gave up and left without any real, honest communication.

Thor, however, seems to be up to the task: he has proven himself, over and over, to be someone who can stand in the fire with me, who can look at his part in things and take responsibility for them as well as do his best to understand and support me. I regularly feel astounded that he is every bit as loving towards me, nearly a year after we first met and after having seen me in my worst, most raw and triggered moments. Everything about our relationship is real, and we've explored depths of intimate connection that I never dreamed possible.

So why am I getting cold feet again? Are my trust issues so deeply rooted that no amount of therapy, self-examination or love will ever heal me?

Maybe there's something else brewing under the surface. Two of my previous relationships ended after I had gone away without my partner.

It's possible that I just don't trust Thor to be there when I get back.

BACK HOME

Maybe I like pleasure pain
Of going and coming back again
What I leave behind
I come back to find
It's no longer mine

~ Laura Marling, 'Little Bird'

The next time I visit Lewes, it's as a stopover before taking the plane from Heathrow all the way back home to South Africa with Jay. I used to feel so uncomfortably open when I was making this transition between van and urbanity, but now it feels normal, just like when I was in London and found myself curiously immune to the vibes. I wonder whether this is because I'm shapeshifting more skilfully between the two spaces or if it's simply that my habitual modes are asserting themselves in the hopeless way that they do.

It's strange how things move on – in a place that I called home for five years, it feels almost like a betrayal. I walk past my old house and there's a family living there; I can hear a baby crying. They've put stained glass up in the window and it's much more tastefully decorated than when I lived there – a trickle of shame before I remember that these folks probably just have more money and time than I had when I lived there.

I walk past a red-headed woman and her son whose paths Jay and would cross every morning on the school-run. We would exchange smiles, then, but this time, she doesn't return mine: it's clear that she doesn't remember me.

I go into a café I used to frequent, and the layout is almost unrecognisable: sofas replacing chairs, mirrors everywhere. Reality check: half a year has passed. Of course, things and people move on, but I feel a lump in my throat, a painful dislocation under my ribs.

Even though it's more sensible for me to have an early night before my epically long journey the next day, I spontaneously attend a small birthday gathering for Rose, the long-term vandweller who gave me encouragement early in my consideration of this lifestyle. It's comforting to be here, in Martin's warehouse, with all its associations with the much larger space he used to co-run: Zu Studios, a hub of artistic and holistic happenings, legendary dress-up parties and 'Light Nights' (conscious, drug-and-alcohol-free dance events).

Surrounded by familiar faces, I feel the sense of 'tribe' that I spent so much of my life looking for, even though many of them are people with whom I've only ever exchanged a handful of words.

But, like Rose and Carl, who are moving out West to start a rural community, I want to expand. By the time I stopped living here, Lewes had become too small for me, too familiar. The same faces on the high street every day. A sense of being stuck and of not moving towards the off-grid lifestyle I longed for.

Every time I try and talk to Rose about their community project, which she first mentioned to me at Carl's fortieth birthday party back in November with a clear invitation to be part of it, we're interrupted by someone else coming to say hello to the birthday girl. Eventually, Rebecca, who I'm staying with that night, laughs and says, "You're not meant to have this conversation, are you?"

I let go much more readily than I used to. Pre-vanlife, I would have tried to force the issue and become stressed about it, feeling I was being blocked from my dream. I know now that my path will do what it wants, will take me where it will. As George Harrison sang: "If you don't know where you're going, any road will take you there."

I sleep badly, more and more anxious, knowing I won't get any sleep the next night on the twelve-hour plane journey either. It's been seven years since I went home – am I returning with different skin and cells inside me? Do we really renew every seven years? And does this mean I'll react differently, not be as drawn into the old dynamics between my parents and me?

The journey is about as arduous as my night-time dread indicated it would be. After Luke delivers Jay to me at the station, we kick off with a late morning rail replacement bus and two trains just to get to the airport. By eight a.m. the next morning, in Oliver Tambo airport, I am snapping apart. I've had literally no sleep and it all feels too much, when Jay rejects a sandwich at the airport despite having chosen the flavour himself.

Out of practice at being 'conscious mommy', I'm turning into 'horrible mommy', blaming and shaming. "Why do you have to make everything so difficult? We're in another country now – the food is different, so deal with it." I'm resentful: he's slept and I haven't. But I immediately smart with guilt.

We spend hours sitting on uncomfortable plastic chairs, waiting for the shuttle bus to the town nearest to my parents' village. There is, unbelievably, still almost another four hours of travelling ahead. I come out of my personal suffering when I see two young black men taking pictures of each other with the Mandela statue opposite, feeling oddly moved by this sight. Then, when I see two women who must be sisters or very close friends, hug each other tightly and cry with joy, that's it: the tears take over. But it feels good, cleansing. "Are you OK, Mom?" Jay looks up briefly from his tablet and holds my hand. I nod and carry on crying.

I notice that unlike in the UK, people aren't all glued to their devices here; they're actually sitting doing nothing, or reading newspapers, or talking animatedly to each other as they wait. What is it with my adopted homeland that everyone seems so cut off and locked into their private screen-worlds?

I'm surprised by how unfamiliar everything feels, how difficult to navigate. I can't estimate prices any more or figure out what's a reasonable amount to pay for a packet of crisps. It's confusing finding my way around the airport, leading to more moaning from Jay as we aimlessly wander with our laden luggage trolley. While some of the restaurants we walk past – especially Steers, a fast-food chain my dad used to run a branch of – stir childhood memories of bubblegum milkshakes and big hearty burgers, the general disorientation reminds me more of when I first moved to England and fumbled over the currency and the etiquette.

The biggest thing I've become unused to is the crime issue. I feel I can't take my eyes off my stuff for a minute, and I suddenly worry about leaving Jay outside the Ladies when he refuses to come in with me – something I wouldn't even think about at a typical English public loo. The precariousness of vanlife back home already seems not at all scary, in fact, it looks positively safe in comparison. Maybe vanlifers are merely pretending at taking risks; this odd blend of third- and first-worlds is the real danger.

We're frequently accosted by people wanting to sell us their services or wares, adding to my on-edge-ness. Why is this experience tougher than when I travelled with a much younger Jay (twenty months old and three and a half)? Somehow, I had the stamina and the tolerance for it then. I was younger and more naïve. Or maybe I was just so switched off from my body that I didn't even know how stressed I was.

But then it's suddenly all OK again. Jay and I start joking and playing a verbal 'guess the animal' game, and the sullen, entitled pre-adolescent who has accompanied me for the past twenty-two hours is gone, replaced by the open, laughing affectionate boy I know so well.

On the CitiBug shuttle bus, I start to relax. There's a certain friendliness and informality about South Africans, which touches me after the bland blank-facedness of the English. Even though I am an English-speaking South African, listening to the Afrikaans around me, I start to feel more at home. One fellow passenger even speaks to me in the Dutch-derived language of the first South African settlers and I understand and respond instinctively, amazed at myself. Twelve years of learning the language at school and attending a bilingual school at one point must have deeply embedded it in me.

Mile after mile of open grassy land dotted with thornbush trees soothe my heart, then open it with their simple beauty. I imagine this all as it must have been centuries ago: plains full of animals and free of people. I feel my love for this country come out of its hiding behind the fear and exhaustion.

Will I have a chance to properly connect with the nature here, in the way I do now in England? To listen to what the trees have to say to me?

The guy who takes my money at the service station on one of the bus stopovers is called Lucky, which I remember being a common Anglo-African name. "Hello, how are you?" he says warmly and genuinely, and I am flooded with pleasure at the connection, even though he doesn't respond to my reciprocal question.

It feels as if I'm rediscovering SA as a tourist but with the background of having grown up here. The lens of apartheid with which I was brainwashed as a child growing up in the eighties is gone – now, I can see it all fresh. I'm able to feel the shared humanity without the pervasive guilt of being a privileged white 'oppressor'.

There's also a new, hard-earned humility in me that I don't remember having the last time I visited. Is it the marginalised status of being a vandweller, the knowledge that I'm only one rung away from the street sleepers that are so much more visible here? The boundary between me and the many people who live in shacks on the side of the motorway is no longer such a chasm.

Getting a mineral water out of the fridge, I see a couple who look Spanish or Italian, the woman with very short shorts and copious black inked tattoos on her legs which I try not to stare at. She gives me a big 'You're one of us' smile.

As we get closer to Nelspruit, where my parents will pick us up, I brace myself: I must not expect my dad to ask lots of interested questions about my life. I mustn't expect my mum to listen to or expand on any answers I give her that don't fit her model of the world. *It's going to be all kinds of things ... you're gonna feel all of the extremes,* I coach myself. *Pleasure and pain, the usual mix. Just like everything else.*

I see them before we get out of the CitiBug, and my heart lifts at their familiar shapes, then clenches as I see how grey my dad has become in the seven years since I last saw him. My mom visited us four years ago so hasn't changed that much, and besides, she always carries her age well, even at sixty-nine.

It's stiflingly hot as we unload luggage and begin the ritual of hugs and hellos. My dad is in tears; he always was quicker to show emotion than my mom, who greets us as casually as if she saw us only last month.

My dad helps us pack our stuff into the boot and off we go. After having to hold the fort with Jay for so long, I'm relieved to be able to settle into the 'in the backseat' child mode along with my son as we chat about our trip.

I'm soothed by how normal everything seems. My dad, as usual, is mostly silent, turning the wheel as my mom talks animatedly. We pass more beautiful scenery, seemingly endless unoccupied land, escarpment covered with trees, so unlike the gentle roll of English hills. Then, acres of covered avocado trees surrounded by barbed wire, with one simple dwelling stuck in the middle of it all. In the distance, through the long grass, I see a scene out of the past: what looks like a family sitting on a donkey-driven cart.

Signs on the motorway offer guidance for preventing wildfires and I remember the airport toilet signs about water, admonishing people to shower for only five minutes daily with the slogan 'Water is life, cleanliness is dignity'. I know that when we go to Cape Town in just over a week's time – where there is a severe drought – we will be subject to heavy water restrictions.

The landscape gradually becomes more urban again until we get to Hazyview, which has multiplied its shopping malls three-fold since my last visit and now resembles a town more than a village. We drive up the rough dirt road, which some of my parents' guests refuse to believe actually *is* a road, ringing them up in puzzlement when they cannot find their Bed 'n Breakfast. The sign reading 'Blue Jay Lodge' with the pretty bird on it announces that we are here. My dad drives us down the steep driveway after opening the electronic gates, which are alarmed at night.

Here we are, in the subtropical green of several dozen species of indigenous trees, all carefully labelled by my dad, surrounded by the thatched-roof guest chalets. This time, Jay and I will have our own chalet, 'Kingfisher', to ourselves, rather than staying in the guest bedroom in the main house. After the van, it feels enormous and luxurious.

After Jay and I have settled into the chalet and had a rest, I join my dad for a drink on the verandah of the house. I'm surprised to sense him as more open in his manner than the last time I saw him. Whether it's me or him that's changed, I don't know, but when he asks me how I am, I find myself able to talk at length about both the pro's and con's of van life without censoring myself. It feels like an adult-to-adult conversation rather than 'daughter reporting back, hoping dad approves'.

He listens attentively and then suddenly asks, "Are you happy?"

I'm not sure how to answer that, but I try. "I'm happy with my relationship and with having removed most of the stress from my life, but I would still like work to go better and to be able to see friends more. But overall, I'm happy." He nods and I realise he's a better listener than my mom, who would have let me get about one sentence out before asking me a worried question and steering the conversation towards her agenda.

But later, when we're watching TV together in the lounge, my mom, looking at Jay, rapt at 'Mr Bean', says, "He's such a beautiful child."

"He is, isn't he?" I respond proudly, my heart melting. It feels like the most meaningful compliment my mom has ever given me. Perhaps this is my biggest achievement in her eyes.

*

On our first night, Jay has a nightmare and comes into my huge four-poster bed, which is surrounded by the mosquito net passing for a curtain. And that's how it is for the rest of the holiday, except for a couple of times when I'm desperate for space and premenstrual enough to insist on it. I'm not without my own nerves: sleeping in a new room in a now-unfamiliar country feels strange, and sleeping on my own is odd too, when I'm so used to sharing a bed with Thor.

I'm puzzled by my lack of courage: haven't I been so brave lately? Is being back home putting me back into my vulnerability in an unpleasant way? But mostly I feel relief at not having to constantly prod and examine every little issue ripple in my inner world. Here, without what I now realise is an ever-present scrutiny from Thor, I can just *be*.

I'm amazed that it feels just like it always was between me and Jay. For a while after he moved out, our dynamic seemed to have changed: he was less demanding and a bit more formal with me, even detached at times. I remember one time, when I picked him up from his friend's house, he barely greeted me or looked me in the eye, and didn't hug me as he usually would. I struggled to hide my tears. Now, it's a huge relief to be back to our close bond, but I also soon start to struggle with the lack of space.

He's there first thing in the morning, leaving me no time to collect myself and meditate slowly into the day. It doesn't help that my mom also tends to burst in at eight a.m. and that cleaners and repairmen are liable to come in at any time. Jay is perky until nine-thirty p.m., way past when I start to flag, so we go to bed at the same time too. There's the now-unfamiliar pressure of keeping him entertained, then worrying when it's impossible and he's on a screen for hours each day. It's the opposite of the van: I have much more physical space, but less headspace and time to myself.

In many ways, I feel transported back into the past – only I'm in another layer of it. I'm strongly reminded of when Jay was littler and much more dependent on me.

Descending the steps in my parents' garden reminds me of our first visit, when Jay was a toddler and I used to walk him up and down those stairs over and over. He was learning to count, and he'd practice on the steps, diligently and carefully pronouncing "One, two, three," as he concentrated on his descent. He'd stop and touch all the rocks and plants along the garden paths, fascinated by everything.

On both trips, I remember reading to him for hours, filling the hours while my parents were busy with guests by reading the picture-filled Richard Scarry book, *Trains and Planes and Things that Go*, countless times. The hours oozed by, and it was up to me to fill them all, without the help of the toddler groups and playdates that helped our Brighton days back home pass so quickly.

Now that he's ten, I only have to do about two hours max of intensive one-to-one interaction each day – like swimming together and reading to him from Harry Potter. Still, accustomed as I now am to resting when I need to and generally taking it easy, I get easily drained by simply having an awareness of him in the background all the time, and he's upset when I eventually want to stop what we're doing and have a nap. He wants more, and of course, he's making up for me not being there most of the time to give him attention.

One morning, I carve out some time for myself while my dad takes him to do a zipwire activity. I buzz around like a bee catching up on work but also treat myself to a long-planned Skype healing session with my friend Alice. She reminds me about being sensitive, being an empath. "Empaths need to have time away from other people regularly, on our own, in order to stay on our path and feel what our truth is. Otherwise, you get very influenced," she says gently but firmly. It's good to be reminded – and I can't help thinking how much this applies to my situation in the van with Thor, where his stronger energy often seems to take over.

After a week in Hazyview, filled with pleasant tourist activities such as meeting elephants up close, going on a guided safari in the Kruger National Park (almost scuppered by a road protest), and riding down a lift into a gorge filled with forest, we embark on a three-day road trip to Cape Town, my hometown.

This is the bit of the holiday I usually look forward to most, somewhat suffering through Hazyview. But this time, I've enjoyed the relaxation of being at my parents' home, with all the unstructured time; they don't seem to be triggering me, and I'm feeling nourished by simple pleasures like basking in the sun in a poolside deckchair after months of cold and snow.

Cape Town turns out to be much harder work. I enjoy watching Jay climb sand dunes on various sunny beaches, but too many early mornings and days out soon take their toll. I'm exhausted and it feels like an effort to fill the time for Jay. One day, I hit a wall when we visit some posh friends of my parents, who live in a gated community.

It soon becomes apparent that I'm not going to be given the opportunity to present myself as an adult with my own life here. After fourteen years of living in England on my own terms, it feels frustrating and humiliating to be paraded around and talked down to. It evokes memories of being seated with my sister and our cousins at a little table for 'the girls and boys' while we listened to the laughter and chatter of the adults at their table. Even then, I smarted at the segregation.

Back at the annexe of another set of parental friends, in the bland beachy suburb of Blouberg, everything is setting my teeth on edge, even listening to Jay crunch his way through a bag of Doritos on the bed next to me. I desperately need to get away. So, an hour before sunset, I manage to escape to the beach on my own.

The beach is only a few minutes' walk away. I throw myself down on the sand and stare at the water, breathing deeply. And within minutes, my soul starts to knit itself back together again. My trust finds me, simply from watching the inexorability of the waves, over and over again, coming closer and closer and surrendering to the moon's sway.

They remind me that it's all OK. That I don't have to bend, I don't have to break, I can be in the allowing of everything through me.

I'm startled as shadows fall over me and quickly turn around. It's just a couple walking past, but my adrenaline has already kicked in. I remember how living in this country is to be subject to that fear all the time. In all my social circles in South Africa, I didn't know a single person who hadn't been mugged, burgled or physically threatened in some way, at some point. And the rape statistics were alarming – I'd had a near-miss myself one time, when my boyfriend and I were surrounded by a gang outside a nightclub and by some miracle managed to escape.

Unlike my friends who continued to live here, I simply couldn't get past that threat. It's sad because it's so beautiful here, and yet, it's clear to me now that this is no longer my home.

REDEMPTION

It's our last night in Cape Town before we part ways with my parents and go to stay with my own friends. My dad and I are sitting at one of the outside tables while Jay swims in the pool naked, although the day's warmth has long since evaporated. He never seems to feel the cold.

Conversation run dry, my dad and I are doing the usual slightly awkward chit chat dance when he suddenly says, "I've been thinking that your sister does want to reconcile. There's an indication of it in the end of her email."

I'm startled by his take. While I'm willing to consider this, all I can remember is the accusations she threw at me; the brutal rewriting of our history together. "I'm sorry, I can't see that." Feeling the pressure to be positive and not leave him without hope, I add, "But you never know. Maybe in the future we can work it out."

It feels jarring, and I wonder where this is all coming from. Then he says, "Your mom and I talk a lot about my own childhood and how difficult it was. It was really horrible." I realise he's choking up.

I remember the stories: his dad summoning his mom to bring all but one of her four children – my eight-year-old dad – to him in England (because she couldn't handle all of them on the long journey by sea), then sending her word *en route* that he wanted a divorce. He'd met another woman, a Danish-American, and she was now pregnant.

They married, and meanwhile, my dad was stuck in South Africa and sent to boarding school. When his dad and his new wife and child moved back to South Africa, they were within viewing distance of his boarding school, yet never came to visit him. I remember reading a letter my mom had found: my dad begging his mom to come and see him. It took his mother ages to save up enough to come back to South Africa – so long that he didn't feel like she was his mother anymore.

Now, his voice clots with tears as he continues: "I know I've been a bad father but I *am* a father, and that one – " pointing towards Jay, who's gone back into the annexe – "That one is an absolute gift."

I sit there, speechless. There's so much I could say, but something keeps me in my chair, nailing my mouth shut. "I know I'm not good at keeping in touch and writing the emails and all that – your mother does that, and I know the level of the conversation may not always be what you would want, but she does do that."

Eventually I do speak. I'm remembering what Thor told me he said to his mom when he heard the admission from her of "I was a bad mum." And the words start to form in my mouth: "Nobody gets it perfect as a parent, and now that I'm a parent I know how hard it is."

His shoulders heave with sobs and he hides his head in his hands. I get up and hug him in his chair. "I'm sorry." I don't know what else to say.

He says, still crying, "You don't have to be sorry."

Just then, Jay comes bursting out of the annexe, interrupting us, and the moment is gone.

But when Jay returns to the annexe soon after, I feel a niggling sense that I don't want to let this opportunity pass to say what I've always wanted to say, what I've countless times imagined in therapy sessions and on my own. I swallow. *Here goes.*

"Well, the way it's affected me most has been my relationship with men."

He speaks in a high pitched, almost strangled voice I barely recognise: "Because of me?" and I immediately feel the child in him, and I think, *I can't put that on him.* It just feels so harsh. Even though it's true. I also realise that I'm scared of his anger, even after all this time, so I back-pedal and say, "Oh, it was because of lots of things in my childhood," and he nods with understanding.

But something in me is determined to be heard: "The thing that's been hardest for me has been just not connecting as much as I would have wanted to." And then Jay interrupts again and that moment, too, is taken from us.

That night, I can't sleep because I keep replaying it all in my mind – the scene I'd always longed for, imagined, never thought could happen. Especially with it coming from him. I always thought it would have to be me sitting him down and saying, "Look, what happened as a child really damaged me" and him either apologising or denying it. But I really didn't expect it to take the form that it did.

I feel exultation and a deep relief. Something powerful has happened, even if it's still incomplete.

CAPTIVE FISH

We shall not cease from exploration, and the end of all our exploring will be to arrive where we started and know the place for the first time. ~ T S Eliot

On my return, my days with Thor fall into an effortless flow. I keep thinking I'm about to do something – like cook dinner – but instead, I find something else happening that is just as essential and delightful.

A typical day: we make love and go for a walk, then Thor walks ahead on the way back and I return to the domestic bliss of him chopping carrots and the wood burner going. I am about to start watching a TV show on my laptop, but the computer is slow with routine Windows updates, so I listen to the Beatles and sing along instead, which makes me very happy. That night, we do a spontaneous ritual on the ridge of Firle Beacon, and it feels like I'm both following the imprints of my ancestors and allowing the thread of my Inner Child through my days.

I laugh at myself for imagining I could know how important an experience is when I'm not actually in it, experiencing it for real. Away from this environment, on my South Africa holiday, I spent a lot of time obsessing about whether to leave the van or not. While I was in the sterile comfort of houses, I'd started to doubt the importance of looking out at hills and sky, clouds and grass, and began thinking work and money and security and knowing what's happening on Tuesday was more important. But the scales have fallen from my eyes once again.

*

It's the first day we've been able to go out wearing sandals and no jumpers. We have to avoid the rapeseed fields because they trigger our hayfever; we started sneezing a couple of days before when the wind began to blow in from the fields. In the hopes of neutralising our allergic reactions, we stopped the van near one of the fields on the way back from our supermarket run on Monday to pick some of the rapeseed for herbal tea in the hopes of neutralising our reactions.

Now, we're descending into the bright valley to play some music together, as we've been wanting to do for ages. It's gorgeously sunny and peaceful and the birds seem to like our tunes too. I decide to do a video of us singing and Thor gets into the whole idea. It feels like a satisfying outlet for my need to express and be seen, and I feel very supported by him in that.

We end up doing lots of videos, including silly improvised songs about how much we want to eat olives and a more serious one about being sensitive. Thor sings about how he has armour, as a crab (astrologically speaking) and I sing about being a fish who could swim away.

Then it goes a bit wrong: I try to initiate sex because we're in a private spot and it seems like a good idea – I like outdoor adventures – but, for once, Thor isn't interested. I get upset and then suddenly I'm tired of feeling vulnerable: I've been so extremely thin-skinned and open since my return from South Africa, and I've seen nothing near as naked from Thor.

I vent for a bit, and finally, he says, "I'm scared you'll swim away, like the fish in your song." I hug him and say, "I'm not swimming away. I love you so much."

"I love you too. I've been concentrating so much on the breathing techniques I'm doing that I've forgotten about being vulnerable. I think you just need me to be vulnerable now and again."

Later, we walk back up the steep bit; we've started taking uphill walks daily, like training back into fitness after the long winter of barely exercising. "It feels special, getting to spend this time of the year together for the first time," Thor says as we walk through the avenue of trees that slowly climbs up towards the burial mounds and across the field to the carpark. "I guess we did spend the other parts of the year together for the first time too, but springtime feels different. Maybe because we're getting closer to the bit where we have been together before. And we've nearly made it to a year without breaking up even once. That's a first for me, since I stopped drinking."

Thor, like me, tended to have long relationships in his years of drink and drugs but shorter ones after getting sober. "It's because every time something felt difficult, I'd just get drunk," he laughs. I felt like it was more complicated for me, because post-drinking also coincided with post-motherhood, and dating as a single mother was infinitely more challenging than before, when I could wrap my whole life around a man and any partners didn't have to be confronted by a little boy always wanting my full attention.

I don't like all this mention of breaking up, but I keep quiet. After a while, though, when he's still talking about it being our first spring, I say, "Do you remember when we talked about our romantic fantasies, last year? Do you remember what I said about Beltane?"

"Yes."

A long silence.

"Are you just going to say that, and not actually ask me for what you want?" He smiles now. I shake my head.

"We can talk about that," he says, referring to the handfasting I dream of having on Beltane.

But I can hear that it's no big deal to him. I'm always so scared of naming these things, but then when I do, he responds a way that relaxes my whole body. "I don't know if we'd get a Druid at Beltane. But I like the way you're so sweet and subtle about it."

I smile. Then he says, "I don't think it would make much difference," and I know he means to our relationship.

"It's not that I want it to do anything," I respond defensively, but it already doesn't feel true. I want to have a handfasting before my sister gets married (and handfasted) in July. I want to have my moment in the sun. I want to stop our relationship disappearing through my hands like all those other relationships I've had.

Back in the van, we settle into another sunset, this one a particularly hopeful, innocent rose pink as the snake of lights begins down in the town, cars taking people home to their boxes. A long Summer Time day, still light at eight-fifteen.

Thor puts our 'music videos' on his laptop for us to watch. We're both pleasantly surprised by how good we sound together, singing old folk songs like "Where have all the flowers gone" and the Beatles classic "Across the Universe". I'm also touched by the interactions between us: the banter, the gentle affection.

But then, on the videos, I notice my periodic nervous grimaces and tense expression, and the inner critic rears her inevitable head. I shove her away: This is a good moment. Don't fucking ruin it.

It's only later, cuddling on the bed, that I realise what an impact seeing the video has had on Thor. "When I watched those videos, I could see how happy I was." I look at him in surprise and see the tears welling up. "I've never seen myself look so happy, ever. Only in drunken moments, and that wasn't real happiness. I'm so scared of losing you. If I lost you, I'd never be able to watch those videos again." Now he's crying really hard.

"Oh baby." I hold him and listen and try not to rescue with reassurance, the way he does for me. But I so much want to say: I'm so scared to lose you too. If you only knew how much I love you, you'd never worry about it.

*

I'm beginning to wonder if the saying that people don't really change might be untrue – if, perhaps, even I can change.

"I think you no longer have that anger against your dad," Thor says a few weeks after I get back. "It looks like you don't need to go into that pattern where you switch off your love after a while. That pattern where you then react by being angry and then I react to that by being withdrawn and being scared and it stops the flow of love even more."

It's true that we haven't been doing that familiar dance – we've caught ourselves on the brink of it a few times but pulled back from it. It was somehow possible to carry on being loving. I don't think I've ever managed to be this close and continuously loving with someone ever in my life. It's huge.

And it's broader than just my relationship. The next time I go and see Jay, I notice that I'm just being myself, that my social mask seems to have completely disappeared. I'm even being myself with Luke as well. When he picks me up from the train station to take me to meet Jay's new pet rabbits, I find myself talking naturally and not editing myself. It's a little bit scary but very real.

*

During the Mpumalanga part of our trip, Jay chose a soft toy rhino at a Saturday market. At first, he wanted to get it for Thor, but with my encouragement he welcomed 'Cuddles' as his own friend.

After our return to England, the next time he saw Thor, which has happened only rarely since he moved in with Luke, Jay came into the van and showed Cuddles the Rhino to Thor.

After a quick mutual glance, together, Thor and I helped Jay to 'meet' our own animals: the ever-growing unicorn family (Snibbles had been joined by 'Sunbum' and a baby called 'Twinkle Sparkles'); my Eeyore; Thor's tiny raccoon, Andrew – who he'd once carried around in his shirt – and Shaun the Sheep, the older, more established members of the family. To my surprise, Thor offered Andrew to Jay – it was clear that he was finished with that part of his process of inner child work.

From then on, Jay would periodically report to me that Andrew was settling in nicely, and whenever he spoke to Thor on our video calls, Thor would ask him how Andrew was doing. "Cuddles carries him on his back," Jay told us.

I felt deeply moved by this process. I knew it was an important part of Jay's integration into his new life, while keeping his connection with me and my side of the 'family' – and with Thor, too – in such a simple and effortless way.

WE ARE CRAZY NOW

April 2018

"You know, the van has really done amazingly well."

We're sitting outside on another warm spring day, still at Firle Beacon. It's the first time we've put the back of the van down, and we're sitting on the newly made 'porch' eating beetroot, avocado on rice cakes, and salad with sprouts, a rare lunchtime effort on my part. I'm in a state which is a cross between ecstasy and smugness: we've finally made it to the 'fun summer part' after all our struggles, and I've proven all the doubters wrong. We are, in fact, in heaven.

"It's provided a home to two people through the whole winter," Thor goes on. There were so many times I wondered if it would make it through. So, I'm thinking of putting more money and time into fixing it up. Like the rust and the alternator."

It's true. Ironic that it's the smallest space I've ever lived in and that I've been living in the most unstable surroundings of my life – yet I've never felt more at home than in the van. Not in all the years of longing for somewhere to live that I could truly come home to and feel comfortable in.

I laugh. "Remember when you said that the van is not suitable for two people? That after a week, we'd drive each other crazy. A week – " I'm really cracking up now – "is the maximum you can do. That's what you said."

He looks at me, totally deadpan. "We did drive each other crazy, and we do, and we are crazy now."

The next day, the weather turns back to rain and we're both feeling a bit down in the dumps; a crash down to earth after the heady reunion honeymoon. We're driving to Ringmer to drop off some recycling on a day of mundane tasks when I spot a sign saying, "Pizza van is here! Five to eight p.m."

"Go check it out," Thor urges, and I say, "But what are the chances they have gluten free pizza? So unlikely."

"Just go and ask".

"No, it'll be too expensive anyway."

But he's firm. "You should go – you felt the urge to have pizza, go and check it out." So, while he does the recycling I go and check the board at the funky blue pizza van. They do have gluten-free options, but it's quite expensive. I come back and report this, but he says, "Are you serious? They have gluten free! You should get some."

I ask the red-headed, bearded pizza guy to give us a wave in the van when our order is ready. "Yeah sure, you gonna eat it back there? What have you got back there?" and I reply, "Our whole lives."

He smiles, and that's it. This whole mission is immediately worth it, because now he's telling me how he met his now wife when she was living in a van travelling around Portugal and Spain. "I thought it was really hot that she was doing that. And now we have kids and another van." I grin back at him. I love this story. "Where are you based? Where are you from?"

By the time I've told the story to his fascinated ears, the pizza is ready. My rainy-day blues are gone, and the pizza is absolutely delicious, crispy thin base with pumpkin, spinach and feta. Before I go, the guy poses for a picture for my Instagram.

"You're all happy and excited and adventurous," Thor exclaims when I return to the van with our goods. "It's lovely to see you like that."

It's true – the inner child in me has been re-awakened. And she's hungry for more adventure. A bit later, he suggests we stop and look at a graveyard of a church where there's a yew tree he wants to see. Happy to go with the flow, with no clear destination in mind, I agree without hesitation.

In the graveyard, we each spend some time communing with two different yew trees before he comes over to me and says, "Draw this symbol. It's a Reiki symbol for creating a channel between things, for opening a channel." He shows me how to draw it on the soil and after I've practiced it a couple of times, he says, "Draw it on the tree".

I wonder why it's me that should do it – why he doesn't just do it himself – but after he returns to his tree, I take on the task. Then, I close my eyes and feel for a few seconds the sensation that the tree's roots are moving underneath me, like the ground is giving way beneath me. I kneel down and put my hands on the roots of the tree, and I remember that quote from Roethke, "Blessed are the roots, body and soul are one."

At that moment, I look up and see that two of the branches have melded together – one of them is growing into the other one. I call Thor over, excited to share this story with him.

After looking at the different yew trees and exploring unsuccessfully for a possible water source, he goes ahead of me back to the van because his shoes are getting wet. When I approach the van a little later, he's pacing up and down outside it. Uh-Oh. I see that the windscreen has been smashed. Instant downer. Why?

Then we find the stone, lying on the ground next to the van. We figure out that it was just a random occurrence: the stone must have glanced off a passing car's wheels. The hole in the windscreen is precisely the shape of the stone, which despite its modest size has generated large cracks right around it. There's glass all over the front two seats.

"I know it wasn't deliberate," Thor explains, "because I actually heard the sound of the glass breaking and saw a car driving slowly by at that moment, as I came out of the churchyard. If it had been done on purpose, surely they would have been speeding away?"

He turns to me with a strange expression on his face. "What did you call in?"

"I asked for connection between the natural world and the human world."

"Well, that's happened in a very strong way."

"Yeah. The power of that little stone just caused so much damage. If one of us had been sitting there, we'd have been really hurt – and Snibbles was sitting on the dashboard." I pick her up and hold her.

"You know, you did that," he says, but his voice is matter of fact, not accusatory. "You did some strong magic there, and it's to show you what you're capable of. Because it seemed as if it happened at exactly the same moment that you were doing that piece of work with the yew tree, drawing that symbol and asking for the connection to be opened between the natural and human worlds."

He pauses, then, "But the thing is, also," he says, "a while ago I considered damaging it on purpose so I could claim insurance to have the windscreen replaced. I had been patching it up for some time where the rubber seal was coming off. So maybe I created this, too."

We both fall silent and stare at the stone. It's almost a heart shape, with a little dent in the top.

*

Two days later, we're still stuck in Barcombe, waiting for the windscreen to be repaired before we can travel properly again. We keep discussing what happened. "My take on it is that this is real and can really happen, that nature can speak to us directly," Thor says. "You did this magic."

His words land in me, in the place where I know that the victim stance I often fall back on is a lie. That I'm more powerful than I know, in touch with forces I don't fully understand. Everything I've ever wanted to happen in my life – really wanted – has happened.

"Look how powerful you are," he goes on. "What are you going to do with that magic?"

HANDFASTING

Here is the plan
It is love
Nothing else is working for us
Nothing else is guiding us

~ *Martha Tilston, Blue Pearl.*

Whose idea was this anyway?

I'm on day one of my period and the last thing I feel like doing is standing up in front of my closest friends and proclaiming my eternal love – for a year and a day – to Thor. Having people look at me, having to look happy … What was I thinking?

Oh yes, it was my idea. First vulnerably expressed last summer, on our Wales road trip, then raised again recently in Firle – and now this tender shoot is blossoming because it's what I wanted: getting handfasted in the bloom of early spring, surrounded by bluebells, at a festival where all my friends will be.

My original vision was much more extroverted than our current situation – I pictured everyone at the festival getting involved, with spontaneity and revelry in the centre of the village green as everyone celebrated with us.

Obviously, a vision for a totally different time of my cycle. Annoyingly, my bleeding time has decided to sync up with every single festival and camp for the whole summer season again, beginning with this one.

I've always been heavily affected by my cycle. The week leading up what most of my friends call 'the moontime' typically encompassed anything from fits of weeping for no particular reason (or every reason) to sharp, uncontrollable outbursts of irritability and deep despondency about my entire life. I dreaded and hated it, and although the arrival of blood itself would bring relief from the emotional rollercoaster, it was only replaced by one to two days of harsh physical pain, usually requiring the permanent plastering of a hot water bottle to my abdomen.

In recent years, however, I've started practicing something called Menstrual Cycle Awareness, which began as a fertility awareness method – charting fertility signs to avoid conception – and became a much deeper interest as I discovered the emotional and spiritual significance of different parts of the cycle.

I started to separate out what used to be just 'PMS week' and 'the rest of it, which feels OK' into much more subtle inner seasons of spring (pre-ovulatory phase), summer (ovulatory phase), autumn (premenstrual phase) and winter (the time just before, during and after my three days of bleeding). With this loving attention, my 'PMS' started to calm down, and was often completely navigable if I simply had enough space and autonomy during that time – which I was more and more motivated to create. My pain had also become more manageable.

Still, all this awareness didn't change the fact that outer circumstances often spectacularly failed to line up with my inner landscape – and the fallout from that was hard. Because my cycle wasn't exactly regular, I couldn't 'sync my diary' with it the way the Wild Power book advised – resting during my bleed and partying during ovulation – and even if it was, I wasn't going to miss exciting festivals that I looked forward to all year, just because they fell at the wrong time of the month!

We arrive at Into the Wild on a Monday full of rain, and in my exhaustion and negligible enthusiasm for life, I am ultra-grateful not to be in Thor's shoes: helping to set up structures as part of the site crew. I can safely stay in the van while he gets on with it, knowing that my ticket-earning job only begins during the festival itself: running a writing workshop and a mother's sharing circle. Maybe I will have recovered enough energy by then to be excited about this festival.

It doesn't matter how many workshops I've held over the past nine years. Whenever I know I have to hold space in a structured setting, I'm plagued by some degree of 'performance anxiety'. It also makes no difference how much I know I enjoy running sessions: I get such a buzz from the inspiration that flies around the room, all the juicy ideas and emotions, and I move into pure flow as I facilitate. I still dread it, every single time, and cannot relax until it's over.

But the fact that we've arranged the Handfasting for Saturday feels like an added level of stage fright that my nervous system is currently ill-equipped to deal with. It takes until Thursday, in fact, to finalise a day and time for the ceremony that suits our celebrant, ourselves, and the friends we invite to attend – correction, who I invite to attend, since Thor would much prefer it to be just us two, the tree and Lynne, the celebrant.

The tension builds. As the festival crew gathers and the punters arrive a few days later, kicking off the festival celebrations, my urge to socialise unsurprisingly fails to make an appearance. I surrender resentfully to the regime of early nights my body fascistically requires, jealous that Thor is out late dancing, doing contact improvisation jams and playing music. He distances himself because, from our discussions on cycle awareness, he understands 'Autumn' to be a time when I need to be alone and independent.

But I feel abandoned.

It's also not an ideal time to grapple with the insecurities that the start of festival season brings. We are moving from the intensity and closeness – with all its challenges and joys – of being just the two of us in the van most of the time, to being surrounded by lots of people with all their different energies. Including women of a stunning variety of beauty.

I'm so used to Thor being right there, rarely more than a metre away, that it's a shock when I suddenly don't know exactly where he is for hours at a time. Underneath is a bubbling cauldron of resentment that I don't get to have a proper wedding day the way my sister will have in July, one worthy of my parents flying over from the other side of the world. And it's more than that: it's the growing suspicion that this occasion of getting handfasted just doesn't mean as much to him as it does to me. In our discussion about logistics, it seems to me that he wants to fit the ceremony around certain festival workshops, rather than the other way around. And in my present state, left unacknowledged, my feelings of hurt and disappointment soon fester into anger.

Fed up with sitting in the van, I distract myself by getting sporadically involved with the Woodland décor team, which is suitably 'fairy' for me and allows me to be around gentle, soothing feminine energy. I get into fascinating conversations with other women about spirituality and connection with the land, and this gives me enough of a sense of who I am outside of the pain of my relationship to keep going.

While helping the décor organiser, Lina, a beautiful fairy-like woman and amazing artist, to set up her little fairy gardens, I hear Gabrielle, a festival regular from Brighton, exclaim joyfully: "The place looks like it's decorated for a wedding!" She's not wrong: white ribbons and heart-shaped willow decorations are everywhere. "Maybe there will be one happening – wouldn't that be exciting!"

I can't help but smile. "Actually … my partner and I are having a handfasting here."

"What? Wow! That's amazing!" They all gather around me, and I feel like it's my one hen party moment. "How perfect!"

"Have you decorated the yew tree? That's where we're doing the ceremony."

"Yes," Gabrielle beams. "Have a look." We all traipse over there. The Yew, where we first connected a year ago and where Thor was guided to bring me, still has that special energy that brings me comfort when I sit against it. Now, it has a beautiful dreamcatcher and occasional white ribbons hanging from its branches. A huge smile catches my face, and I even allow myself to be romantic for a moment.

"He's handsome," says Lina, the head of the décor team. "I was talking to him a bit around the fire, and I suddenly realised – oh, yes, you're cute, underneath all the beard and hair and stuff." I laugh, secretly pleased. The beard and hair never fooled me.

But that's only an interlude. An hour before the ceremony, which we've set for Saturday, the fifth of May, things come to a head between me and Thor. My bleed has now started, and we've spent all day in and out of arguments in our usual, entrenched positions on the van sofa.

Right now, I am very far from the emotional zone I imagined I would be for this ceremony: excited, celebratory, in love. Right now, handsomeness or not, I don't find anything about him even remotely appealing. I just want it all to go away.

I'm cursing myself: how horrifically optimistic I was to schedule this when we'd already called off one Handfasting, back in the autumn, because I was in the menstrual zone and not in the right space, suddenly finding Thor wrong in every way – and for his part, he was hell-bent on criticising me.

But the shame of having to text all my friends and the celebrant, Lynne, and tell them it's off, coming off as total flakes, dooming our relationship with a second cancelled commitment, is just not an option for me. So, we grind on through.

Thor admits that behind his distance and seeming nonchalance about this commitment are his feelings of mistrust and hurt at being 'left at the altar' at Stonehenge over the Equinox. "I'm only going to do this if we can manage to connect before, even if it's just for a few minutes," he says, and I know he's right. Somehow, with sheer determination, we manage to find our way back to each other for a few moments before we go to meet the others in the woods.

"You look beautiful," Kristen says as she and Graham greet us at the archway leading into what's known as the 'Owl Woods'. I've opted for a dark blue strapless velvet dress that I know accentuates my eyes and my tattoos. Thor is wearing goldy-brown hippy gear as usual, and Lynne is in forest green, as we requested. "You look beautiful too," I tell Kristen, who I'm touched to see has made a real effort to dress up for the occasion in a red dress, and Graham has too, wearing a smart-casual shirt and a waistcoat. She puts a wreath on my head, and I tear-up for a moment. Wendy is there too, looking as Mermaid-like and stunning as ever – everyone so punctual.

As we assemble under the Yew, Thor and I touch the tree and connect with it, though it's harder for me to really feel it through my self-consciousness. I'm aware of Kristen snapping away with her camera and am both grateful and embarrassed.

I get through the ceremony one painstaking moment at a time. Thor tears-up more than once and I feel ashamed that I'm so disconnected from my loving feelings, especially when he says, "You're so beautiful," in an emotional voice, at one point.

Speaking my vows is a powerful moment, though. We've each chosen our own – I wrote mine down and memorised them, but of course they don't come out exactly as they did on paper. As well as promising to be there for each other, in our own ways and words, and love each other, we both commit to reserving intimacy only for the other. I'm surprised at what an impact it makes on me to hear Thor say those words in front of everyone, even though he said it outside the stones back at Autumn Equinox. I realise this is the essence of what I want: that specialness, and for that exclusivity to be spoken aloud in front of others.

Lynne's contributions are sensitive and heartfelt, and I'm glad I chose her to do the ceremony. My favourite part is when we exchange our necklaces as symbols of our devotion, kyanite set in a 'his and hers' frame by my dear South African friend, Nicki. We chose kyanite because it is a self-cleansing crystal and Nicki told me it would help protect us energetically. When Lynne binds our hands together with my Indian scarf, we turn to the yew and place our hands against it. Lynne reads one of her poems, a long one that I've heard before, about being the 'all and the everything'. Graham plays a couple of gentle, sweet tunes on his guitar, sitting under another tree.

A random guy comes to watch the last part of the ceremony from a little distance, and at first, I think, who the fuck are you? But then it turns out that Thor knows him, and they hug, and have pictures taken together with Graham. As everyone else present is primarily my friend, invited by me, it feels right to have one of Thor's connections there.

We share the apple juice Graham has gifted us and my jitteriness starts to calm down. Now for the good part – enjoying that it's over and sharing the news and the photos. Always my comfy spot.

Attempts at being in a honeymoon space don't last, though. When we attempt to make love that afternoon, my necklace breaks – the kyanite splitting off – before we even get going. Thor is so upset by this that he pulls away. It's clear that he thinks it means something. I try to minimise the situation, but I feel uneasy, too.

*

It's two days after the end of the festival and almost everyone has gone home. We're still here – something that certainly eases the 'back to real life' pain I used to get after festivals. I'm sitting under a tree in a state of oneness that is visceral.

I feel like I've been on a descent into the Underworld. It feels like the strongest one I've had for a very long time. I've gone through so much resistance, struggle, and self-judgment – wanting to change everything around me. Now I've returned, Persephone with the pomegranate seeds grown into the most succulent fruit imaginable. I seem to be experiencing what Wild Power says about the 'effortless altered states of consciousness' and 'spiritual deep diving' that can be experienced during menstruation.

I've been walking around in a state of awe for a couple of days now, reeling with the embodied truth of things I've often read in spiritual books, things like "There's nowhere else you could be in this moment that would be better than where you are." And "Everything is just happening, you're not doing any of it and yet you are all of it". I have a stunning clarity about the identifications of my mind, seeing them for what they are, and I feel, for possibly the first time, how without those, I'm just pure, flowing bliss and love. And that's something that we can all be.

Inspired thoughts have been cascading through me as I walk through the woods, too many to possibly write down, but even that feels OK. The tide has turned from acute suffering, emotional overwhelm and physical pain, to bliss.

It wasn't our handfasting that was responsible for this shift. It was my Wild Writing workshop on Sunday afternoon. I was crying just a few minutes before, after yet another big, emotional discussion with Thor in the woods, but, of course, I had to show up anyway and deliver.

And what I was dreading turned out to be the biggest blessing.

The vulnerable state I was in only enhanced the richness of the workshop, as everyone present came with me into that space of rawness and realness. Within the first few minutes of the workshop, a woman was crying as she read her potent, heartbreaking words of longing to be one with nature, to live in harmony with the land. A man shared writing about his longing for family and freedom. Several participants came up to me afterwards to thank me or rekindling their love of words and their connection to themselves. I was on a high, yet totally grounded at the same time.

Sharing my gifts and being in my purpose healed me in a way that continually seeking love and affirmation from Thor never could.

From this space, reconnected with myself and my power, I can see that being with Thor, as painful as it can be, is such a powerful self-development tool for me. Because, really, relationship is spiritual growth, or at least it's my path to it, anyway. In this often agonising, yet ultimately liberating, opening of the heart, I simply can't get away with my bullshit the way that I've always been able to in more superficial, mind-based relationships.

In this relationship, as soon as I am in any kind of pattern, there is pain, and the relationship shows that immediately. We have a perfect feedback system: with his energetic sensitivity, he responds to any nuance of my issues arising, and then I respond to that. Things go well between us when I'm in the flow, moving with appreciation and gratitude in the zone of love; when I'm in my feminine, in balance with my masculine. If I'm in any other state, it's a bumpy ride. Our connection is calling me into greater and greater alignment and presence – what a gift. Intense and crazy-making as it can be sometimes.

I've also received some powerful medicine for my broader life journey.

I've been trying out Thor's method of finding answers from the yews, coming with the question: How should I approach this thing with Jay? The contradictions of wanting to keep up a relationship with him and the difficulties of seeing him have been weighing heavily on me: the practical issues of finding somewhere to stay each time, the financial strain of the travel expenses when I have no regular income, the exhausting travel and draining city-vibes that have been starting to give me a headache again.

I sat with the yew where we were handfasted. There was only one white ribbon left.

I was quiet for some time, and then it came: "Be who you are".

That was all.

RAINBOW: THE ANARCHIC UTOPIA

When I was thirteen, my best friend and I, both unpopular "nerds" at school, used to pretend we were hippies from the 60's. We dressed up in bell-bottoms and scavenged items from our mothers' wardrobes – not realising that the rainbow-coloured dresses were, in fact, 80's 'retro' fashion, rather than authentic Flower-Power items. We decorated ourselves with copious beads and medallions from my grandmother's treasury of jewellery and wore our hair in long braids.

We adored the song 'Aquarius' by 5th Dimension and used the line 'Let the Sunshine in' as a password to our secret garden hideaway, where purple morning glory flowers climbed over a brick wall. Alienated by the rap and early techno music popular with my peers, I pored over biographies of John Lennon and the Beatles and learned the poetry of Jim Morrison off by heart. I was convinced I was born in the wrong decade and wished I could have gone to Woodstock and taken part in peace protests. Later, I decided that in a past life, I probably did.

Fast forward to May 2018, and memories of these songs and dreams come vividly back to me when Thor and I spent eleven days at a Rainbow Gathering. 'The Rainbow Family' had a history in our acquaintance already, of course, one of their camps having been the setting of the Big Hippy Blowout between him and Dylan nearly a year ago.

The Rainbow Gatherings originally grew out of a huge peace gathering in the U.S. in the 1970's and developed into seasonal camps all over Europe and, eventually, in England too. Wikipedia describes their ideology as one of 'peace, harmony, freedom, and respect.' By the end of our time with this particular incarnation of 'The Family', I come to the conclusion that 'freedom' is the primary value. The camps, in their European/UK form, exist for twenty-eight days, from New Moon to New Moon, usually on squatted land. When I dropped into these gatherings briefly before and saw people lounging around on the grass or playing with hula hoops, I had the secret thought, "But what do they *do* all day?"

This particular 'Rainbow' is taking place in the beauty of the Ashdown Forest on the Sussex/Kent border. It's an essentially Utopian micro-society which is also semi-anarchic, in the sense that there's no 'leader', explicit organisation or control, and the few rules are all decided by consensus. Within the larger umbrella of 'Rainbow Gatherings', there is a subtype called 'Healing Gatherings', which are intended to be both substance-free and technology-free.

In stark contrast to the pre-booked, organised, often expensive, and 'closed' community camps (where you commit to stay for the whole time period) I've participated in for the past eight years, anyone who is in the 'know' via word of mouth or the Facebook group can attend a Rainbow Gathering, and you can come and go as you like, staying for an afternoon or a month. You don't need a penny to your name, and in fact there are a couple of homeless people (as well as us houseless vandweller folks) at the camp, yet this isn't at all obvious because of the absence of the usual social hierarchies and structure. Mainstream, disconnected-from-nature, commercially driven society is referred to as 'Babylon' and funds for group needs are raised by a Magic Hat voluntary contributions system.

On arrival, we are greeted with the customary words "Welcome home, brother / sister" at the signposted 'Welcome home' fire. A little way off, there's the cooking fire and a Sacred Fire, where cooking is forbidden – it's the site for communal gatherings, singing and dancing. The 'facilities' are extremely basic, with a 'shit pit' in the ground for daily toileting. Due to the lack of running water (all water is sourced, at great effort, from the nearest stream), 'washing up' is achieved by rubbing bowls and pans with ash from the fire.

One night, I find myself cooking a meal which includes creamed coconut donated by a guy who claimed he'd "tried it out as deodorant but it didn't really work". I graduate to a whole new level of simplicity and basicness, way beyond the van and previous camps – in fact, the van feels like luxury. There are no chopping boards or work surfaces, pocket-knives need to be borrowed from individuals to prepare vegetables, and there is no way to wash anything.

Let me introduce the human characters at this particular camp: Rob, one of the 'family' who seeded this particular camp (the 'Focaliser'), an intense Scorpio who takes everything very seriously and frequently clashes horns with Rolf. Rolf is a large, over-enthusiastic and puppy-like German who follows the camps all around Europe, is permanently attached to his weed and his guitar ('Healing Gathering' rules or not), and soon develops a hero-worship relationship with Thor. Larch (so named in a recent ceremony), another guitarist and weed chain-smoker who swings between humour and bitterness, telling us how he has been denied access to his young son for years by his evil ex. Self-proclaimed 'Green', a perpetually cheerful former bus driver with a barely concealed anger underneath, who constantly preaches at us that to be happy all the time is to be totally in the moment; Bryan, a long-term rough sleeper with a colourful and often-told history of environmental protest who spends most of the camp polishing the deer's antlers he found.

River, a near-silent Eastern European woman and blissfully smiling 'earth goddess' who wears long Victorian skirts despite their impracticality and who all the men are clearly in love with – but "She's in love with Mother Earth,"

Larch despairs around the campfire one night, "She has no time for me." River's friend, Tunya, also Eastern European, unspeaking but scowling. Hhuw, a 60-something devout Welsh nationalist and moon-goddess worshipper who I've often seen at festivals over the years, perpetually wearing nothing but a loincloth.

The first day of camp, for me, is a struggle between my civilised self and the wild one inside, trying to break through. It's my first time camping since last summer and on a physical level, I'm almost intolerably uncomfortable. I'm worried about stuff like smelly breath, and I feel oppressed and stressed by group dynamics. I want to retreat to the safety and familiarity of the dynamic between me and Thor alone together in the van, intense and challenging as that can be.

For a week, I wake up itching all over from mosquito and midge bites, tired, hungry, dirty, and feeling skanky. Yet I have seldom felt so spiritually fulfilled. It's almost as if we *need* a certain degree of letting go of the physical body to reach these places.

It's only when I reach some level of surrender that I get relief from my physical discomfort, or, rather, it just fades into the background of my immense connection with the earth and with the ecstasy of being alive, of somehow reaching the essence of it all through literally getting down into the dirt, letting go of the rules, and seeing what comes through.

The days have very little structure, yet they are full. Everything is purely spontaneous: sometimes, meal-making doesn't even happen, something which would have challenged me much more in my pre-van life. Time flows by in a stream of nature communion, hanging out by the fire, laughing, fetching water, chopping wood and building structures, talking circles, regular cathartic shouts as people release their feelings in a way that's impossible in urban life without the police being called, and near-constant singing and music-making. We start to learn a large repertoire of 'Rainbow songs', earth-based, nature-loving, 'peace 'n love' type songs.

At first, I can't quite take in that at Rainbow, it's really OK to be however you are. Even the aspects of people's personalities that could be a challenge are part of the liberating atmosphere. When I interact with Tunya, who never seems to smile and barely says two words to me – and when she does speak, it's very abrupt – it's easy to imagine that she dislikes me. But eventually I realise that the very permission she has to be unapologetically herself without being 'nice' or 'polite' is the same permission I have to be clumsy, hairy-legged, sometimes babbling nonsense, and to sing my heart out in whatever way I want, without being judged.

The usual social conventions and niceties are starkly absent here. For the first few days, this makes me feel lonely and un-integrated, because usually I get to know people by asking them questions about themselves and being asked these in turn. But chit-chat doesn't seem to exist here: no-one asks what you do and who you are. There's often silence as we peel vegetables together or make the fire, or else there's talk about social issues and protests, which I don't get involved in because they feel negative and draining.

Perhaps the usual polite yet insincere 'essential behaviour' is yet another mask for reality, for what really connects us. After a while, I no longer desire conversations that require me to define who I am; when these do occasionally emerge, I find it distracting from simply being in the moment.

Surrender moves in spirals. I find myself dealing with my usual 'group dynamic' stuff: the pull to be seen and included, and yet not always feeling particularly nourished by my involvement, many times feeling that I'd be better off alone with a tree. This was easier to do in the van because there was no risk of missing anything. When I stay on, sitting by the fire way past my capacity while Bryan goes on about chaining himself to a building, I wonder if I'm trying to keep my place in the family, the way my place in my own family felt precarious.

When I get more involved with making music and cooking, I find more connection and fulfilment in the group. But I feel insecure when Thor, my usual 'go-to', seems more independent – suddenly, it feels like it's always me approaching him for cuddles rather than the other way around. I comfort myself with the closeness to nature, which is deeper than I've experienced in van-living or even the community camps. I wake up to direct birdsong outside the tent, feeling no gap between my body and the earth as I lie there, camped in a circle of beech trees who shower us with their little catkins.

Thor and I have a freezing cold but refreshing dip in the nearby stream, and when walking alone one day, I see six deer ahead of me on the path. One of them immediately runs off, but the others stay and share a moment with me, locking eyes, until the other deer, probably the leader, comes to fetch them. Later, when we move sites, I spot the glowing eye of a frog in the hollow of a beech tree in the healing area. I call others over to watch in wonder as it breathes, its throat moving rhythmically.

Although at times, I feel left out by Thor's endless jamming with Larch and Rolf (a technical musician I'll probably never be), we gel as a musical couple at a level beyond my imagination, from our times playing and singing together in the depths of winter vanlife. It's the first time we've shared ourselves with others, both as a couple and as musicians playing together, and the mirrors we receive are strong.

One especially potent moment is on a hot afternoon, sitting naked opposite each other in the sacred fire circle, playing drums fast and furious and singing our hearts out. Our drumming comes to a stop in perfect synchrony, and there is an impressed silence from all present before Larch pronounces in awe, "Twin flames." Then he turns to us and asks, "When did you know?"

"Right away," Thor answers without hesitation, and I nod.

People join in with our songs and seem to be entering into spaces of inspiration, even ecstasy. It feels like a dream come true, yet it's happening so naturally. "We're enchanting people," Thor tells me, and it's true. Rolf and Hhuw are very taken with us, and we see that our way of singing while facing each other is more powerful than we realised. When Hhuw invites us to sing kirtan, a form of devotional chanting, at two small festivals after listening to us lead it once, I'm taken aback: this is the first time we've even done this publicly.

As we jam together with the other musicians, I go so deeply with my singing at times that it starts to feel like it's just *happening*, like I'm channelling. This is the first time I've experienced this through voice, though it has happened through dance a few times, at 5Rhythms classes or workshops.

I now know that I, too, am a music-maker, a musician, and a proper one at that, according to Thor's definition: "A proper musician can move into that space whenever and whatever is happening, whoever is around."

*

I find myself strangely drawn to Larch, with his blonde stubble, long-suffering expression, and frequent witticisms. There's a brotherly love there, but I'm wary of it, because that's how it started with Dylan, too. There are other similarities: like Dylan, Larch is not allowed to see his young child.

I realise that both he and Dylan represent a 'path not taken' in my own life. I came so close to doing what Larch and Dylan's exes had done – stopping Luke seeing Jay unsupervised when I was concerned about his substance use, and I didn't. The legal advice I got at the time said I didn't have a strong case, because alcohol is so normalised in British society, and I didn't feel able to live with separating my child from his father and facing a fallout down the line. I imagined Jay hating me when he was older, and I didn't think it was worth it. But unlike Dylan and Larch, the situation has been turned around: now I'm the one who doesn't have my child with me.

When Larch starts saying things to Thor like, "If your woman gets any more beautiful, I'll have to come and steal her one night," I hear the alarm bells and take a step back. I don't want to create another destructive triangle.

Like any group, the dynamics at Rainbow can be a total mind-fuck. Against the backdrop of obligatory 'chilled'-ness, there is an ongoing conflict between Rob and Larch around a perceived lack of contribution to the camp wellbeing (aka smoking a spliff and just lying around all day). A talking circle on group unity has been unable to resolve this problem, with everyone merely getting more entrenched in their positions.

When this tension is at its height, we are all affected by the negative atmosphere. The frequent lack of adherence to one of the very few rules for Rainbow Healing Gatherings – no weed smoking – as agreed by the

European Rainbow Family, is also starting to get to us, particularly Thor, who strongly dislikes being around stoned people since he himself stopped using substances.

All decisions are made using the Native American custom of the talking stick, using the consensus method. Consensus is notoriously difficult to reach in Rainbow Gatherings, but this time, we do reach one – about not sharing recordings someone had made of the music being played around the fire, and not making such recordings any longer, since the use of electronic devices is forbidden in line with the 'get back to nature' ethos. However, shortly after that consensus, members of the group are being rather loose about it.

Though emotive to some, this is a relatively minor issue, but I worry: what if something really harmful or dangerous was going on? A few of those who'd stayed at previous gatherings have told me about aggressive and sexually harassing men whose behaviour the group had not been able to resolve, resulting in others, particularly the targeted women, feeling unsafe.

I'm troubled by the implications. I imagine that in a gathering that draws people very much into their own path – perhaps rigidly attached to their independence, and their right to individualistic self-expression – it could be a challenge for the group to step up as a whole and put the greater good above personal liberty. And the fact that there are no fees undoubtedly makes the camps more accessible to those whose 'society dropout' status is due to mental health issues – something that could increase their vulnerability to being on either side of the attacker/victim polarity.

The sense of anarchy and edginess due to the squatting nature of the camp – the fear that our camp could be discovered at any time and we could be moved on – is not unlike constant threat in our daily vanlife, yet I feel much more insecure than I do in the van, where the two of us make the decisions. There are more unstable elements here.

And then the day comes when the fears come true: Thor and I return from a walk to find a disconsolate group sitting around the community fire. Larch informs us that the camp has just been discovered by a hostile rambler who threatened to call the police if we don't move. As a group, we elect to relocate from public to private land nearby, where it would take twenty-eight days for an eviction to be enforceable – and by then the camp would be over anyway. This time, the circle decision-making process is swift and efficient: our survival is at stake.

Thor and I have both had enough and after a private chat decide to take twenty-four hours out; we're not sure if we'll come back. But then we remember that Richard, who is to be the didgeridoo player in our upcoming improvised music space at Colourfest, is supposed to be turning up, and we need to practice playing music with him.

One of the reasons for our withdrawal is that we're a bit fed up with the inconsistency of the group around rules. Thor feels that the consensus-rule against the sound recorder is too dogmatic, especially considering that Rob, along with most of the camp, totally disregards the rule of no weed smoking which is just as much part of the European consensus as the no devices rule.

Still assessing whether we'll go back, we visit Tesco to pick up some bits, and to get rid of some rubbish. Suddenly, a member of staff snaps a picture of me putting a bag in the bin outside. Incensed, Thor walks straight up to him, threatening him with legal action if he doesn't delete the photo, while I watch from a distance, terrified. "It's OK, it's OK," the Tesco guy says, walking off.

Later, once Thor's calmed down, he realises what a mirror he just received. "That anger and aggression that came up in me – I'm no better than Rob, getting angry about electronic devices!"

We decide that our journey with the Rainbow family isn't yet complete this time around.

We return with fresh energy to the new space and become more proactive in creating the offerings we want to see happen. Thor starts an official Healing Area under a beech tree, I offer a women's circle and co-facilitate a cacao ceremony with Marion, who arrived recently with Zeb, and we play some powerful music together with Richard the didge-player, which feels like a real sound healing session. Again, I notice that when I step up and give to the group in an active way, I feel a much greater sense of belonging and satisfaction. It's strange, but I've filled my cup through filling others', when my usual understanding is that my own has to be filled first.

The tension between Rob and Rolf hasn't shifted, though, and things come to a head when a rage-filled Rob, triggered by what he perceived as Rolf's continual laziness and non-adherence to the music recording rule, pulls down the healing area bell tent while Rolf is still in it. We are all horrified, and I feel frightened: only minutes before the incident, Thor and I, along with some others, had been making music in there.

Inevitably, my initial happiness and relief at being back, seeing everyone and being back in nature freely, wears off and I find myself feeling like the tentative, uncomfortable, excluded girl again. I'm being tough on myself for not being able to stay with or integrate the expanded, spiritually blissed out place I had reached by the end of Into the Wild.

"Stop trying to change things. There's no point in trying to get somewhere else and be better," Thor tells me, but I'm so stuck in my negativity, I can't see a way out. At one point, he holds me up against the Healing Area beech tree in a gentle yet firm way and that's it: the emotions come flooding out. Along with the tears, there's a surge of body memories and visuals: witch burnings, whether from the collective unconscious or my own past-life memory, I don't know. I connect with the frustration of all that lost wisdom, the grief of it, and I let it all course through me. Afterwards, it's like a storm has passed, but a vague uneasiness remains.

*

The newly relocated camp has the unfortunate new feature of daily visits from the land agents who, of course, are keen to get rid of us. Knowing that legally they can't do anything yet, they still want to make their presence known on an ongoing basis. At times, these meetings are tense, and I avoid getting involved.

The first time the officials arrive, they walk straight up to our Healing Area opening circle under the beech tree, which I find very disturbing, instantly going into fight or flight with a racing heart. But to my surprise, the group just carries right on afterwards as if nothing has happened. I wondered if my strong reaction is just a symptom of my authority issues, having grown up in an era and a country where police violence was commonplace. To my surprise, when the police themselves turn up one day, they're very pleasant, much more easy-going than the land agents, happily following Rolf on a guided tour of our setup. I smile, watching Rolf's cheerful oblivion to any threat.

While I feel compassion for the landowners, who might feel threatened and afraid of unknowns camping on their land, my primary feeling is moved by the ancestral stirrings of grief and rage that the land of the people, once free for all to use, has gradually become the property of the very wealthy and privileged few. Those who genuinely respect and love the land and take good care of it are unable to live in the way that is natural to us as beings of this planet. The Rainbow family have a tradition of minimising their impact on the site and never use the same site again for seven years, allowing the earth time to restore itself. Later, after we've left, I'm pleasantly surprised to hear that the owner of the land himself (a Lord) eventually visited and was completely approachable and understanding.

In the background, all the time, there's a sadness in me. There has been a drop in contact from Jay since he stopped using his tablet, which I used to message and call him on, and I feel frustrated that prompting Luke to facilitate contact isn't always effective. The happiness of having Zeb around, seeing his natural and enthusiastic participation in the camp and the connection between him and his mum in this environment, is touched with poignancy that I'm not able to share this with Jay. When I asked him if he wanted to come to Rainbow with us for a weekend, he said "No". In fact, he no longer wants to come to any festivals with me. Mostly, I accept that we have very different interests in life now, and I've always subscribed to the 'your children are not your children' Kahlil Gibran philosophy, but our divergence still touches into some deep places sometimes.

*

When another German guy, Michael, says in a heart sharing circle towards the end of our time there, "I'm not here on this earth to be happy, I'm here to have experiences", I relate deeply. I realise that on this path, I'm learning to have trust in the unfolding rather than trying to control, manipulate or worry about how I'm going to ensure my happiness. And the payoff: synchronicities abound. Magic happens daily. I'm no longer trying to make anything happen except exploration, opening and finding out new things about myself and life.

At Rainbow, being given complete freedom to express and who I am, along with everyone else, has taken me deeper into a surrender to who I am, what I'm meant to do here, and what's coming through me. I touch into new depths of wildness: for the first time in my life, I allow my full-on hairy legs to be seen by others apart from Thor. There's something so liberating about it: I'm just being natural, I'm not changing my appearance to suit you or make you more comfortable, and it's really empowering.

Of course, at Rainbow, this is totally acceptable, and most of the women are the same here, but I know that at Colourfest I'm going to feel more vulnerable. After we leave to go to Dorset, we have a little shopping spree in Sainsbury's – "Babylon!" – and at Thor's prompting, I try on a pair of Native American-style fringed shorts, showing them to Thor in full view of the attendants. "This is the next step," I tell him. I would never usually wear shorts, least of all with unshaven legs.

Full of the Rainbow spirit, we have a lot of fun on the supermarket round, skating around the shop in joy and silliness, bringing in the joy and the playful child. The 'Babylon' that Rainbow people go on about is exposed for the illusion it is: our spirits are always there, and we can always access that, even if we're surrounded by commercialism. And we can connect with others in that place. When I see a woman coming out of Asda with an enormous unicorn balloon tied to her trolley, I'm captivated. Instead of suppressing the urge as I usually would, I follow her out and say, "That's a really great balloon, where did you get it?" She's the kind of woman I wouldn't normally talk to, overweight, wearing a tracksuit, but she smiles at me, and we share a moment of both really liking the unicorn thing.

Will we be able to bring this energy of freedom, innocence and wildness to Colourfest in the space we intend to create there?

Thor and I were both touched when Rob gave us a piece of the sacred fire to take with us. Maybe it will power us on.

*

As the post-Rainbow high starts to fade, the contrast of being in the van is strong: I find myself suddenly paranoid about being hassled and moved on by authorities, convinced that the woman who frowns at us from her car as we park up is disapproving, when in reality she's probably only annoyed because we've blocked her view. Although at the time I felt unsafe at Rainbow, too, because of the illegality and the tensions, I realise now that there was something reassuring about the solidarity and support of the community. Now, it feels like just me and Thor against the world.

But Rainbow is only a moment in time, not a sustainable way of life. Even this attempt at a Utopian society doesn't work, because of drugs, unresolved trauma coming out as aggression, and embedded sexism.

Listening to Xavier Rudd's 'Spirit Bird' song, I let the tears come again, feeling the deep poignancy of knowing that with all our best intentions, we can only ever approximate the dream, here on earth, on the material plane.

Give it time and we wonder why, do what we can, laugh and we cry
And we sleep in your dust because we've seen this all before
Culture fades with tears and grace,
Leaving us stunned hollow with shame
We have seen this all, seen this all before

Many tribes of a modern kind doing brand new work same spirit by side
Joining hearts and hands and ancestral twine, ancestral twine
Many tribes of a modern kind doing brand new work same spirit by side
Joining hearts and hands and ancestral twine, ancestral twine

Slowly it fades
Slowly we fade

Spirit bird she creaks and groans,
She knows she has seen this all before

~ Xavier Rudd, Spirit Bird

COLOURFEST

May / June 2018

Divine Longing

I'm lying on the floor at the back of a near-packed marquee called 'Emptiness', which is situated opposite another structure called 'Bliss'. I've carefully placed myself where I can easily leave if it all gets too awkward. A dark-skinned man with a vaguely American accent, a spiritual teacher called Matteo who arrived fifteen minutes late for his own talk – or 'satsang' – is speaking into the microphone in encouraging tones: He's encouraging us to feel the longing we have for God and our pain at being separate from the divine.

"Feel how difficult it is to live without God, *feel* how much you long for God," he says over a backdrop of angel-choir music. "Really feel it, let it through, feel it fully." The room soon erupts into moans, cries and sobs. "Whatever pain you feel in your life, let it be a doorway to your longing for God."

Suddenly, having managed to momentarily bracket my self-conscious cynicism – *Who is this guy? What kind of music is that?* – I find the bottom opening out from the trigger city I've been in for days. Of course … It's *this* that has really been playing out in my relationship with Thor.

At first, it was much easier than I thought it would be to make the transition from Rainbow to Colourfest. I realised that I was, finally, 'living the dream': I was co-creating with people, making music, spending most of my time in nature, travelling, getting into festivals for free … and now I was about to co-host a shamanic woodland space for music improvisation and ritual. It was one of those times when I felt like pinching myself with the amazing-ness of it all.

But then, my inner Autumn hit, and I stepped into another uncomfortable crucible of change. Yes, the perfectly aligned festival-bleed again. For the first time, Thor and I decided to experiment with having space from each other during my inner Autumn while we're still together. Previously, we've endured this difficult time while having to completely co-exist in the van, with neither of us able to have what we need. Or we've had time completely apart, like when I escaped to London in March.

Now, we are sleeping apart and being independent in our movements. He's staying in a tent in the woods, wanting to be close to nature so he can be in the right zone for what we're offering. I've taken ownership of the van, and after only two nights of me sleeping in it, he's observed it now feels like 'my van': "It feels softer and more comfortable."

There's something significant about the fact that now, all the time we spend together is through choice: I feel more powerful, having more control over how I conduct the space I live in. And, somehow, it's all connected to the fact that we are, for the first time, consciously creating a space to share with others, extending our 'field' together to other people. To play music most powerfully together, we need to be both stepped into our power as individuals *and* connected enough with each other. We corral our sexual energy, our couple energy, into our music, and it works. I feel good about following the advice Marion gave me when I consulted her about my lack of libido during my premenstrual phase: "If you don't feel to have sex, that's because the energy is supposed to be expressed in some other way. Find the way. Find what's not being met."

This seems to be the answer. And sometimes, we've ended up making love anyway, out of choice and genuine attraction rather than the habitual physical proximity of the other. Perhaps this is the rebirthing place of true desire.

But then my abandonment triggers inevitably rear their persistent heads: Thor has been going out and partying till late, and unlike previous festivals, because we're not sharing the van or a tent, there is no 'coming home' to me. I feel awful when, two mornings in a row, he doesn't turn up to the van for breakfast, as we arranged – the first morning, he overslept; the second, he'd left his phone in the van so had no idea what time it was.

Hard as I try to reason it away, every time he goes off to do his own thing, I'm confronted with my father wound. My dad would go off at nights without telling my mother when he'd be back – and occasionally not come back at all. Now, it hurts when Thor wants to go and connect with other people because I'm not, in that moment, in a space to connect the way he wants to. I feel judged, frustrated, rejected, and furious.

Frustratingly, it's the same as it was at Into the Wild and at Rainbow: the vulnerable parts of me feel lost without the one reliable and secure source of love that Thor represents. I want to stay 'plugged in' and I furiously battle surrendering to the natural separation of this point of my cycle. The fact is, I really *need* to separate so that I can go within, but the busy festival setting makes this impossible. I have to hold space for others, showing up to set up our woodland music area and rehearse, whether I feel like it or not. This was all supposed to be fun, but in my current space, it's just *work*. I can't drop fully into my own space, and there aren't enough women I know here to have a safe, gentle hang out 'posse'.

But then, I start carrying Snibbles around again. At first, I'm offended by Thor's "I don't see you holding your vulnerability" comment. But doing it more outwardly really does make a difference. As I walk around with Snibbles, I start to connect with my vulnerability, to gain comfort from stroking her, holding her, and feeling her tenderness, curiosity and magical playfulness present with me wherever I am. I get to a point where I can go to bed and spend a whole night without any abandonment triggering when Thor isn't there.

I still feel as if I'm constantly staving off an undercurrent of pain, though. It's hard work.

Now, in the Emptiness marquee, as I follow Matteo's instructions to ramp up the pain and really feel it, it becomes crystal clear to me that my life-or-death clinging to a connection with Thor is actually a manifestation of my pain at being separated from God. I now know this longing to be continually reassured of his love for me as something else: a desire to be deeply rooted in being loved by the Divine.

Something glimmers through the pain, and I let it in, because maybe it's that love that Matteo is talking about. The relief is instant. There's a softening, a ripening, a tentative green over the dark hills of my inner landscape. And I let it in more. My body becomes relaxed and open, pulsing in what I can only imagine is a kind of bliss. I've broken through. My pain has become, as Matteo keeps saying, the way in.

I've arranged to meet Thor at the oak tree in the healing circle after this session. I'm eager to show him what I'm like when I'm open and loving. He rewards me with a 'You feel lovely', but after a few minutes of holding each other my anxiety creeps back in. *Am I open enough? Will he move away from me again because I'm not open enough?*

I start to feel unsure whether I am in the right space to be with him. The truth is, as soon as I wonder that, I'm not, because I'm in fear. What I keep experiencing, over and over, is that whenever I am in fear, he doesn't want to be around me, and of course that's tremendously painful and I attach lots of stories to that: I'm not being loved or accepted as I am; this is conditional love. But Matteo's satsang showed me something: that I can choose to see my moments of insecurity as a spiritual opportunity. A moment of *Yes, I'm really just having to face my stuff here and be the love that I am, regardless of what's going on with my partner.*

It's then that I start to turn the corner.

That night, we're dancing at the Woodland Cathedral, which we 'space-cleared' the day before the festival started, at the request of the organiser. We're going deep with the music; the DJ is Will Softmore, who weaves a lot of spiritual stuff into his music, both in the tracks he chooses, which take you to certain places, and in the words he occasionally says in-between.

I feel the pain nudging its way into my consciousness: Thor is dancing near me but not connecting to me. I keep dancing. And I bring in my 'loving myself' practice but it's not doing it; I feel like I'm just going through the motions. Then suddenly, something shifts. I break out of the automaton way of doing self-love, into a moment of loving myself so much, loving myself in my pain. It's no longer just a concept but an actual, embodied feeling: a knowledge that life really loves me because if it didn't, I wouldn't be breathing, I wouldn't be here, I wouldn't be given this body or this life.

As I really embrace how much pain I feel, and at the same time see that the love is there, that life is loving me through the shit, gratitude and love pulse through me in waves. I see that all these things I've been suffering from are nothing more than practiced patterns of thought, unreal as graphics on a computer screen.

As we continue to dance, I occasionally observe a trigger thought – "He's dancing with that woman, I should be feeling worried about that" – and notice that there isn't an accompanying emotion. I'm not actually feeling threatened by what's going on; I can see there's no erotic energy flowing between them, but I have this pattern of thought that tells me this is a threat. And I can see that that pattern of thought, if I indulged it, would sooner or later arouse some emotion in me which then makes it all feel very real, true and convincing. I see now that it was just a practiced thought from the past, and I don't need it.

I can trust, I can choose love, and I do. And as soon as I do, I see all his behaviour in a different light. I see that he *has* been very consistently loving to me, and not negligent at all, but just not willing to be my father, psychologist or safety blanket. Because that wouldn't be helping me. Because I need to be love for myself.

We start to hug, and it feels joyful and loving. I can feel we've both gone very deep. When we go back to the van together, he really wants to connect intimately from that awakened state, but my physical needs are niggling. I'm hungry and tired, but I know that if I make a snack, it will break the energy for him, and the moment we could have had will be lost. I sense his tension and start to feel anxious, but I still need to take care of myself, so I doggedly spread hummus on rice cakes. Suddenly, he gets up to leave, saying, "I feel vulnerable."

"What do you need?" I ask him, facing him with as much love as I can muster.

To my utter surprise, he says, "For you not to be angry with me." Immediately, my heart softens as I realise that he's as afraid of me as I can be of him – that he can also feel rejected.

We do end up being intimate and it's beautifully vulnerable: he's crying, and a couple of times I slip into comforting him. "Don't meet me in the mother energy", he says, and I rejoin him in vulnerability.

What happened at Colourfest cracked the shell of a lot of co-dependent patterns we had become mired in: habits of caretaking each other's needs without checking in with ourselves as to what we really wanted to give. It's one thing to ask for your needs and give the other person a chance to give a clear yes or no, and, if it's a no, decide what to do to take care of yourself or meet the need elsewhere. It's another thing to just automatically say 'yes' to everything and give up your own freedom without realising it.

For the first time, my abandonment agony unfolded to become a discovery of the advantages of freedom. The freedom that we are giving each other. The story that's been running in my head throughout our relationship, that I'm the one who's always having to give him this freedom – a freedom I deny I need myself – is exposed for the bullshit it is. I can now *feel* that the freedom is great for me too: I see how precious it is for me to be able to follow my own flow, my own speed of movement. To not have to consult anyone about where I'm going next, to get into conversation with a friend I bump into for as long as I want.

The whole of the next day, with everyone I look at, I feel love. It's like a deepening of what happened at Into the Wild, where I found my belonging and my connection again but then went into grief afterwards about losing it. Now, I have touched on a deeper layer, one where I know that 'it' can't be lost. It is always there.

The Real Workshop

I'm in a hot, sweaty marquee. I'm roasting and uncomfortable and all I want to do is take my top off. The space is full of shouting men on the one side and women making 'Goddess-y' sounds on the other. I'm not feeling it.

The day before, I went to a workshop for women with Jewels Wingfield, whose work centres around 'rewilding love, earthing soul' while Thor simultaneously went to one for men, led by Jewels' partner, Mark. I absolutely loved the women's workshop. We howled and catharted and held space for each other as we moved through all kinds of emotions. It felt safe and precious and healing.

This one is the mixed-gender sequel and the culmination of the work we've done to heal our gender-related wounds. Thor and I have long talked about doing this kind of work together, with a view to perhaps eventually leading our own 'healing the masculine and feminine' stuff, together. We both committed to seeing this whole process through and coming to both workshops.

But as we walked in together and went our separate ways, I immediately I felt resistance, even though I'd been up for it just minutes before. Mark is getting the men to tap into their inner warrior power and it's all that beating-chests and roaring stuff that alternately makes me want to roll my eyes and to run for the hills in terror. The energy is so intense, and the worst thing is, the women aren't in unity the way the men seem to be. We're all shuffling around self-consciously and only half-heartedly expressing with our vocal 'celebration' of our femininity.

After Jewels and Mark talk about the gender war and the way we're trying to heal it now, we're invited to walk around the room and make eye contact and 'feel' the individuals of the opposite sex as we walk past them. It's uncomfortable, but that's what you expect in workshops like this. Most of the men look shifty and not very open, and I feel self-conscious and worried about looking like an angry female, but occasionally I meet the eyes of a man who's in his vulnerability and it touches me deeply.

Then we're asked to pair up and do a mixed-gender exercise. Now comes the crunch: no-one chooses to work with me. We're asked to put up our hands if we don't have a partner. I'm one of four women who congregate in the centre of the room and stand there like wallflowers at the school dance with our hands up in the air. One of the women is joined by a man and off she goes, wallflower no more. Then, as it becomes clear no other men are coming forward, the other two look at each other and decide to pair off, leaving me alone.

That's it. I go to the side of the room and sit out the exercise, watching with a churning of pain in my gut. I start talking quietly to a woman at the door who was refused entry because the gender balance was out, and she needed to have brought a man to be allowed in. "It's totally reinforcing the patriarchy thing," she says softly but with fire. "You can't come in without a man." That decides me. This is bullshit. I'm out.

"Should we go somewhere else?" I ask her. "Yes, let's go to the Woodland Cathedral."

The afternoon DJ at the cathedral is predictably chilled out, and I'm not motivated to dance very much, but I sit against the trees and talk with Hannah, my new friend. She spreads out a blanket and lays out sacred items: "This is what I do. I make an altar everywhere I go." But it doesn't seem nutty when she anoints me with an essential oil blend and smudges my aura. A couple of her friends join us, and I feel jolted, unsure of my place in the group.

I reflect on the way that, yet again, the workshop showed up my abandonment wounds. "I'm not being chosen" goes right to the core of me: all the times I was excluded from friendship groups at school because I was too nerdy or didn't have a tan, all the times I wasn't picked to dance with at school socials. Until I was sixteen, and suddenly boys noticed me. But by then, I'd learned to play a game.

Now, I choose not to distance myself from the other women because of my past stuff, because of a belief that I'm not wanted. I end up having a lovely time, dancing around between the trees like a carefree fairy in a band of many. Any time a man approaches our group, he quickly moves off again, intimidated by our self-contained magic.

The pull of loyalty is soon activated, though: as the time of the end of the workshop approaches, I go and wait at the tree outside the marquee for Thor. Of course, he's angry that I'd left. "I had this profound healing experience with the feminine, and then when I turned to see where you were, I realised you were gone. I was devastated." Later, when he's calmed down, he declares that I'm an elf. "Maybe that's why you're put off by things like the gender workshop – they're just too human".

The Birth of Treenity Portal

The first session of Treenity Portal, our woodland music improvisation space at Colourfest, turns out to be the best one. It's on the full moon, and several enthusiastic folk turn up in response to the board we've put up: a violinist, several guitarists, and a few drummers. It's fun, it's powerful, it's free flow.

For the rest of the festival, holding this space is a mixed experience for me, with a quality of 'fake it till you make it'. We're playing with Thor's didge-playing friend Richard for the first time – and we've only made music with him twice before, at the Rainbow Gathering. Exposing our musical duo for the first time to another musician feels like an edge for me, but mostly, Thor's hope that Richard would be the neutral, holding space between our 'couple' polarity seems to bear fruit. Richard is a very intuitive didge player, definitely tuned in to the mystical.

Still, within this new configuration, my ability to 'bring through' the sounds in my singing is difficult at first. Although Richard doesn't at all try to assert his ego – he's clearly happy to serve our vision – I feel more self-conscious when he's around, and it takes me a while to get used to his presence. It's also twice as hard to project my voice loud enough to be heard, since the didge is quite an overpowering instrument, but I know this is a good challenge for me to work with.

But then Richard doesn't turn up to one of the sessions – in classic hippy style, he refuses to wear a watch and forgot the time – and we struggle to hold it together. "It's because our polarity was weak, and we didn't have a third to hold it together," Thor says, and it feels true.

As the Treenity Portal sessions continue, though, I rise to the challenge of stepping into voice and my power of letting go in front of others, even when I'm not feeling like it because, of course (and again), I'm now on my period.

The menstrual zone, of course, does have its perks: greater access to depth and magic. During a rare practice session when Richard, the didge player, isn't there, I have an unexpectedly strong experience of singing with Thor. I sense my female ancestors stretching in a long line around me and next to me, singing with me in solidarity, in joy, in power, in blessing for all the women who are to come and are already blooming in this world.

The singing, which I've been struggling with since we got here and left the fiery creative womb of Rainbow, now comes naturally without any strain to my voice. I feel I've tapped into something again.

It seems to me that the music flows more liquidly when it's spontaneous. When we have a sing-song outside the van on the last night, people join in, and it goes on for ages. Later that night, we have an incredible jam with the crew and hangers-on around the sauna fire, each making up songs on the spot – so connective, so beautiful.

One night, around the fire of our sacred woodland space, Richard tells us about a dream where several figures appeared to him in turn: the Manitou, the Tyrannosaurus Rex, the warrior/knight, and an unknown male figure with regal clothing – "but not a king." Thor's interpretation is that these are all the creatures who ruled the earth at different points in time – and the final figure is the unknown one who will come in the future.

And then, I have a big dream of my own. Thor is standing in front of me with that steady holding-gaze he has, where he calls me into presence with him, witnessing me in all that I am in that moment. In the dream, I have the knowing that he is calling me to power, to the equal power I have with him. I have a strong sense of clarity that we have danced a version of this dance in past lives, that we have committed to each other to play these roles: for him to support me to reach my power.

When I wake, everything feels charged with the question: *How do I live this and know this, without giving him the power, without giving mine away?* Just because he has attained it already and can teach me something, doesn't mean I'm not teaching him something, too.

By the end of the festival, I find myself again where I was as Into the Wild rumbled to a close: I've been through an enormous crucible of change and growth, and I'm coming out the other side feeling so much more connected, landed in love and in the sweet centre of myself. I'm very grateful for that – but, my god, it's been a rough ride.

After festival take-down, we spend a day or two parked up in the area and go walking to look for the source of a stream Thor's spotted. "It's so strange," he says, "how we're living this way, just doing what we want and working when we want. Somehow it feels more real, living this way, when you do it with someone else." I smile at him and take his hand. Butterflies circle our heads, and the smell of yarrow and marigold is thick. "When I was travelling on my own, I often thought that I wished I could share it all with someone else." I think about the scene in the film *Into the Wild*, when Chris McCandless, after weeks alone in the far North, underlines "Happiness is only real when shared" in his journal.

We visit a Neolithic henge and gather some elderberries. Later, Thor tells me that the yew tree he speaks to at the church told him, "She's the one. Keep following her."

OSHO LEELA

June 2018

I'm working in a kitchen with a team of four others, preparing food for about fifty people. Chopping veg, making bread dough, washing up as we go along. Only, it doesn't feel like work: for nearly two hours, I've been involved in fascinating discussions about astrology and Human Design while listening to good music. I have discovered that one of the women is almost my astrological twin. My brain is buzzing, and my heart feels open and connected.

I come out into the garden on my tea break and sit there in the midsummer heat, inhaling the roses. In the background, the stately house; in front of me: a lawn surrounded by well-tended flowers, herbs and shrubs, extending out into a field with the hills of Dorset in the background. It feels like heaven. When I get back, I'm asked by the chef, a plain-talking but kind Australian woman, to collect rose petals from the garden to adorn the salad.

When preparing food for myself, this kind of delicate touch would not be something I'd 'waste' time on. Cooking is a perfunctory means-to-an-end that gets in the way of more important activities, like writing. But now I enjoy every moment of it, loving the feel of the smooth pink and purple petals, picking out the bruised ones with care.

Thor and I have been at Osho Leela Personal Development Centre in Dorset for a week. It all started with a weekend Tantra workshop called 'Being Total', held at Osho Leela, which my tantra teacher friend Marion, with characteristic generosity, gave us free places on. When we got to Sunday evening, we decided we didn't want to leave yet – that we wanted to experience the community and volunteer there. We impulsively signed up for the Community Experience Program (CEP). Exploring communities had been one of our intentions from the start of our vanlife journey, and we were excited to finally begin this part of our adventure.

My long-held dream of living permanently in community had whittled away from loss of faith over the years, as several meetings with others to try and create this came to nothing. Lack of financial resources stopped me from joining already existing communities that required buying in. Strangely enough, Osho Leela was the only community I had ever seriously contemplated joining. When Jay was three, and we attended the child-friendly

Kundalini Yoga Festival there, I loved the setting and atmosphere so much that I asked one of the residents, Tarisha, about what I'd need to do to live there.

I remember asking: "Do you have to be really into Osho?" to which she replied, "No," and made it sound possible for me to make the move. But when I got back home and emerged from the festival bubble, I didn't seriously consider uprooting my life: I couldn't face trekking Jay across the country every second weekend to see his dad.

Really, though, I wasn't ready.

Gradually, as Jay got older, the need for community living became less urgent. I found my groove as a single mom, accessed more support in other ways, and generally coped better with it all.

Now, I get the chance to explore community life from an entirely different vantage point. The Community Experience Program, to us freelancer vanomads, involves an almost unthinkable amount of structure and work: six hours on a rota, six days a week, plus three compulsory group meditations a day. The days begin at seven a.m. and end between seven and eight p.m. each weekday, depending on whether you're washing dishes for lunch or dinner. Coffee, tea, and lunch breaks are precisely timed and ordered. CEP's, as they are called, stay for a week at a time.

The centre is founded on the teachings of the controversial, radical guru Osho (formerly known as Bhagwan Shree Rajneesh) and incorporates many of his practices, as well as the therapeutic approaches developed by the therapy school Humaniversity, which was founded by his disciple, Veeresh, and the body-based practice of Bioenergetics. As well as running their own in-house workshops, programmes and festivals, the Osho Leela community also hosts outside events.

On my first couple of days on this intense regime, especially when changing sheets and hoovering an entire flat, I honestly have no idea what people are talking about when they say, "You can just feel the love here". I feel grumpy, tired, resistant and socially shy. Yet, I am here, for reasons I can't yet understand.

But after I settle into the work and start to bond with the women I shared a dorm with – yes, there are compulsory single-sex dorms, although you can also book one of the highly competed-for private 'dating rooms' – and get into the 'morning meetings', which involve dancing and hugging; after experiencing how landed in my body I feel after being given complete permission to release sadness and anger in the safe, supportive format of the weekly AUM meditation; after the group hugs at the end of each dishwashing session, and standing together for long moments of meditative silence watching the sky awash with the most stunning sunset, I'm beginning to see what this 'love' is.

It's a tough love, in many ways, a no-holds-barred facing of your issues, where everyone tells it like it is. But there is also a genuine meeting beyond the masks, a sense that everyone, however much of a misfit in the outside world, is accepted here. It's a chance to feel part of something, to be held by this belonging as we stir up the shit of our conditioning and our past, of everything that's limited us – and attempt to break through it.

As someone who has often struggled with groups, taking a while to find my place in them, I'm intrigued by the difference between my group experiences at Leela and what I had found at Into the Wild and Colourfest, where I struggled so much to belong and connect. The key to the unity I feel at Leela seems, very simply, to be the regularity and structure: I'm doing stuff consistently with the same group and, rather than having to figure out the social aspects, connection is 'built in' through the practices we share. This gives no room for the clique-ness that I've come across in even the best-intentioned group set ups.

On the surface, Leela is so completely opposite to our experience at Rainbow, where there was no structure at all. But the surrender to the flow of life that I experienced so strongly at Rainbow was, in a strange way, preparation for a different kind of letting go here at Leela: releasing any control over my own schedule.

Rainbow also paved the way because I was invited by life to integrate the 'working me' with the 'playful me': I had to attend to my freelance editing work even while living in a forest with the barest of amenities. This meant, for the first week of the camp, often missing out on the sheer spontaneity that was going on, resentfully stalking off to the 'signal spot' while I could hear others in full musical swing or laughing around the fire.

At Leela, this skill of dropping in and out of different selves with fluidity is very relevant, because throughout the day I need to move between deep, often emotionally intense spaces and physical, grounding work.

Unlike Rainbow, where anger often seemed to come out sideways or was hidden behind calling each other 'brother' and 'sister' through clenched teeth, at Leela there are socially sanctioned, organised, and structured ways of releasing anger and other negative emotions, through dynamic meditations taught by Osho and through the AUM meditation developed by Veeresh with Osho.

From my first AUM meditation, I feel the shift. As we journey through the whole human emotional spectrum, from anger to craziness to sadness to sensuality, expressing each feeling fully, I release so much. My whole body is buzzing with energy afterwards, even as I feel completely wiped out.

Rather than the well-intentioned anarchy of Rainbow, at Leela, responsibility is equally balanced with self-expression and permission to 'be'. There is an unabashed, clear hierarchy, set out on the photo board: at the bottom rung, CEP's like us; further up, Team Leaders, who have more responsibility and are committed to be there for three months continuously;

and at the top, the twelve long-term core members, including a few directors. The power dynamics are explicit: CEPs certainly do the 'dirtiest work' – toilet cleaning, laundry and bed-making – but the support available to them is also very good.

We have weekly sharing circles and if you have an issue with anyone, you can call for a mediated Friendship Meeting, something Thor and I end up making use of when we get stuck in a negative dynamic at one point. Each new CEP is also assigned a 'buddy', a more experienced long-term CEP who checks in with you regularly. Both Thor and I bond well with our 'buddies'.

One of the things about being at Leela that really works for me is that my need to 'do', so often frustrated in the van, is satisfied. The surprising result of being so busy is that I'm more able to grab the gaps, to make full use of them to relax, enjoy the moment and feel peaceful. I make a point of breathing with one of the eight yew trees in the wooded meditation area, or of relaxing in the hammock or grabbing a few minutes with Thor.

I realise that it just isn't natural for me to try and 'be' all the time, as I felt compelled to do in the van. My energy simply needs to express itself; I need to exert and exhaust myself. At Leela this is naturally built into the day, so I don't have to even think about it or seek it out. At seven a.m., I'm jumping up and down and running around the room with my arms in the air during Bioenergetics, a practice aimed at getting you back into your body and releasing any unnecessary 'armouring' you've developed due to past trauma. Or I'm thumping a pillow or shaking all the tension out of my body in a Dynamic meditation.

Don't get me wrong: sometimes I absolutely *hate* the thought of getting up at six-forty-five and want nothing more than to roll back over in bed. But I always feel fantastic afterwards, tingling, fully alive, energised, and spacious in my body and being. I also enjoy the relief and ease of so rarely having to decide what to do at any given moment. Having my day planned out for me makes me feel held. While two hours in vanlife could pass with me barely noticing, on the CEP I squeeze the most out of the day and go to bed feeling satisfied – if a little exhausted. My longing to work with people, to be part of a team that is creating something together, rather than always working alone, is also fulfilled by 'Leela life' as the regular CEP's call it.

On the Wednesday of the first week of the program, a Biodanza Festival gets going. I've always been a bit skeptical about Biodanza, a South American-created dance, based around the human need for connection and gently healing the nervous system, because it's very structured and I prefer the free movement of 5Rhythms. But I decide to have a go anyway, since it's here, and I'm rewarded with a touching and powerful experience at one of the workshops. Dancing with Thor within a group of four, tears come as I realise that I feel totally included here: I belong, no less than any other individual in this group. That it's the exact size of my family group is no coincidence.

On Friday, when it's time to leave Leela to visit Jay in Sussex, I'm surprised at how much grief I feel about leaving the holding energy of the community there. I've already fallen in love with waking up to hear the sounds of people and music in the kitchen, so touching and satisfying after years of living in various states of isolation. During my single mom years, struggling to create every experience for myself and Jay, I so often longed for an already-existing momentum to sweep me up like this.

Thor suggests we spend a longer period at Leela after my return from Sussex. Despite my already emerging feelings of attachment, I find it so hard to just say yes to this. Can I really allow myself to have this – this family, this home? Where, after only a few days, I feel I belong?

On a rational level, this feeling of belonging doesn't make sense. Living in a stately house and working full-time seems a huge divergence from the nature-based, nomadic, pagan path I'm on. I'm afraid of losing my own track, but I also know that Leela is meeting my long-held needs for community and for a spiritual growth that breaks through my patterns. I feel that real change is possible here.

But as I consider what it would be like to live at Leela permanently, I wonder how meaningful it would feel to me. While I would be on board with supporting personal development workshops that enhance people's lives, I know from experience that working on things that aren't part of my own vision doesn't feel rewarding to me. Could there be room for my own ideas if I stayed?

*

I board the train feeling blissful and expanded. Something big has shifted: on the train, instead of feeling irritation or overwhelm at the sound of a screaming little girl, I sense her free expression as a powerful primal force and feel nothing but empathy for her parents. When people get onto the full train and have to stand because there are no seats available, instead of numbing myself to them, I really *feel* where they are at.

I also notice that my usually very-present Inner Critic has quietened right down and there is more space in my body – a body I feel much more aware of than usual. Could it be that through the practices at Leela, space has been cleared in me for compassion and joy? To come out of my self-obsession enough to truly sense others, instead of being wrapped up in myself, with my energy held inside?

When I arrive in Lewes, I'm still in a total 'love space'. As I walk down the High Street in the sunshine, past the boutique shops and the mothers with their pushchairs, I wonder what it would have been like if I could have experienced motherhood in this state of love and openness. How come motherhood didn't open me in this way, and in fact often seemed to cause further contraction?

I walk to the riverbank and sit for a long time, stroking my own feet. There's a new sensuality in my body. I feel a rush of love and exuberance and gorgeousness. But it doesn't feel like the temporary 'high' I've often experienced after so many yoga and personal development workshops. It feels grounded and real.

When I move from being alone to being with Jay again, however, I soon start to feel uncomfortable. Suddenly, everything is painfully reminding me of the emotional states and habitual mindsets I used to occupy in my single motherhood days.

Coming from the expanded openness of an intense, embodied spiritual practice within the holding of community support, I feel the vividness of the contrast intensely. *Wow, I just really didn't enjoy life very much back when I was living in Lewes.* So often, I was just in survival mode.

That weekend, at the notoriously busy Level Park in Brighton with Jay, watching others parent is a surreal experience. So much of the personal development work at Leela is about unravelling the conditioning we've had so we can be our original selves, free of the bullshit. But now that I'm here, back in the situation of actively being a parent, around other parents, I remember the awkward contradiction of this approach. As a parent, if you want to give your child a chance of reasonably coping in the world, you *have* to condition them to some extent.

You can't raise them to be a totally free self-expressive person, or you close off their chances of being able to camouflage and make it in this strange (some would say sick) society we have. It's just so difficult – how do you live that way, freely and free of conditioning and repression, while being a parent? Is it inevitable that we all have to end up at centres like Leela, working so hard to reclaim our essential selves – if there even is such a thing?

Of course, my role as parent has changed drastically. I'm no longer there to oversee everything and to ensure that the conditioning is as un-damaging as possible. This time, it's been four weeks since I last saw Jay, and I'm struck by how much he's matured in that time. I feel both proud and moved when he initiates a conversation about impending adolescence. "I don't want to be a teenager," he says. "I don't want to change like my cousins did."

*

At the end of the visit, I'm in tears at leaving him after what feels like way too little time together. He seems to be feeling a similar way – on the last night, as we massage each other's feet at his request, he tells me, "Sometimes I miss living with you."

Through my feelings of grief, I'm starting to, slowly but surely, let go of my ideas of what my being an involved parent looks like. I'm no longer attending school plays or helping with homework. But my time at Leela has helped me to see that I have a role which is just as important as the daily holding-the-fort that I used to do. I can be there for Jay, emotionally holding space for him, showing him different aspects of life, and having fun with him.

When I expressed my guilt at doing so little actual 'parenting' to Fiona, who we're staying with that weekend, she reminds me that I am the one who did what she calls 'the hard graft' – the broken sleep for 2.5 years, the breastfeeding, and the early, painfully difficult socialising. And I did it alone, whereas Jay's dad has, and always has had, family support.

Fiona also reminds me of this key fact: after Jay came on the scene, Luke was in a position to continue his life exactly as he had pre-parenthood while I, of course, couldn't. What would be the point of having my freedom, now, if I didn't fully take it and live my life as I want to?

Sometimes I imagine moving closer to Jay, getting a job and a room in a town and letting go of the dream of living on the land for now, but everything in my body and soul shouts an unequivocal no. And I remember what the tree said to me at the Iron Age Hill fort in Cadbury, Somerset, when I got right inside its hollow: You're on the right path.

*

I return after my weekend with Jay to do another five days of the Community Experience Program. Leaving Thor there during the weekend of the Biodanza festival, especially on a 'Sexuality' themed Saturday, felt edgy, but I trusted him, and when he tells me he felt empty after I left, wondering why he was there, it feels like a good remedy for my stories that he has a better time without me, that I stand in his way when he wants to be free.

Walking through the big red front door, I feel my whole body relax. But the next morning, Thor accuses me of being disconnected again, of not being in my body. "You were only riding off my good waves because I was at the Biodanza weekend," he says, and I prickle at this: I put a lot of effort into my practice during my days away, continually bringing my attention back to my body.

But I have to face the fact that in my short time away, I have indeed gone into my head: the anxiety is back, the heady-ness of a weekend of talking a lot has taken its toll. I try to do a love practice from David Deida but it feels like just another thing I am doing with my head and not a real energetic thing that is happening. Another effort.

As the week goes on, though, things continue to move. I get closer to the women I'm sharing a dorm with and also bond with some new arrivals – the flux in the community is near-constant. Thor and I also have some big breakthroughs in our relationship due to the work we're both doing there, getting to the bottom of patterns that have been sticky throughout our time in the van, such as my (inaccurate) belief that he only wants me for pleasure and the way he gets triggered when I withdraw from connection.

But I'm getting tired. I know, as I approach my inner Autumn, that the need to slow down and rest more will be impossible to meet in the relentlessness of Leela's schedule. Despite the beauty of the gardens and fields, I've also started to miss being in the wilder nature that's possible in our vanlife. I long for open space.

HEALING CRISIS

I'm waiting in the van while Thor is at a doctor's appointment to have the sore on his nose checked out. We've decided to go away for a few days to take a break and assess whether we want to come back to Leela. Thor has mentioned the sore from time to time, noting that it's been getting bigger, and I've tended to shrug it off as a pimple gone wrong or something harmless like that.

I'm feeling the strangeness of being in a town and, wanting desperately to be in nature, I go and sit with a tree I can see opposite the surgery, even though it's overlooked by a row of houses. Just as I'm getting comfortable, expecting Thor to be a while because doctors always run late, I see him walking back from his appointment already.

Something very uncomfortable awakens in my solar plexus.

He doesn't look at me, just hands me a piece of paper which has 'basal cell carcinoma' written on it. He looks ashen. His words come out in a blurt: "I really thought she was just gonna say it was nothing, but she was quite concerned. She said it could be this thing, which could be cancer. She's referred me on to a dermatologist and she's fast tracked me."

I don't know what to say, so I just take his arm and we go back into the van together. He drives us to a park up by some woods so we can have some time to digest this news.

He starts crying. "I'm scared." I hug him, feeling strangely detached. After my initial reaction at seeing him come out of the doctors, there isn't even a hint of dread, fear or anxiety in me. I don't think he's going to die.

But we continue to talk about it, and I listen to him share about his feelings and cry for a while. Finally, he says, "I think you probably have something to express about it too," and his words unlock something in me: a huge terror of losing him. A wave of tears cascades from me.

We hold each other and cry and he says, "You shouldn't depend on me too much." I know it's true – Right now, I feel like I would be so lost without him. For the rest of that day, everything is surreal. It's as if we've entered into a space where these might be our last precious days together.

It feels totally clear to me that I just want to love him as fully and embrace him as completely as I can without all the difficult stuff that comes up between us. I want to appreciate every single moment I have with him.

"If I knew for sure I was going to die, would you have a baby with me then? Something to keep of me so you won't be alone?"

My 'yes' comes without hesitation.

But inevitably, practicals take over from dramatic emotional resolutions: we end up having an argument about whether to stay in the area so he can get the referral that will come via Leela.

I need to get some fresh air, so I go for a brief walk. Thor declines to come along. The peaceful appearance of the woods we've chosen turns out to be deceptive – one of the first things I see on emerging from the van is a sign warning that some of the trees are diseased and must be felled.

I continue my walk through the constant buzzing of bees and flies around swampy water, none of which feels inviting. My mood becomes deflated. Maybe we should have stayed at Leela. Maybe we're just resisting the process of change that's been unleashed for us both there through the excavation of long-buried emotions. And now, this health crisis. It's probably a sign.

I soon turn back, and as I approach the van, I notice two butterflies dancing around each other outside. It makes me smile, but I'm dismayed as I enter to find Thor crying in bed. "I didn't really want to be alone," he sobs, and I feel dreadful. *Why didn't I see that?*

"I was in a pattern", he goes on, "but I only saw it after you went. … a pattern of pushing people away from me when I actually need them. I think I was doing that by leaving Leela, because I was just getting close to people and then I left." He pauses. "I need your help. Will you give me some healing?"

"Of course," I say.

"Let's go outside," he says, and we go for a walk, discovering some pleasant woods opposite the tainted ones I explored earlier.

We spot two butterflies interacting in an interesting way. It looks as if they're about to mate ("I've never seen butterflies making love before", he says, with a childlike innocence). But then we notice that one of them isn't moving. "Is it dead?"

The other butterfly keeps prodding it gently and persistently, then it flies around it at a distance. Suddenly, the prone butterfly begins to move. It feels like we are witnessing a miracle. Thor turns to me and says, "I give you complete permission to give me healing in whatever form you want and feel guided to."

A bit later, as we're walking back in the direction of the van, I feel an intuition to have him lie up against me as I sit with my back to a beech tree. I send healing energy from my womb, which is close to its releasing time and feeling powerful. He feels it strongly, and I do too.

But after this healing, a few days pass without me feeling called to give any more – and without him asking for any. Eventually, he gets upset with me: "I asked you to do healing for me."

I sigh. "I thought that you would ask me on an occasion-by-occasion kind of basis, like, "would you do it for me now?"'" I protest. "In the moment."

"No. What I meant was, I want you to give me healing. You can do it whenever you feel to."

On one level, it's a simple misunderstanding, but it also feels like there's some deeper stuff going on there about trust and self-esteem for me – especially when he says, "If you heal this, it's a real opportunity to show to yourself what a great healer you are."

I feel the pressure inside me. I know that I have healing abilities, but I don't seem to be able to tap into them at will to the same strength as Thor does. Sometimes they are strong and accessible, and sometimes they're not, and I can't figure out how to control that. It totally depends on where I'm at. And this is a potentially life-threatening health situation. I don't know if I want to be responsible for healing that. Not that he's asking me to solve it, but still …

Later, I give him some healing again on the bed, using crystals. He's becoming very concerned about his heart, now, focusing on the chest pain and cough that have plagued him intermittently for years and have already been checked out, with no result.

"There's something wrong. I think I'm going to die of cancer."

I don't know what to say.

*

After these strange few days of limbo, the urgency of the health crisis seems to fade into the background as we resign ourselves to awaiting the referral. "We can't know anything, and we shouldn't worry about anything, till we know what's actually going on" is the standpoint we settle on. Thor rings Leela and asks them to look out for a medical letter addressed to him.

Right now, though, we need to make a decision: should we go back to Leela – we're still in Dorset – or travel on to Glastonbury, to sing at the kirtan gathering Hhuw invited us to? For no reason that we can name, though, neither of us feels drawn to returning to Leela right now. "Are we just running away?" Thor asks me.

"I don't know, maybe."

"I think we might be escaping from getting closer to people," Thor suggests. "Maybe we're scared of forming relationships with people who are really emotionally open?" I think there could be some truth to this. Is the risk, without the commitment of an intimate relationship such as we share, just too threatening because of the transitory nature of the community?

I know that there's more potential to connect on a heart level with the people at Leela: connection is so woven into the daily activities, through working and doing the practices together. Also, the people drawn to Leela on a repeated basis tend to be more open. Every time I hugged a particular woman, who had come on CEP several times before, all the way from Israel, my heart would almost explode. It felt as if she was embodying love, and we became a sort of love-field together. It was so beautiful.

Yet, it's also true that having my freedom felt safer.

I wonder if we're continuing to pursue external freedom – the freedom to move, to not to be told what to do, and to have our day be ours – over the internal freedom we could gain through commitment to the program at Leela. Doing the deep transformative work there.

In the end, we decide that we just can't do it. Something is saying 'no' at this time. On a practical level, we need the space to do our own work, anyway. But we agree to not 'waste' the inner work we've already done: to continue supporting each other to keep coming back into our bodies when we leave them.

We do spend a few days near Glastonbury, but Thor's voice is so ragged from all the cathartic shouting during an empowerment workshop at Leela that singing at the kirtan festival becomes a clear non-option. He has too much work to do, anyway. I find myself with plenty of rest and space, but there's no denying that I'm not as happy as I was in a community setting. I feel stuck in the middle of nowhere: unable to access a Red Tent women's gathering I know is happening in Glastonbury because Thor is too busy working for me to even consider asking him to drive me there.

Even though, on the surface of things, my life as a nomad is dramatically different from my former incarnation as an urban single mom, this feeling of isolation is oddly familiar. I remember a single mom friend asking me to help her do a deep clean of her house and feeling unable to offer that support, even though I really wanted to and was totally on board with the principle of single mothers helping each other out. I was just too drained and stretched myself. Now, although I'm not tired and overwhelmed, I feel I'm coming up against the isolation of fragmented living once again.

Being there for each other is important, but not enough. We need the holding of community. I felt the power of this when Thor and I had our ups and downs at Leela but were able to have the space from each other that we needed, as well as other sympathetic ears to confide in. We weren't so reliant on each other for our emotional needs – and this felt much healthier.

Yet, committing to any community involves allegiance to certain ideologies, even dogmas, whether explicit or unspoken – and this can mean compromise beyond my integrity. On my Sussex weekend, I was given pause when I spoke to a friend and her partner who had both stayed at Leela before and encountered what sounded like some dubious power dynamics there. It brought up fear that my relationship with Thor would not survive there; that we would both be confronted beyond what we could handle.

On the most basic level, I know I would struggle with the lack of space for us as a couple, and with balancing the needs of our relationship with our own individual needs in the very limited time available. Thor did book one of the dating rooms for us once, but unfortunately it coincided with me having a day when I really needed 'me time' and was in no mood to connect – the pressure of having such limited time to do so did me no favours, either. An argument and a stand-off resulted, and I ended up sleeping alone in the beautiful red-themed room.

*

The changes set into motion at Leela do seem to stick for some time, though. We both notice that I'm more spontaneously expressive, moving from one emotion to another freely, like we do in the AUM, without getting stuck in any one feeling. When we discover that the current heatwave has killed the mineral water supplies actually swear in Lidl in full hearing of a staff member, which is, as Thor points out, highly unusual for me. The PMT that usually plagues me seems practically non-existent when that part of my cycle comes around this time. Maybe I've released some of the tension that usually comes up.

As for Thor, the critical and angry sides of his nature seem to have calmed right down, to my enormous relief. Is it possible that two weeks of emotional release could have shifted things so much? For the first time in the van, I don't feel like I'm walking on eggshells.

Still, being back in the small space of the van after a fortnight is a surprisingly hard adjustment. While I'm appreciating the lack of structure and the beauty of the nature around us, it's proving harder to let go of the autonomy I had at Leela in relation to Thor. We seem to have forgotten how to navigate around each other physically in the confined space and keep bumping into each other. I feel frustrated at having to run everything by him, negotiating when it's OK to work on my laptop.

My thoughts run wild: *Well, I'm not happy like this so I should change it, but I'm not happy at Leela either so I need to find the perfect situation …*

But there are moments where I break through. Yes, it's a heatwave, it's too hot to be in the van, I'm miles from anywhere nice and Thor is watching football, for fuck's sake. Yet somehow, it's all, strangely, OK. Perhaps I'm learning, at last, that there isn't a perfect situation. Learning to make the best of it, accepting that however it is, it's temporary. And that my external circumstances don't matter so much.

SCRUFFY BOX

As time passes, the sore on Thor's nose continues to grow, along with his now obsessive worry. He finally gets his referral to the dermatologist, but he's afraid that it will take a long time before the lesion can be removed because it has to be biopsied first. Then, the night before his appointment at Yeovil hospital, after a long and tiring drive to find a park up in the area, we get into an argument.

The accusations come thick and fast: "You're just not supporting me. I do so much for you, you don't do anything for me." We've parked up outside a river, opposite a bridge, and he suddenly gets up and walks off. I'm furious: he's left me unable to lock the van and go for a walk myself because he's got the keys. As I continue to fume, I wonder if tapping into the anger the way we do at Leela is always such a good thing.

One night, after the AUM meditation, a row had escalated to the point where I ended up throwing his belt at him – not deliberately intending to hurt him, but still, it nearly hit him in the face, and he was really upset. "If that had hit me, I don't know what I would have done – I might have got out of control, because I was hurt." It scared me, because I never used to do stuff like that. Had I taken the lid off something that was now proving to be uncontrollable?

Now, I find myself in a very inhospitable environment: signs everywhere saying 'private property', 'no public right of way'. I ignore one of them to climb over a wire fence, desperate to try and relax by the river, to connect with nature, always my go-to. But it's impossible, of course, I only get more and more wound up, sitting there, having to glance at the van every few seconds to make sure no one's breaking into it, while feeling like I need to have eyes in the back of my head on the lookout for an angry property-owner.

After forty minutes, Thor comes back to the van. I approach him, still furious. "Do you want to talk?"

"No, but it looks like you do." His eyes are red from crying – so he's not angry anymore, he's upset. Something in me says, *this is not the time,* but I railroad over it because I'm just so angry and I have him as a captive audience right now. I begin to share with him how I'm feeling, and I really give it to him. His eyes well up but rather than it evoking my empathy, I only feel manipulated, which winds me up even more, so I carry on listing all his faults. He finally says, "Are you done now?" and when I nod, he gets up without a word and climbs into bed.

I try to walk off some of my anger, but the road is busy and noisy. I return to see him lying there on the bed and something sparks off in me. "Oh yeah, that's right, just lie there being sorry for yourself!" I cannot believe the words coming out of my mouth. It's like I'm channelling my mother, or maybe his mother.

He leaps out of bed, jumps down from the bunk and stands in front of me, absolutely heaving. "That's enough!" he shouts, and he's livid. His face is streaming with snot from all the crying; he looks a total mess and more than a bit insane. There's a look in his eyes I've never seen before. He shouts at me, "That's enough. No more. I will not allow you to talk to me like that." He moves his arm and it's not exactly that I'm scared of him – I don't think he's going to hit me or anything, but I feel the power of where he is in this moment, and it silences me.

"OK," I say.

He lifts his arm to make another movement and then suddenly he's clutching his nose and going, "Oh fuck, oh fuck." Blood is pouring from his nose, mingling with the snot and the tears. He climbs up on the bed, gets some toilet paper and tries to mop it up: it's bleeding so much, and I'm terrified. Is this another symptom? Maybe his nose is bleeding internally!

He curls up on the bed and starts to cry in the most deeply primal way, like a baby. It's so intense. I feel like I need to comfort him, but I feel numb. Eventually, he lets me hold him and we somehow get through it. I realise that all that's happened is that the sore has been knocked off his nose, and after a little while, the bleeding stops.

When he's more coherent, he explains what's happened from his perspective. "In that moment, when I confronted you, I was finally standing up to the archetypal feminine – which in the form of my mother was always criticising me. I was basically saying, no more, this is my boundary, and it's when I did that that the lesion on my nose ripped off."

At the dermatologist appointment next day, he's told that he did a good job of removing it. However, there's still the gauntlet of the biopsy ahead, and the dermatologist is also concerned about another mole on his head.

As the next days unfold, we watch as the sore on Thor's nose, which we both hoped was now gone, starts to grow back, and at a rapid rate that frightens us both. Thor is obsessed with the thought that he may have cancer. I try to reassure him, but my words feel as insubstantial as air

What is clear is that it's my turn to give to Thor in the way he's so often given to me. The onus is now on me to suggest, from my intuition, things that could be supportive on his healing journey, like 'go into the sea' or 'express through your music'. I also give him healing, often spontaneously. I'm so accustomed to focusing on keeping myself on an even keel that I'm surprised how good and empowering it feels to simply give. And this crisis seems to be bringing us closer. When I give him healing, I feel an unconditional love force come out through me into him and around us both, and it continues afterwards for some time. I feel resourced and energised.

After a while, we settle back into vanlife and start to enjoy sharing the space again. We're finding better park ups and it feels like we've once more coalesced into the joint energy that's essential to making this situation work – affection, closeness, and humour have returned. We're also both managing to find a way to work. taking turns to sit in the van and in the cab. We have hot chocolates, chat, and chill, and I relish doing simple things for Thor like trimming his beard, always with this background awareness that it could be one of the last times I do it for him. I'm haunted by a post on Facebook about a programme following a man in his last months of life after a terminal diagnosis.

We have a fun evening walking on Chesil Beach, playing music, which we've not managed to do since Colourfest. The Chesil Beach day is one of those days where I wonder if it's possible, after all, for us to be together *and* express our creativity and autonomy. As we step across a line of rocks outside the van door to get onto the pebbled beach, we start joking about how we now have our own stairs from our scruffy box to the beach. The name 'scruffy box' sticks.

Autonomy is still an issue, though. I need Thor to drive me somewhere with signal so I can fulfil an appointment with a client. If he needs to get water to wash his hair, that can potentially delay me with a deadline, and I feel fidgety and powerless. The conflicts we have over phone use continue; Thor feels that we need phone-free time, which in theory I agree with, but I also resist being externally controlled over it. I battle with being a social creature, with a need to hook into networks, to share pictures of my experiences and to be seen and heard. I know this breaks me away from the deep feeling of peace I get when I'm sitting in a circle of trees or gazing out at the sea from the hills, but I can't seem to help it. I need both.

BUDDHAFIELD

July 2018

Blasé

This is odd. We're driving up a dirt track onto the farm that marks the last bit of semi-civilisation before we enter the timeless land of Buddhafield. I can see fields and the beginnings of structures half-way assembled, a few scattered tents, and groups of people moving around, working, chatting. And the weird thing is, not one bone in my body is excited.

Since my early twenties, I have almost *lived* for festivals and community camps. They've given me access to community, outdoor living, ecstatic and transformative experiences, and a sense of myself as I really am. But after nearly eight months living off-grid, it's just not the same anymore: the contrast isn't so great, and the sense of relief at 'arriving' in freedom is missing – my life is so untethered already.

Come to think of it, Into the Wild and Colourfest didn't excite me as much as they usually would, either. Feeling zero sap rising as we approach Buddhafield, however, really hits me. It's been my dream to be part of the set-up of this festival since I visited Thor while he did it last year and stayed with him in the van. I remember seeing the crew playing music late into the night around the fire and longing to share in their sense of togetherness, to be a part of creating this legendary five-day event, the biggest, most popular alternative summer festival.

This is the festival my sister and I fell out about. But now, I feel blasé and jaded. I just want all these people to go away.

My experience last year of hanging out by the van for a week before the festival while Thor did the electrics, not talking to anyone apart from him, turned out to be pretty isolating, so this time I've resolved to get more involved. But I was turned down for all three teams I applied for: décor, the Women's Area, and stewarding. All were already full. Probably the same people who always did it had taken the few places available, again.

So, I organised my free ticket by volunteering to work at the same café I worked at last year, during the festival itself, although I would have preferred to enjoy the programme of events without working, along with Thor.

Still, with his encouragement and characteristic "It'll all work out" approach, I've turned up nearly two weeks before the start, on a wing and a prayer, trusting that I'll be able to find set-up crew work once I'm there in exchange for meal tickets. It's a risk: I've brought only minimal food, which is unusual for me, given my food scarcity issues.

I'm arriving on a deficit, exhausted after the past two months of non-stop-ness (Rainbow, Colourfest, and Leela). Even resting for whole days hasn't improved things. There's a fair amount of anxiety around, before I even start: will I have the energy to do the tasks required of me? And will I be able to do them, or will my dyspraxia expose me for a fool?

Part of me wonders if it's even worth it, since I seem to be not as bothered about festivals anymore. My grumpiness is augmented by the fact that I've recently failed to properly read Jay's school report, sent on by Luke, which seems like a massive motherhood fail. Jay's reading levels are this, his comprehension is that... Bizarrely, it all seems to have nothing to do with me. All I can think is: *Is this the creature that I've created?*

Trying to Sew

I'm sitting cross-legged on the floor of a marquee, surrounded by half-finished creations of bamboo, wool and sticks. Several women and a couple of men apply themselves diligently to the painting of masks for the 'Dance of Life and Death' theme of the festival. I hoped to be given a mask to paint, but because I'm not on the core team and have joined 'on the hoof', I'm asked instead to sew bamboo onto the scrolls I decorated yesterday with poetry.

Sewing has always terrified me. I have vivid memories of being shouted at, aged nine, in Miss Johannesson's sewing class. "But you're a clever girl, I don't understand why you can't do it!" she would exclaim in despair and disgust when, no matter how many times I was shown how to stitch something, I still couldn't grasp it.

I remember the paralysing feeling when my brain just wouldn't allow me to do something that seemed so effortless for others. Eventually, I managed to sew something passable for presentation in the end-of-year-assembly, but it was half done by the teacher. As soon as I could, I turned my back on all traditionally feminine crafting activities – with the exception of knitting, which for some reason I had no problem with – and stuck to what I could do best: make up stories, write, listen.

Now, here I am, despite Thor telling the décor team leader that I was dyspraxic when he got me this volunteer role, being expected to sew. Writing the quotes yesterday – extracts from my own poems and from others', the sayings of Buddha about life and death – was enjoyable, especially painting one of my 'darker' poems onto a piece of wood. But because the scrolls have to be hung from trees around the festival site, and need to be secured to bamboo, they have become my bane.

At first, I employ my frequently used strategy of pretending to myself that I can do something and getting on with it as best as I can. It sometimes works because a lot of my dyspraxia is anxiety related. This time, it doesn't, and the tension builds as time passes and I spend most of it unpicking what I've done and starting again. The stitches keep ending up in the wrong place and I can't figure out the principle behind why they sometimes do and sometimes don't.

Eventually, I try my second strategy: ask for help. The décor team leader intimidates me, so I won't risk a re-enactment of Miss Johannesson. I ask a kind woman who I connected with the previous day, Jane. She's paused her mask painting and agrees to do one scroll for me and thereby show me how to do it. And to my amazement, from her patient instruction I grasp the task and am able to carry on – a little messily, and it takes me a long time, but I'm doing it.

I'm exultant: I've broken through my barrier of self-imposed exclusion from practical teamwork. I can do it!

It's been a long journey to get here. The first three days of set up, I was on the sauna team, which mostly consisted of sitting around having cups of tea in the blazing sun with occasional banging in of marquee pegs and rigging up of changing room divisions. No-one was critical, but I felt inept, often getting the angles wrong and being reliant on the others to get a handle on how things worked.

The biggest struggle I face is not being an official part of the site crew. This brings up a lot of uncomfortable feelings about belonging and worthiness, and it doesn't help that Marion, who I actually got on to the sauna team, has securely entrenched herself there in her characteristically effortless extrovert style. She's ended up with a week's worth of meal passes and what seems like everyone's friendship, while I, as a floating support, have to extract my meal tickets from the team leader each time, feeling like a beggar and an outsider. I move from sauna to décor to the women's area and back to the van again, where I feel safest. I know it's probably mostly in my head, but I can't seem to settle in myself.

Then, when I have a sudden rush of copywriting work, I'm forced to plough on despite my exhaustion and take a step back from crewing. I survive on the inadequate provisions of baked beans and eggs in the van.

There it is: I'm back on my own again, working in the van, and my feeling of separation deepens with the knowledge that I'm here for different purposes than everyone else. All the others on the field – growing numbers as the week goes on – are united in the co-creation of this festival, while I'm only dipping my toe in because I have other goals and need more rest than others seem to. I long to be 'together' and get involved, but it feels like such an uphill battle.

It wasn't like this at Leela. Although it took me a couple of days to shift from a focus on Thor to connecting with others there, the way things were set up with such structure and organisation made it easy to seamlessly integrate into the worklife and into the shared purpose of making the centre run. Here, I've not come in on an equal basis and it shows.

By nine days in, my patterns are showing themselves clearly and painfully to me. My battle for meal tickets, with crew leaders often forgetting to give them to me or saying they don't have enough, seems a clear reflection of my belief that I don't deserve to receive. It shows up my lack of value for my own work, and the way I therefore don't expect others to value it. When both Thor and Marion tell me I'm talking about my copywriting work too much (Marion more kindly than Thor), I realise that I have a tendency to prop up my identity by being busy, to derive my worth from my writing work. It's as if this gives me some validity, but it's not something I need to bring into this field. The only reason I do is because I feel inadequate with the practical tasks that everyone else seems so effortlessly busy with. Ouch.

It helps, temporarily, when people – usually women – share in the site crew morning check-in that they feel 'less than' with some of the tasks. But soon I feel like I can't even go to those check-ins anymore: I'm not site crew, and when I ask if I can join the décor crew check-in while I'm working with them, I get a hesitant response from the leader: "It's just getting so big." But I push on anyway, because Thor has encouraged me to integrate myself into as many teams as possible. And the check-in is rich, and deep, and I'm glad I went.

Then, when I step outside the décor marquee for a pee break and see a group of women singing together in the area marked 'Rituals', my heart lifts with recognition and longing. I feel like I've found the team I belong with. Ceremony, singing, sacredness – what could be more up my street? I even say to one of them, "I think this is the team I want to be working with next year," but she completely ignores me, and the shame flushes my face. Still, I bravely persist: I later talk to one of the members of the group, a woman I know from my old Lewes choir, and ask if I can get involved. She's enthusiastic and invites me to join the rehearsals for the big ritual performance on Saturday.

I'm excited, but as the festival begins, I soon realise that this is an invitation extended to everyone, both crew and festival-goers. My need to contribute something valuable and be recognised for it is a source of both frustration and shame. Is it not enough for me to have my poetry scattered around the site? But when I have to pick up one of the scrolls for the third time from where the wind – or a person? – has scattered it to the ground on the 'Faery Path', and notice that the wooden sign I put so much love and attention into has also gone, there's a lump in my throat.

I dutifully turn up to the chaotic first and last rehearsals, but I don't make it to the ritual itself. When I hear that we have to be barefoot on the cold ground for the entire time it takes up to a thousand people to place tealight candles on an altar, something in me snaps. I feel premenstrual, fed up, tired and totally devoid of the stamina this ritual will require. I feel a powerful yearning to ditch the ritual and go to the kirtan I know is happening up at the Beloved's Arms café. I haven't made it to one kirtan yet, the main event I enjoy at festivals. But surely it's a terrible thing to do, to back out at this point.

"Go," urges Katie, a woman from choir who I've always had a sweet connection with, when she hears my grumpiness spoken aloud. "Go to the kirtan. We'll be fine. We have enough people."

"But shouldn't I tell Vicki?" I say, like a naughty schoolgirl.

"Don't tell Vicki." She's firm now, obviously picking up on my need to be Given Permission from the Headteacher. "Just go." So, I do, with a mixture of guilt and liberation, and later, on the way back from kirtan, which never got off the ground anyway, I hear the ritual team chanting with the thousand onlookers. It's a Buddhist chant whose meaning I've forgotten, but the sound of their voices together in the night brings an unexpected sadness. Once again, I failed to be part of something that mattered. Even when given the chance.

The Elder Tree

"I want to be led to the elder tree and to meet the fairies. I want you to take me there."

We're sitting on the sofa; we've just had Green n Black's hot chocolate and Thor's looking at me with that intensely burning look in his eyes. "I've been hearing that it's a spiritual thing and a powerful energy, but maybe I just need to have a moment of experiencing you in it, to understand what it is. If I understand it, I think I'd be more motivated to nurture and protect that. You see, I have to wonder, what's the benefit of it to me? What's the benefit to me of supporting it?"

It all started with him asking me when I'm next bleeding; he knew it was coming in the next few days but wanted to know roughly when. When I told him my estimate – my cycle is never entirely regular – he acknowledged that he struggled to fully put his back behind supporting my need for sacred space at my bleed because he didn't know what it really was.

"The thing is," I say now, carefully, "do you remember the last time my period started? And I asked you to stop the van so I could rest, and it was so difficult?"

At first, he can't remember. Then the light dawns: "Yes. I was really angry."

He was taking me to Gillingham Station from Leela so I could go back and see Jay. My period, threatening for days, suddenly descended with full force in the front cab of the van, complete with the usual intense cramps. But instead of feeling pain, I felt ecstasy. Yes, my womb was contracting, and it hurt, but I felt, emotionally and spiritually, on a different plane.

I had read, in the *Wild Power* menstruality book, that this portal to other dimensions was possible, and had experienced it briefly at a menstrual-aware friend's house when given enough time to rest and be in the presence of another, conscious, woman. It was an experience I wanted to dive deliciously right into. So, I said nothing for some time, as we drove, assuming that as there was no hurry for me to get a particular train, we'd soon be able to stop somewhere nearby.

But then I realised that Thor was heading straight for the station, on a mission. I had forgotten that he never liked protracted goodbyes. So, I summoned my strength and voiced my needs, from inside the bubble, explaining that I just needed to lie down for an hour or so before getting the train. I knew I was in no state to navigate buying a ticket and getting on a busy carriage right now.

Thor was taken aback by my request, but I could see him configuring it as a reasonable request, given our discussions about him supporting my cycle and my need to rest at bleeding time. But his attempts to find a place to stop off were disastrous. There simply weren't any park ups near the station and he realised we were fast running out of fuel.

He ended up having to reverse down an extremely narrow country lane when an agricultural vehicle came towards us. It was at that point that he started shouting. "I'm not your taxi driver! You take me totally for granted! I'm not just here to drive you around!"

I sat there in mute terror and anger, unable to defend myself. Eventually he parked up in a supermarket car park and I went to lie down. After sending a few venty texts to Marion, I resolved to be with my feelings as best as I could. The ecstasy was still there, flitting around at the edges of my shock like a fragmented supernova. And after an hour, sure enough, the process had run its course and, though still tender, I felt able to function reasonably well in the outside world again.

Of course, we discussed the whole event to the point where I could leave peacefully. I realised that I had been so spaced out I hadn't clearly asked for what I needed until it came to the crunch, when it became abundantly obvious to me that this was a strong experience that needed attention. And I was surprised that he didn't feel it, being next to me, because he's super sensitive to energy, but he was driving and not particularly tuned into the subtle sphere at that point.

Now, in the van at Buddhafield, he acknowledges my point. "Yes, I felt this huge rage. Maybe it was about more than just the situation of feeling pissed off with driving you around. Maybe," he suggested, "maybe we both have blocks there. Maybe I don't feel what's there because of the ancestral stuff of men feeling threatened by women's power and trying to suppress it. And maybe on your side, as a woman, you're not really claiming this cyclical thing fully and standing up for its importance."

"Yes. I definitely do struggle to believe I deserve to be honoured for that … for the altered state during bleeding to be seen for what it is. And the thing is, I think I've been expecting you to understand this gift of the bleed when I've only recently begun to really step into it myself. I mean, I've been practicing cycle awareness for years but it's only very recently that I've started to experience this visioning side of it. But there's also this backlog of frustration at the masculine for not understanding it and women having that understanding taken away from them … so they pass the ignorance and hatred of the bleed onto their daughters and don't celebrate their menarche. My mother was totally oblivious to it, like most mothers. I remember a woman crying in Jewels' workshop yesterday about her daughter having this raw wild power which is not acceptable in our society, yet it's the power we're desperately trying to get in touch with as women, now. It was so moving to hear her share that."

He takes all of this in. "Take me to the elder tree. I want to experience the magic."

I know instantly what he means. 'The elder tree' is a symbol for the magical realm of life, which he's called the 'faery tree' ever since we connected with one in our first days of travel in Arundel. A big part of me, the part that was silenced by an ex-boyfriend saying "None of my previous partners ever made a big deal about their period" when I mentioned I'd need space on a particular Sunday, thinks, *Yes, thank you, I really appreciate you supporting me with this. Thank god, finally a man is doing that.*

But there's another part: one that's scared of my cycle, as a women's mystery, being co-opted, like so many things taken over by men and turned into a pressurised thing. Like, *well you've got to perform now, you've got to produce a vision — where's this vision? How is this of benefit to us?* And part of me is really angry about that. That part is screaming, *Why does it have to benefit you to be useful?*

On another level, I know it *is* useful, to the collective. It is useful to the man you're in a relationship with if this is honoured, because the woman is then much more in tune with herself and in alignment with her purpose, able to serve from that resourced place, from being in the web of wisdom. And maybe, if he understands it, he can help other men understand it too.

The Supportive Girlfriend

On the last night of Buddhafield, the life and death theme of the festival strikes much too close to home: it's time for Thor to leave so that he can have the early morning surgery on his nose. He's elected to go alone; I was so painfully awkward when he went to his dermatologist appointment that he'd had to ask me to leave the waiting room and sit outside.

I feel vulnerable and exposed without my 'shell' of the van, staying in the tent. Even though we hadn't spent that much time together at the festival, the removal of his presence is palpable. It's like a holding I wasn't even aware of is suddenly gone.

Despite my intentions of participating more in the fireside music-making, I go to bed quite early, too tired to make the effort. But just before I turn in, I take a walk in the Glade, a small clearing of high grass, solemn oaks and friendly beeches. It's the first time I've visited it at night despite it being so close to the van and having been a frequent sanctuary for me by day. The light installations move me deeply: the fragile, beautiful bits of plants in light bulbs, the sphere on the ground lit from within by many-coloured lights. I find myself crying, staring at a piece of fern glowing as if it was the first thing created by God.

When Thor returns the next day at noon, I don't notice him or the van at first. After a tiring morning of copywriting work, I'm intent on making my way from my tent to the Glade to lie down under my favourite oak, armed with blanket, sheepskin, pillows and sarong.

"Hello?" I hear the familiar voice. I stop and turn and there he is, his nose and head bandaged, looking like he's back from a war. My eyes fill and I turn towards him over enthusiastically, dropping my stuff. His half-accusatory, half-vulnerable words, "You didn't even see me or the van," fall to the floor as I go to hug him. But he fends me off gently and folds me into his arm on his right side – "Careful". Of course, in my eagerness, I was in danger of bashing one of his wounds.

"How are you feeling? How did it go?" I clamour at him. I'm conscious of playing the 'supportive girlfriend' role: the familiar anxiety to get it right seems to crowd out any genuine empathy, as it so often does. Of course, he wants to tell me the story of the surgery, but he makes it clear that it was a Big Spiritual Process and will require my full attention. I'm feeling exhausted, but I gather myself because I must. We go to the Glade together and set up camp under a tree.

"There was a doctor and two nurses, all women. They were so kind. The surgeon explained everything she was doing and was very gentle. The only thing that really hurt was the anaesthetic going into my nose. That was extremely painful."

He goes on to explain that the way he sees it, he has experienced a healing from the feminine. That his attempts to get rid of the lesion on his nose by ripping it off – albeit accidentally – didn't work, but this time, 'the feminine' was making him better. He is blown away by the experience.

I'm trying to be present with his story, which goes on for some time, but it doesn't go well. I'm trying too hard. I haven't taken care of my own needs first – I thought he'd be back much later than he was. And, of course, with his super-sensitive antennae, he picks up my anxiety – and being in a particularly vulnerable space, he doesn't react well. "I knew I should have stayed in the area longer afterwards and just rested in the van."

After the operation, he parked up at Castle Neroche, the beautiful Blackdown Hills spot we stayed at before Buddhafield. "It was so peaceful there," he goes on, "It feels strange coming back here. You're not in the right space."

Here we go again, I think angrily and despairingly. Why couldn't I just be with someone who would accept my going-through-the-motions as genuine caring and let us just get through it without a drama? *Because you wanted something real. Because you wanted to strip your skins away.*

Once again, nothing less than total authenticity will do in this relationship. I admit I've been feeling tired and wanted some time for myself after work, that I was really looking forward to seeing him and hearing how it all went but wasn't ready for it yet. That I was sad to have done a crappy job at helping him re-integrate into the field after such an intense experience.

We manage to listen to each other and work through it all, even though there are moments when it all feels truly horrible. Once again, I have to accept that a situation is beyond my control. I also glimpse another, more hidden aspect: that I can be less than perfect and still be loved.

THE OLD LANDSCAPE

Dance Camp East has been an integral part of my history and annual seasonal landscape with Jay for seven years – only one year missed in that time. It feels good and right to be with him there again, especially in such a spacious way: we have ten whole days.

The normal experiences of pitching a tent together and reading by torchlight feel even more precious now that we no longer live together. Every year, he's that much more independent. We do parallel reading and writing now and then, and the rest of the time he's off playing with his oldest friend, Noah, who we started to 'bring along' to DCE a couple of years ago.

The practical side of being here is hard work, though, with one obstacle after another, and I'm soon exhausted. Intense rain, high winds; my tent breaks on the first day; the food situation is tricky. Finding myself again in that internal premenstrual zone in a festival type setting, I notice a lack of willingness on my part to engage socially. The initial social ease of arriving on the field and being greeted throughout the evening by so many people I know, all happy to see me, soon wears off as I realise I've ended up in a circle full of drinkers-from-noon who are incapable of a conversation without talking over each other.

I seek refuge in the spiritual singing sessions each morning but find myself hiding out on the Healing Field more and more, where nothing is expected of me. While Jay plays with Noah all day, I lie in the sun or under the trees with the other sauna devotees, hidden behind the awning that protects sensitive teens from our ageing naked bodies.

It seems that the festival jadedness I noticed at Buddhafield has well and truly set in.

I start to feel prickly and critical, actively avoiding my circle and hanging out in other circles when I do any circle time at all. *They're all so totally unpresent and disconnected,* I fume. I'm sad to not be in a circle with Brian and Cathy, who are followers of the spiritual bible 'A Course in Miracles' and embody a timeless, gentle presence. Brian's endless repertoire of 60's and 70's songs are like a hammock I gratefully ease into every year: but this time, their circle was already full when we arrived, and I've ended up in this hodge-podge of people I don't resonate with at all, apart from Fiona, who's in the same zone as me and regularly shares a bit of a gripe.

My heart is pained regularly by Jay's refrains of "I miss you so much,

Mom". Guilt and sadness – but also, somewhere in there, a happiness at realising he does love me and need me. His requests to be with me, once an intrusion on my adult social time, are now welcome: I embrace his desire to talk at bedtime and hang out in the tent, relinquishing my desire to have a 'camp nightlife'; I give him foot and back massages while we read and chill out.

A year ago, at this camp, I was seven weeks into my whirlwind relationship with Thor and so in love. It was the zone of absolute obsession: I'd hide in the tent away from everyone and spend an hour on the phone to him every day.

This was when we first talked about getting a place together in the countryside. We were deciding which villages we'd like to live in, and even, incredibly, talking about having a baby together. How far away those dreams seem now.

Finally, the camp comes to an end, and we drive back with Fiona and Sophie to spend a few days with them in Shoreham-by-Sea. It's a soothing time: I feel in touch with the simple pleasures of life, soaking up the vividness of the sea's colours and the delight of watching Sophie and Jay squeal as they swim. Everything is suddenly beautiful and fresh and fun, in the way that camp life used to be. How peculiar that suburban life is now looking so fresh and appealing, while camp life, once the utopia, has lost its allure.

Walking back from the beach, Fiona and I have a conversation about the pressure from society, as a parent, to be a certain way. "It's like we have to put on this face for society. When we become parents, we have to interface with society in a more conventional way even though we may not agree with those values. Because if we don't, we prejudice our children's chances of fitting in, having friends and having all the opportunities. That's what you're moving away from, in your new life. There doesn't have to be any more compromise for you – Jay can now be with a family who effortlessly embodies these values and actually agrees with them and has no inner conflict about it. And he can see you living your life exactly as you want to and being free. No more inner conflict."

When Jay, even though he's been showing every appearance of having a good time with Betty and me, asks to go home nearly two days early because he wants to be with his dad, I let go gracefully, with only a small, sharp corner of sadness.

THIS ISLE

"What's happened to the reservoir?"

It's new moon, heading towards mid-August, and I've travelled up to meet Thor after two weeks with Jay. He's just done another Enlightenment Intensive at Spirit Horse community and we're driving towards a special spot where we parked last year: Mid-Wales, in the Cambrian mountains.

Excited to return to the wild and reconnect with Thor, I look out the window, waiting for the reservoir to become visible, the one where we canoed illegally last year. But gradually, I realise with horror that most of the water is gone. For miles, there is just grey, like the surface of a deserted planet.

"Wow, the lack of rain has really affected things here," Thor remarks, and I can hear his shock and sadness too. We get out of the van and walk down, over the raised squelchy earth with its cracks like the pads of elephants' feet. Thor goes ahead of me to test the ground for safety first, and I appreciate the way he looks out for us.

When I catch up to him, we stand looking at the desolation for a long moment. I can't help it: I burst into tears. Suddenly, the whole world feels totally fucked.

"The water will come back," Thor says kindly, unperturbed at my tears.

"It's not just that. The whole world is wrecked." It's as if I've fallen out of some kind of bubble. Maybe it's because I was so bored at Dance Camp that I started falling down the portal of Facebook, reading too much bad news. But everything feels unbearably doomed.

"The world will change as you change," he says in his Zen way. "No, it won't," I say furiously, despairingly.

"You have to experience it, you can't get it from me saying it," he says patiently.

"Remember when we took all those photos, we were so in love," he says, smiling and hugging me gently. Last summer, on our first trip together in the van, we took dozens of photos of each other and of ourselves kissing, on top of one of the hills surrounding the impressive reservoir.

But remembering this only adds to my grief. *Things were so different then.* I feel the parched nature of the earth beneath my feet.

Eventually, I calm down and we walk back to the van. After our long time apart, we're both oddly tentative around each other, and confess to each other a fear of saying or doing the wrong things. I admit that some insecurity was triggered for me when he reminisced about the photos. I thought he meant that we weren't in love like that anymore.

"I was thinking that I was feeling the same way as I did a year ago," he says, and I relax.

Later, back in the van, Thor tells me over hot chocolate about his first communication with the ancestors, years ago. "They were the first ones I'd ever connected with – I didn't really know what I was doing, yet. They told me very clearly to 'do something about the destruction of the planet'. I didn't even recycle, before that. The way I see it, the way you change things is by being how you would like things to be. So, I believe the world is fucked up because of disconnection from nature, that's at the root of it, and the reason why we are destroying things. But the only thing you can do about that is to *be* connected to nature so strongly yourself that others feel it when they're around you, and you carry that energy with you. For example, at the Empowerment Intensive workshop at Leela, I was called 'tree person' and 'wild man' by the facilitator, even though he didn't know anything of my history. He could sense my connection with nature, and how I bring that."

I think back to our first Glastonbury trip together, when after looking forward to being around people and 'community' for so long, I ended up feeling overwhelmed and repelled by the energy of the High Street. When I shared this with David over our controversial coffee, he responded, "You don't need that anymore. You're more attuned to the energy of nature now, you're on that vibration, so a town just feels wrong to you."

I think about how many of my friends have gone to Bali, Thailand and India to find their spiritual roots. It's clear to me now that this vanomad journey is about travel on *this* land, on this Isle – that there's no need for me, right now, to go to any of those exotic places. It's here, on this land where my ancestors originate, that the work is – my work to connect with the spirit of the land, and to find out what is needed for healing.

Things get more philosophical and we're soon in a complicated conversation about masculine-based vs feminine-based religions. Thor insists that my interest in Buddhism, as a woman, will lead me nowhere useful. I've always been intrigued by Buddhism but was ultimately put off by the hierarchical structure involved in the local groups and the unfriendly demeanour of some of the practitioners. But every now and then, I read something that sparks my interest again. "You won't get anywhere following the enlightened male. Women have their own way," Thor says in that calmly certain way he has.

"The moon cycle is maybe the closest thing to the feminine religion that has been lost but I think it's like meditation is for men – both are only starting points." Then, suddenly, he says, "I think you'd get more out of going outside and looking at a flower than from having this discussion."

Naked after our reunion-love, I wrap myself in a soft grey blanket and go outside into the wind. He follows me shortly after and we sit wrapped together in the blanket, listening to the wind, watching the mountains and the dance of the reeds. It feels like I am again dropping into that deep, timeless, blissful space that was so much a feature of my last time here.

We walk down from the road a bit and curl up on the 'beach', the high grass near the stones leading to the reservoir. "What does the earth underneath feel like to you?" Thor asks me as he joins me in the blanket.

"Melty, deep, pulling me in. How about you?"

"All the words you said, plus friendly and kind." Kisses and cuddles under the blanket soon turn passionate as a massive, soft, loving feeling seems to rise up out of the earth and envelop us both. We are both completely connected in earthiness, lust, love, and vulnerability, love, and vulnerability, as if the earth were making love to us through each other.

SPIRIT HORSE

August 2018

Wild Eyes

"People seem to get these wild eyes after they've been here for a while," Thor says as we turn the corner past the fierce farm dog who always tries to stop us driving past. "Like, a little crazy. I've seen it in Rebecca and Mark, and now Ben has it too."

I laugh. I know exactly what he means.

We're on the 30-mile drive to the nearest supermarket after six days at Spirit Horse, spent either stepping around Thor's tools in the van – he's doing some electrical work for the owner, Shiv – or climbing up hills and sitting by the river.

"You don't have it, though. Maybe you're already so much like that, it doesn't make a difference," I tell him.

"Yes, probably," he laughs. "And Shiv doesn't have it either. I reckon that's why his girlfriend left. She was expecting some kind of kingdom, but it's just a bunch of people going slightly mad."

There's definitely something of the otherworldly about Spirit Horse, and the people who've been here all through the summer reflect it. When I first arrived in this Mid-Wales valley overlooked by the moody, purple Cambrian Mountains, I took in the winding, characterful paths and the candle-lit rickety bridges connecting the structures made with loving hands – the Women's and Men's Lodges, the two Temples, the kitchen, the Roundhouse and the Sweat Lodge, all conduits for the continual song of the river – with the soul recognition of a wonder from my childhood, when I used to visit with the faeries in the garden.

I've been aware of Spirit Horse for years but somehow never made it here. Thor has come here annually every summer for three years to do the Enlightenment Intensive Retreat, followed by a work exchange, doing electrics for the co-founder and 'chieftain' of the village, an Irish storyteller, Tantra teacher and ceremonial guide called Shivam. Finally, I'm here to experience this sanctuary myself.

The quiet and solitude of the place lends itself to deeply satisfying moments of simplicity: chopping veg for dinner, something I've done night after night, suddenly becomes a holy moment while Thor is taking apart an electrical component on the sofa. Only a few hours earlier, I was in a bit of a tizz about how we'd live through another winter and it all felt too much. But right now, my view from the window is an old man we know from Stonehenge sitting outside his green van, reading in his deck chair as if it's midsummer, his grandson whittling beside him on the green open field. So soothing. So right.

Thor and I take daily walks through the beautiful, wild mountain terrain. He tells me about a strong experience he had with a particular butterfly up on a hill when walking alone. "When I got up close to it, I saw its eye in a way I've never seen before." He wells up. "They were your eyes. I've never seen that before."

We've talked before about adopting the butterfly as my symbol in our relationship, but I said I wasn't comfortable with it because it had been Lila's symbol. Now, he asks me again if we can use it. "You see, I said goodbye and fully let go of that relationship when I went and sat under a tree that was 'her tree'. And when I did, when I said, it's finished, and really meant it, this butterfly flew up to me and then flew away. I know that I really let her go then."

But that night, I wake up from a bad dream. I go to him, and he holds me. I imagine my Inner Child with me. I let her feel the love I'm receiving, telling her, "It's for you, you deserve it". I let her be held by my inner Mother and Father and my King and Queen too. I feel so happy that I can now do this work for myself.

Emerald Pool

It's my Emerald Pool Initiation. I'm being led, barefoot like a mountain goat, along narrow cliff-ledges above a roaring river for what feels like a very long time, to meet the place where so much of the wild spirit of Spirit Horse is embodied.

Eventually, I graduate to rock-walking in the river itself: slippery brown-red rocks that remind me of dolphin's backs or prehistoric creatures or the corrugated surfaces of far-away planets. An abundance of moss, coming away in chunks just when I start to treat them as handholds, like the moss on the side of the van that I like to pick at, to Thor's annoyance – "I've been growing that for years. I like having those bits of nature with me".

"Go in spider mode", Thor instructs often: this means going down on hands and knees.

"We're nearly there now," he says as we crawl along the slick black and grey rocks. Thor takes a piece out of a huge quartz crystal that was already crumbling off, with the intention to give it to 'someone'– that person will turn out to be the Ecuadorean shaman we will meet later.

Finally, we reach the rich green pool and it's as magical as I imagined it. I face the waterfall in all its raw, unstoppable, primal power. The fact that I can't see how deep it is feels both mysterious and frightening.

We strip off and stand right under the torrent of water, giving in to the way it takes the breath, the sense of skin. You have to swim right into the pool to get your head under the waterfall; you can't simply walk into it. Your surrender must be complete.

It feels like a continuation of the time we stood staring at an enormous waterfall at Fernworthy Reservoir on Dartmoor, back in the winter, and I let out some of my fury in the face of that unstoppable cascade, when it could barely be heard against the backdrop of the spray. But that was a man-made construction, and this is pure wild. And we're getting right up close to it.

Thor goes straight in and under, whooping and exulting at the shock of the cold. I bend my back into the fall and let the water beat against me, making me gasp and shiver, but I cannot bring myself to dive in. Still, I feel triumphant; I made it, and it feels like I've been baptised.

The slight drizzle – a near-constant feature of the Welsh countryside – has been steadily developing, but it now morphs into full-on rain. I feel a pang of fear as my euphoria recedes. It's a long, hazardous and slippery path back over the rocks and along the mountain edge, and I keep seeing myself falling and smashing my head on the rocks below.

I suddenly remember a scene from 'Into the Wild' where 'Alex Supertramp' canoes on a fast-rushing, wild river. It planted a seed, as so much about his wandering, free-form lifestyle did: every one of the ten times I watched it, I was taken by the aliveness and exhilaration of that scene. But I also doubted I'd ever have the courage to do something like that.

After we eventually make it back and curl up on the sofa with a reward of hot chocolate, Thor says, "Can I tell you something? I don't think you are dyspraxic. You did that walk so well, you only slipped once and it's very dangerous and tricky. Lots of people don't manage it – they stop and go back before they reach the Pool." He smiles. "You were singing on the way back and you were happy. It made me happy to see that."

I nod, pleased, but I'm also aware that I didn't put my head right under the waterfall, although Thor did, twice. I was scared of not being able to breathe.

The Shaman

A shaman is arriving, and he's not one of those British twenty-something people who run monthly Ayahuasca ceremonies in Brighton. He's a genuine shaman from Ecuador (though based in London now). Thor has been rattling the path he is due to arrive on for some time and has also rattled the river. I accompany him for a while, wading through the river past the scattered pink petals, relics of earlier ceremonies.

But when he reaches a point where it gets too slippery for me, I step out and make my way to the women's lodge. It feels so warm and safe: the paintings of bears, the diffuse orange patterns in the material and the stones in the centre; the atmosphere created by all the women who've been in ceremony in here before.

The shaman was expected at seven p.m. but it's now eight-thirty and still no sign of him. We join the vigil on and off: dark gathers as we all hang around in clusters near the bridge. The women have created a colourful flower drawing on the ground to welcome him. Two of the men – with wizardy hoods and hats – start playing with martial art staffs to pass the time.

Finally, after nine p.m., as my stomach is growling with hunger, the lights of Spirit Horse's co-founder, Erica's, car can be seen from the carpark. Collective sigh of relief. We all line up solemnly in rows facing each other and Mary goes to the bridge to do the initial greeting. I feel the awkward agitation of nerves I always get when anything ceremonial is about to happen.

The shaman is indeed the real deal. Dark-skinned with traditional garb, a fringed-jacket and a ponytail. I hear Mary welcome him in her gruff voice. As he appears at the head of our greeting line, he holds what looks like a bundle of tied-together plants above his head and begins to swish it from side to side, singing. Then he walks through the middle of our human tunnel, continuing the movement and the song. I'm not sure where to look.

He thanks us for our welcome. "Now, I'd like to hug each of you." Mary mutters loudly, "We've all been waiting for two hours and we're hungry," and I try not to laugh. But, of course, everyone ignores her, and the hugs begin. I wait for mine with a mixture of nerves and excitement. When it comes, it's friendly and warm and I feel myself relax. After some prompting from Shiv to 'go and eat', we finally make a procession to the kitchen for the evening meal of shepherd's pie.

When Thor announces his decision to have a healing session with the shaman, my heart sinks a little, even as I have hope it will help him with the ongoing health issues he's been facing. I know it'll be Something Big, and take a long time to integrate. And I'm right.

After the healing process is complete, he tells me that at the height of it, he was lying near the waterfall, thickly covered in ginger from head to toe, his eyes burning from chilli. The shaman had applied all of it himself, even to his private parts. "So, I was lying there, making all these weird sounds, and he was leaning over and sucking on the area right above my head to get the dark spirits out." I'm sincerely glad that the shaman was booked up by the time I considered having an appointment myself.

The shaman felt that Thor had picked up some dark spirits because he's so open. He said it was a tendency for that to happen in England. "Maybe it's because in our culture, shamanism is not the consensual worldview so it's harder for us to know what we're tapping into, and because of the history of our land. So much has been buried, spirituality and earth connection destroyed: the ancestors are still upset."

"You know," he goes on, "I think these spirits have been present with me for a few years. The first time I was consciously aware of them was when I led a men's group about two or three years ago and summoned something that felt so powerful it seemed to just take over. I never suspected it to be anything bad."

"Hhhmm. But remember at the Being Total tantric workshop at Leela? In the massage session?" Thor had only been lying there, being touched gently on his chest by myself and another participant, but he started to arch his back, thrash around uncontrollably, and make strange sounds. "Yeah, I think that was probably the dark spirit struggling to not be released. At Empowerment Intensive, it also caused me to cough almost to the point of throwing up."

It all sounds very alarming to me, but hopefully things are now on their way out. Thor creates a kind of retreat camp down by the river to support his integration from the healings. He's surrounded his tent – a precarious few steps from the water, and definitely a flooding risk – with a circle of quartz stones and an improvised standing stone. He spends his days playing guitar, making fires and drinking tea, impervious to the fact that the lively 'Cauldron of Plenty' community camp is going on up in the Spirit Horse village.

Sitting with Thor in his stone circle, merging with the perpetually winding water, the never-ending let-go, I start to feel like I'm shapeshifting into a mermaid. I've been bathing in the river most days, a cleansing ritual which leaves me tingling with new life, however resistant I am when I approach it. The dreamy Pisces Full Moon brings out my Neptunian energy and amplifies the wateriness. We make up a song together about the moon and the water.

Hermit-Crab and Hogwarts

I'm enjoying living in the van again – I joke with Thor that I've become a hermit crab, like him, wanting nothing more than to be holed up in there, even though there are social things going on at Spirit Horse. When a mutual friend, Greg, a some-time vandweller himself, asks me at dinner if I've reached a wall with vanlife lately, I say that I've hit the wall so much that I've come out the other side again.

What's turned the corner is two things: a new, hard-won harmony between me and Thor, eight months in, and the fact that most of the day he's out working on electrics for Shiv, so we have natural, built-in space.

I feel really pleased with us. I think this is the longest we've gone without a significant disagreement – and it's my inner autumn, too, usually a very challenging time. I'm no longer experiencing regular anger and judgment from him. The Enlightenment Intensive seems to have cemented the work started at Leela: at Leela he released a lot of anger, and at EI he experienced the person in front of him during inquiry dyads as being 'him', releasing him from the need to judge them.

Periodically, I break out of the hermit mode and wander up to the main 'village', even though in my introverted mood I'm still a bit wary of the jolly, cider-drinking banjo-playing folk and Shiv himself, a fiery Aries who tends to stride around in regal gear: big yellow kaftans over medieval-looking jester-type trousers, barefoot underneath to underscore his affinity with nature.

One night, I find myself hanging out with a group of young people in the lavish Red Temple – a contrast to the more oriental, green-and-blue temple with huge tree views. Outside, people are juggling with fire and playing flutes and drums. In the cosy, warm interior, I meet an astoundingly wise sixteen-year-old girl impressively called Merlin. I talk to her friends, two young girls whose astrological charts I did a couple of years ago as Christmas gifts from their aunt, my favourite 5Rhythms teacher, who's also here. They are a stunning match to their star-gifts.

Before I know it, all the children and teens are asking me about their starsigns and we're discussing which Hogwarts houses we all belong to in the world of Harry Potter. It can take me ages to 'break into' an adult group, and I feel touched at being so instantly included in theirs. The evening moves on to some storytelling, including stories told by the children, who all blow me away with their maturity and creativity. "The woman who had a story and a song inside her" feels like it is spoken straight to my heart. And when Erica ties threads of red, orange, green and yellow around my wrist to symbolise that I am now part of the village, I can almost believe her.

I'm struck by how much easier it is for me to be out socially and be myself without Thor present. It's like I've stepped out of his shadow and things happen that wouldn't normally happen, synchronicities, new connections. I would guess he probably has the same thing when he's out without me. I know we need to do this more often.

*

The next day, I have a video call with Jay where, inspired by an article I read recently, I suggest we each choose a symbol in nature that whenever we see it, we send love to each other. I brace myself for him being sceptical and even derisive, like the time we were lying under an oak tree on a recent visit, and he said to me, "Stop singing," which silenced me. When he went on to say, "I just want to hear the wind in the trees and I like watching the leaves move," I felt really pleased that he does appreciate nature after all, that maybe I'd taught him that. But later, he told me, "I only said that to make you stop singing."

Now, when I tell him I won't be able to see him again till early September because of being in Wales, he says, "Sadness" and huddles in his duvet. I know this is my moment, and I broach the idea of nature 'message carriers'. To my surprise, he goes for it, agreeing that I could use the butterfly to send my own messages. "I'll look at the mommy bird who sits on the top of the tree outside my window. When I see her go and feed her baby birds, I'll send love." Imagining this baby bird, I feel happiness take wing in my own chest.

Where to Next

"So, where to next?" Shiv asks us, as we stand in the drizzle outside the community kitchen, sipping from earthenware mugs of tea, on the day we plan to leave the village. I've been here three weeks, and it feels almost as if I live here now. Getting involved in Cauldron Camp take-down has integrated me a bit more, but it's mainly the land I feel an affinity with, rather than the people, who I've barely interacted with.

We've dismantled Thor's riverside camp together, taking down the tent, casting the river stones one by one back into the cleansing place from which they've come. We left just two things behind: the protective stone circle and the white feather he stuck into a big moss-covered stump. The white feather is the same one that I left in his tent after an argument during the tumultuous Buddhafield Festival in July. It feels to me like we're leaving something of ourselves there, a relic of this watery journey we've both been on.

As we sat for one last moment beside the river, Thor was thoughtful: "I don't know if I'll come back here again because this stuff that's been going on with me, this dark spirit that the shaman identified … I think it started with my first Enlightenment Intensive and I think these processes … I no longer know if they are what I should be doing, if I should follow this path. Because it might be connecting me with stuff I shouldn't be connecting with."

Now, outside the community kitchen, Thor tells Shiv, "I don't know," in an unconcerned tone. We genuinely have no idea if we'll travel more in Wales or go somewhere else.

Shiv turns to me: "And you're going with him, wherever he goes. Is that the appeal?" and Thor and I both smile at this astute observation.

"You know, you should just go and be with an enlightened master," Shiv tells Thor in that kingly way of his. "There's this person my ex-girlfriend Mari goes to see, in Spain. He's the real deal."

This conversation makes me uneasy: will I lose Thor to a wild goose chase after enlightenment, around the world? It also gets me thinking about my purpose. I feel pulled in two directions – do I devote my life to my relationship with the earth, learning how to live with the earth, to grow food, to protect it and connect with it, to help others do this too, living on the physical plane but with spirit – a sort of grounded spirituality? Or do I go the way of seeking enlightenment experiences and getting off this wheel once and for all?

"I'm scared you'll go off like Mari, to follow a path that leaves me behind," I confess to Thor.

"Well, why would it be me and not you?"

"I just don't really seek those things in the same way."

"If I get enlightened," he says matter-of-factly, "it won't change my patterning, and you're adaptable enough to be with me even if I change."

I feel relieved.

That morning, I went out for a walk up one of the many hills, alone. Along the river path, I ducked under the low-hanging branch like I was doing a Limbo dance. There were spiderwebs coated with dew everywhere, each one a little masterpiece. The river was rushing inexorably through the landscape, and the light glanced off a little sea-green pool at the top of the rocks.

At the summit of the hill, I sat under a magnificent lime tree, sinking into the burble of the river below and the hopeful chatter of birds all around me. The tree was so huge that the boughs were reaching down in front of me with the mountain as a backdrop. For some reason, I was deeply moved by the trees halfway up the mountain, steadfastly clumped together on the vertical incline. I felt a great longing to be on one piece of land through all the seasons, to see it through all the changes, to love it through all the relentless death and rebirth. Will I ever have such a relationship with a piece of land?

Yet there was also something that scared me about it, about the inevitable change, decay and loss that we face in our lives as ephemeral beings. Even my joy in nature was tainted by the shadow of sadness, of the ecocide that's going on, and I felt the terrible weight of not doing enough about it.

But do we all have to be rising as warriors? Don't some of us weave the changes from a gentler, quieter place?

As I descended the hill, I saw huge clouds of what looked like smoke rising from the river. They disappeared as soon as I got close enough, like magical upswirls from a cauldron.

*

After our conversation, in a surprise turn of events, Shiv invites Thor to stay on for the winter to keep up the electrics, or at least until he finds another job – his remote programming job of the past eight years has abruptly come to an end when the company ran out of funds, and we're at a loose end financially.

We're both tempted by the beauty of this land, but we know it'll be too isolated, too windy and cold in the winter, and too far for me to travel to see

Jay regularly enough. And although Spirit Horse has values that I deeply align with – nature connection, rewilding, healing, awareness – it's a transient, revolving community, where even the co-founders, Shiv and Erica, only live part-time. People come and go for retreats, courses, camps; no-one stays.

So, our search for community continues.

The magic of Spirit Horse remains with me, though, as the location where I've spent the longest period during our wandering van travels, and a seed of inspiration of what is possible when you marry the mythical with the human.

The Return

Now that Thor's lost the convenience of his long-term remote job, he's facing all his money issues – the stuff that he himself admits he was basically avoiding through vanlife. My erratic freelancing income can't sustain even our low-cost lifestyle on any long-term basis, so I put on my problem-solving hat and start searching on Diggers and Dreamers, the virtual noticeboard for intentional community vacancies and rural voluntary work opportunities.

We've had WWOOFing (worldwide work on organic farms) on the back burner since the start of our journey, and it feels like a good time to try it out – maybe we can get some autumnal apple-picking work or something. We decide to go for an interview for a voluntary job (bed and part-board exchange) at a farm in Somerset, one of our favourite regions in the UK. A filming location, it looks like a beautiful place, and we're excited. It's a minimum of a month-long commitment with the prospect to continue afterwards.

On our slow winding way from Wales back to the South-West, we visit a special yew tree at a place called Defynnog. Thor tells me it's actually two yews which have been separated. We go and sit with them, but I'm distracted, pulled out of my body in the present by all the planning and thinking of the past days. As much as I try, I can't drop in as deeply as I usually do. It's like I left the wild part of me back in Wales, the part who knows "this is what it's all about, being by the river and the fire". The other parts want to work everything out and don't see much sense in the wild one's priorities.

Thor encourages me to eat one of the berries, but I don't feel to. I know I'm failing some kind of test, but there's a stubbornness in me that has roots unknown to my mind.

Later, Thor tells me about the message he received from the Defynnog yew. "It said that you're not ready. That you're not the one."

What am I supposed to make of that?

The truth is, I only know I'm the one for myself. I don't even know if there's such a thing, anymore, as being 'the one' for anyone else.

*

When we reach the Somerset/Dorset border, we do some serious discussion on our future plans while walking along a lake near a Norman church. We're both wondering, once again, if this is the end of our van journey. As well as the fact that I need more space to work in, we're looking at some scarier stuff, namely, the long-term direction we're going in.

He doesn't want to get a job in a city, but he may have no choice. "I don't want us to just end up doing stuff by default. We need to be sure we're still working towards our vision. What do you really want, long term?"

I stare at the sign saying 'fishing only'. It feels more unclear than ever, but I try. "I want to live in community, on the land, growing our own food ideally."

"OK, so let's break it down into the steps to get there."

As we do so, we get stuck on Money. As ever. The reality is, neither of us wants to work seven hours a day, six days a week as most of the rural communities without big buy-ins require. "So, then, we need to start our own community," he concludes, but I feel a bit despairing. I wonder if we just are too lazy. Maybe we have to just suck it up and work hard for a while. The thought makes me miserable.

The interview goes well and the accommodation – a little cabin – is very charming, but it turns out the farm owner already has a very interested couple he's considering so we're only second on the list. We urge him to contact us once he's clear, but of course, we don't hear from him again, somewhat to our relief. Did we really want to work such long hours outside in the cold winter months?

Then there's the note of exploitation in the whole WWOOFing thing, especially when it's not a community you're becoming part of, but a business you're helping to make profitable with unpaid labour. It feels frustrating to have the freedom to explore so many options but to still feel blocked.

The question of how to build the life we dream of – living in community on the land – feels as baffling as ever.

NEW BOX

We're lying on the bed at two p.m. because Thor wants to connect before I go away tomorrow. I want to, as well, but my heart and mind are scattered across ten different tabs. I've gone into full mission mode with getting us a park up for winter and a place to put the lodge, I have paid work to do and my own book to work on, plus the weekend ahead to organise. And I don't feel sexual at all, or even sensual. I resolve to be honest about how I am but also open to letting things develop.

Of course, he immediately knows I'm distracted and without judgment (how far we've come), asks me what tabs I have open and what I'm sad about. It takes me a while, of gentle stroking and hearts touching, but then I know: my sadness is about not getting to see the newest member of my family, who was born two days ago and who I may never see, because his mother, my sister, decided to stop speaking to me a few months ago.

I am sad because I'm not getting to gather around and share the joy of him being born, I'm not able to hold him and welcome him and to take my place as an auntie in the history of my family. That is denied to me. And suddenly the absence of Jay is a hot, open wound: suddenly it seems as if children, everywhere, are denied to me.

I have been surprised by the amount of affection I feel for this baby I have never seen, just from the photograph my mother sent me. It's much more than I've felt for the babies of even close friends: it must be something of the blood bond, still there.

This is my family, I think, as I feel Thor's arms around me and remember how my mother has shown no interest in anything I've said in my messages lately, and in fact, hasn't got in touch at all for nearly two weeks. Obviously expecting a grandchild is more important than the fact that I'm communing with some land in Wales; but she could ask about whether we've had Thor's biopsy result yet. Does no one in my family care that my partner might have cancer?

This, here, now, is the person who takes care of me, cares how I am, provides a home for me.

*

So, we carry on driving, because there's nothing else to do. Eventually, we're back at the start, where we began our journey in the van, at almost the same time of year: the Barcombe Mills car park.

I feel a longing for the person I was in the first phase of our vanlife journey: when we were staying in places like Exmoor during the winter and everything was so fresh and new. I was so deeply connected with nature, so immersed in the spontaneity of everyday life. Now, I get occasional little glimmers of it, but it just isn't the same.

The carefree, liberated frame of mind I was in last winter, having been recently released from my urban life, is gone. I had no immediate need to work because I had money to live off for several months. Now, while I've built up a good amount of money from working hard since July, I don't feel that relaxation anymore: there's a constant pressure in the background, an awareness of something I should be doing at any given time. Even if there wasn't, I'd feel like I need to be working on my book or my blog. I crave that blissful time when all the pressure seemed to have melted away. Why have I slowly mounted it back on myself again?

There's another undertone, though: since the shaman told him he had a bad spirit, Thor has closed the door on his channelling stuff, turning away from magic. One day, as we're driving along, I'm touched by a moment of the old wonder, a feeling that anything we drove past could be the clue to the next magical thing. I turn to him: "Aah, remember when that was how we did everything, we were just constantly being led by these synchronicities and intuitive impulses."

"Yeah, I've really stopped that now," he responds, "because I realised I could have been being guided by that evil spirit all this time."

I'm sad that the energy's gone out of it. I still have a longing to be a hedgewitch and to know about herbs, and I want to do it in real life, in an immersive way, not in an online course, yet another thing to tether me to my screen.

I come across a metaphor in an article that I resonate strongly with: in life, when you find yourself in a box you want to climb out of, you grab something from outside the box and you step out and change it. At first, everything is great – exciting and new, and you're relieved to have escaped your box.

But eventually, whatever the new thing is becomes part of the box too.

Maybe I could just go back to living for moonrises and sunsets and being with Thor in the van. But the one who did all that feels like a different person now. I've lost my innocence; I've come back from the heroine's quest and I'm trying to integrate what I've learned back into life, but it feels like he's not willing to come back from the journey. He wants to stay on the hero's quest – but looking for what?

I'm also less motivated now that the co-creation part of our journey as a couple has taken a back seat. Our music-making was fulfilling that function, but that dissipated once the festival season was over and Thor's health problems took centre stage – and our attempts to find a new home together have gone nowhere.

Then, in September, I decide to go back to Leela for a week. We always intended to go back in the autumn, and Thor wants to come too, but he has too much work for the travel company at the moment. We part with difficulty, but as soon as I walk through that big red door, relief rushes through my body. I immerse myself in the body-based practices, the emotional release, the female friendship and the land there, sitting with the oaks and the yews. Being away from the hothouse created by Thor's and my combined auras feels like just what I need.

When he comes to visit me on my day off – he's still parked up nearby – he looks, smells and feels almost like a stranger. I feel affection for him, but that irresistible pull between us seems to have vanished. It's like the energy has just gone, and I'm terrified.

What is happening?

*

I'm walking on a beautiful hill with abundant trees and rolling hills in Dorset, many miles away from Sussex, where I felt stuck for so many years – and yet I feel trapped. And it's not a literal feeling, because of course I can go somewhere else. I have more freedom to do that than I've had in the past eleven years.

It's a feeling deep inside, probably rooted deep in some childhood wound. As I walk past the dying blackberries and the thorns on the ground, I suddenly just stop. I stop resisting that part of me that feels really depressed. I invite her in and say, *Yes, you feel really sad and empty and lost. You feel alone and lonely. I hear you and I feel you and I'm not going to make you wrong for feeling like that. I love you.*

I don't feel any lighter, but something settles in me.

*

My visits to Leela become a regular monthly rhythm, in addition to my three-weekly visits to Jay. Sometimes, I even stay at Leela for a whole fortnight. Thor's health takes a downturn so that even when his work eases off, he can't join me at Leela because he's not well enough to take on the punishing regime there, which somehow, I've managed to adapt to. My repeated absence when he needs my support and is feeling isolated on his own in the van begins to be a problem. His resentment builds and we start to argue more.

But I just cannot bear to be in the van full-time anymore.

Unable to let go of the thread of our joint destiny, we still play with the idea of doing something together that's in alignment with us finding a joint home. After a long phone conversation with Thor on my bed in the room I share with two other women, I apply to a full-time voluntary position taking care of a forest garden in Rodmell near Lewes. The deal is that we would receive food and yurt lodgings for four months plus valuable experience in sustainable food production – something that's hugely relevant to our long-term plans.

But in the end, after several more phone discussions, we decide not to go to the interview: it sounds like a nice dream, but driving all that way on the off-chance for an interview, only to be turned down as we were for the Somerset WWOOFing opportunity, feels too risky. And although being based in Sussex also has the advantage of me being able to see Jay more often, it would restrict us so much – we'd have to be on location all the time and not be able to travel. I wouldn't be able to go to Leela.

The benefits of my time at Leela are starting to become more and more apparent. After a few visits, I notice that there's been a massive improvement in my blood sugar difficulties and my related need to eat frequently and urgently. This wasn't an issue I had set out to heal but it seems to have been naturally selected by a mysterious process.

An unfortunate side effect of the healing process seems to be that I have so much less faith in my relationship with Thor. Through my inner work at Leela, I've stepped into my own power, getting in touch with my own needs and feelings. A lot is moving: sadness, relief, fear, excitement; a sense of being on the brink of something new again, something unknown. This is reflected when one of my new friends at Leela, Lalita, tells me: "I have a feeling you're about to embark on a whole new phase."

I am both terrified and excited at this prospect. I want change. On a swimming pool outing in Lewes with Jay, I find myself in a time warp, wondering whether I have, indeed, come full circle. The swimming excursions were something we did weekly through most of my single mothering years, and now I wonder: when this van phase is inevitably over, will I just end up like I was before, with this routine, mundane life, no closer to my dream of living on the land?

At the same time, I'm feeling how nice and grounding and normal it is. Maybe I'll end up just living in a house and having a normal life like nothing unusual ever happened. One of my closest friends at Leela, Sue, tells me that after living there for several months she is longing for a 'normal life'. "Wouldn't it be great to live somewhere and just go to your dance class on a Wednesday? To have your contribution and the things you do on a regular basis." But when I hear that, literally nothing in me lights up: How fucking boring.

Has anything changed in me at all? And if it has, how do I get this to reflect in my outside life circumstances? In other words, how do I integrate these changes?

*

Jay and I are sitting on Marion's spare bedroom bed in London, doing an exercise called 'Thirty-six questions to fall in love'. The aim of these questions is to get closer through self-disclosure. One of them is to list the positive qualities you see in the other. "You're good at loving things," Jay says thoughtfully. "You don't let spiders die, you let them out. You're forgiving – you forgive me quickly when I've done something to upset you or done something wrong. And you're nature-y and creative. Also, you're good at talking about things – like yesterday, when we talked about screentime."

I smile. We'd had a really adult conversation about his (in my view, excessive) use of his tablet, in which I listened to him and gave him space, took his opinions seriously, respected his views and agreed to give him freedom and trust around this issue.

Tears well up in my eyes. I want to skip the next question, the one about what your relationship with your mother is like, because I think it's not appropriate for someone so young, and, of course, it feels strange when I'm right there. But he insists we do all the questions and answers this one with an enthusiasm and honesty that brings even more tears to my eyes. "Oh, it's great!"

I wished I had been able to say that about my own mother.

*

A feeling of desperate exhaustion, a 'got to go to bed right now' kind of feeling, is making it increasingly hard to endure Jay's chatter. It feels like I want to go completely inside myself and I've got out of practice with doing two things at once while listening to him so things like food shopping and cooking feel overwhelming. When we return from Tesco's, I sink desperately into a nap and just as I'm falling asleep, I have a strange experience.

I wake up and feel for a few split seconds that I'm my much younger self waking up in bed during one of the many times when I was sick at home. It's a vulnerable feeling, and although the depths are fleeting, the echoes linger for quite a while. And in its wake comes a thick tide of realisations around how my trauma has affected my relationship history.

I see suddenly how I have two distinct traumas. One is abandonment: being afraid of being left or rejected – which makes me scared, hypervigilant and careful about doing anything to push the other way. The other is abuse: having shaky boundaries because mine were so regularly and painfully invaded; finding it hard to be true to myself; playing it safe to avoid others' anger.

In my most recent relationships, I've been enacting the abandonment part most consistently, by either choosing addictive, emotionally and physically absent partners, or partners who would emotionally abandon me by ending the relationship suddenly or withdrawing after a certain period. Partners who wouldn't shout at or hit me, but nevertheless hurt me with their absence. The boyfriend I had before Dylan was the first one who was really a mixture of both: critical and abandoning, unavailable and attacking, embodying these two distinct aspects of my dad very well.

With Thor, I feel like there's been quite a lot of progress in the sense that he's been consistently loving and not abandoning, although some of his behaviour has triggered my abandonment trauma. But previously, whenever I'd get involved with someone who showed a fierce anger like my father, I'd run a mile. Maybe I have got stronger in myself to be able to deal with that.

Another insight is that I have a repetitive pattern of seeking family, either a family I can join, or longing to create one: the Leela community; my friend Neve's family who are very familiar because they have a father figure like mine; Al Anon and the other 12 step groups I joined ... Trying to create a family by having a child, and the strong family feeling I've had with Thor. Only this seems suddenly to have fragmented, causing a lot of grief and disconnection.

There's a strong feeling of let-down: I can't create a future with this person, I'm not able to have what I need in this situation. Once again, I'm on my own, ultimately, I'm fending for myself. Which is all a recreation of that feeling from childhood of no one's going to help me and support me, I have to keep on struggling on my own.

The lightbulb really came on when my friend Wendy told me, "You know, it's really been important for me to have someone who can hold down that side of life, like earning the money and holding down the stability, so that I can heal."

Yes, I thought, I really haven't had that, I haven't had an environment or people who held that for me. And when I got together with Thor, I thought I had that for a while, because he was giving me a home and that meant so much to me. I was released, for a time, from the burden of having to earn money and pay all those bills. From the constant tension of holding all that responsibility with a traumatised nervous system.

I did do a lot of healing in that time – but then something happened. I can't put my finger on it, but the same loop started running again, and it reminds me of something Luke once said to me, "Can you even be happy at all?"

Maybe I just keep recreating the way that there was no respite for me as a child, apart from going into my books and my music and visiting my best friend. Home was shit, school was shit – I was bullied in both places and didn't feel safe anywhere. I belonged nowhere. I believed I was wrong and defective. It's as if this has come clear to me for the first time.

And then the realisation drops. It comes when I'm thinking about my oldest, best friend, Laurel, who seems to always be winning awards with her business and comes across as a serious, respected professional businesswoman. Not only that, but she actually loves her work and it's not like a chore for her – her work is her fun, her relaxation away from her children. And this has never been the case for me. Work has always been just another thing I have to do, that I can relax when it was over, even when there are aspects of the work that I enjoy.

There are plenty of logical reasons why I didn't create that kind of career, like having way less confidence than Laurel because of my childhood – she had a mother who constantly told her she could do anything she set her mind to. Becoming a mother from an earlier age, as I have, also gave me less of an edge to establish my career.

But it's deeper than that – it's that, over I over, I have always chosen freedom over success and money and security.

And maybe that's something to celebrate, something that's just as valid. Lately, I've had critical thoughts surfacing about the way Thor doesn't really make money. I know he has done it in his life before and working full-time wasn't right for him, so it's not like he can't do it or is too lazy to.

The thing is, I'm the same. I also choose freedom. And there is no one else I can blame for that.

HOME

"Now's the time to be strong and powerful. Make a choice."

Thor stands facing me on the path, holding my hands and looking into my eyes with love, but also with a strength that calls me to match it.

We've talking about the issue I'm wrestling with within myself: Do I go to Leela for the fourth time to do a week of CEP – my third time alone, without Thor – or do I stay here, having quiet time in nature, going for long walks? Thor and I have been connecting so well, so in a way it doesn't make sense to go.

But something else has been stirring, and he senses it too: a fear we both have that I'll again get closed down, triggered and feeling trapped, if I stay in the van. And I know Leela will keep things moving in the process of healing that's begun. So finally, I say, "I'll go."

Just before leaving the van, a huge flood of tears comes out, and he holds me. "I'm so tired of packing suitcases and going to other places. I just want to be home," I wail.

He meets me in my vulnerability. "You live there now, not here anymore," he says, with his 'little' face on.

*

It's the first time I've come here that I've not felt a palpably warm welcome on arrival. The foyer is strangely silent and empty; the whole air of the place is quiet, in recovery from the intensity of the recent Sacred Sexuality Festival, I imagine – which I've dodged, terrified at the idea of being around that much random sexual energy.

I don't see anyone I'm close to, and when I go into my assigned room – Zanzibar again, to my relief – the only other woman in there ignores my greeting and merely gestures irritably when I ask which bed isn't taken, without looking at me.

I don't take it personally because I know people here are often in their own processes, but it doesn't exactly make me feel good about being here. And for the first 24 hours I do, indeed, feel like it was a mistake to come here. I don't feel connected and although it's good to see some familiar faces, the work feels like a struggle and I feel generally uncomfortable and anticlimactic.

I resent the early morning meditations, feeling sleepy and grumpy when I drag myself into Zorba. This week, there's no Bionergetics, because there's a 21-day Dynamic Meditation challenge going on. I enjoy 'bio', as it's affectionately called, because it gets me into my body and I feel much clearer and more relaxed afterwards. With Dynamic, it's less obvious what I'm getting out of it, since my mind just whirs the entire time and all I feel is the discomfort of the exercises – jumping up and down repeatedly for 10 minutes, holding my arms in the air for fifteen.

Within a day, though, after more hugs and a dose of surrender, I find my groove again and start feeling the relief I've come to expect from being here.

Thor has been talking on and off since the summer about wanting us to connect from a 'different place', not just in our vulnerable spaces. Rather than a desire to push the vulnerability away, he said this was about a longing for us to meet when we're both in our power. When he first raised this topic, at Rainbow, I was too triggered and premenstrual to explore it, but at Colourfest I stepped into this zone for the first time: and it didn't look like I thought it would. It was soft power.

At Leela, as I scream and shout and activate my belly strength, it's a harder power that comes into play. A power that has me feeling outraged at all the things I've been putting up with in my life: suddenly, in this context, where I have so much more headspace than in the van, the lack of autonomy in my relationship is glaringly obvious.

I know things have to change.

WHEN A DREAM CHANGES

When a dream changes, you don't notice it at first. You don't know what it's changing into. Sometimes, it turns into a nightmare before you can see the new dream.

At Leela, I'm visited nightly by intense archetypal dreams. One of them is so strong that it haunts my daily life. I'm driving the van and trying to get it through a multi-storey carpark. The van is always too high for multi-storey carparks, yet I'm having a go at it anyway. Every time I move up a level, the ceiling looms closer to the van's top and I freak out. It's sheer terror. What the fuck is going on? Why am I doing such a crazy thing? And why am I even driving the van? I've never dreamed about driving it before. Yet, there is no way I can stop.

Another time, I dream about driving the van as it swerves around huge, steaming hot craters towards the side of the road. There's a sense of both urgency and a certain exultation – like being in a video game where you keep escaping death and stay on for another round. Again, I can't stop. When I share the dream with Marion, she says astutely, "Sounds compulsive."

VANIVERSARY

After the helter-skelter of Leela life, I'm ready to enter another short-lived 'honeymoon' phase of van life, even though I know, deep down, that these days are numbered. After all the early mornings, I'm keen to get lots of sleep, reconnect with Thor and relax with long walks and hot chocolate.

We park up at a field we've stayed in before near the Wiltshire/Somerset border. The first time we came here, I remember our own activities being interspersed, somewhat bizarrely, by army personnel doing some kind of training, their walkie-talkies buzzing intermittently. I found it disturbing and sought out the sanctuary of the sheep.

As we set off for a walk, I'm in a slightly silly, child-like space. "I want to see a rabbit," I say, for no apparent reason.

We're walking down one of the burial mounds, hand in hand, when what looks very ilke a rabbit runs down the hill between us and disappears along the path ahead. "It's a hare!" Thor exclaims. Excitement courses through me.

"What does it mean?"

I know something big is on the horizon.

*

It's nearing our vaniversary. And anniversaries of a kind are happening all the time: It's six months since our handfasting, halfway through 'our sentence', I joke to Thor when he says, "Has it been that long already?". My Leela-inspired empowerment to move on from van cohabitation has receded in the face of a new phase of contentment: we're visiting places from our first van adventures, like Arundel in West Sussex, and it feels nostalgic and lovely.

This time, Swanbourne Lake is partially dried up and there are 'No Entry' signs at the gate, which of course Thor ignores, climbing over the fence anyway. I gingerly follow, hoisting up my skirt. We sit in silence near the elder tree we visited last time, that magical early winter day when I was so high from my newfound liberation. Now, the leaves are smoky, celebratory shades of orange and yellow and there is change in the air. I know I'm more grounded than I was then, but also less innocent, more deeply acquainted with my shadows.

As Thor lays out a circle of wood stubs he collected at Stonehenge, on the ground, I say, "You're connecting up the pieces of the jigsaw again." He's often talked to me about how he joined up the different sacred sites during his travels. And there is something sacred and magical about this site, here, even though it's nothing official, like a burial mound or a Neolithic monument. Just a sense of quiet, ancient peace that takes a strong hold in my bones.

After a short while, we realise it'll soon get dark, so we walk up the steep hill towards the path into town, following my inspiration to get fish and chips. The town is as cute and quirky as I remember it, with its low-hanging bookstore shopfront and winding streets; the trees surrounding the castle like solemn guards.

It feels easier for me to relax into this time with Thor, since we've been trying out a new change in routine: we've agreed that my time in the morning is my own and I can walk and work on my own. Then the rest of the day, we are either doing stuff together or doing parallel stuff that doesn't disturb the other.

I can't believe it's taken us a year to get to this place. But it gives me hope.

*

Of course, we soon bump up against our usual problems – my need for autonomy not being met, his needs for deep connection not being met. It's boringly familiar. Our new 'schedule' only lasted two days before it all crashed down again. I realised that it was ridiculous for me to attempt to cram my spiritual practice, alone time in nature, breakfast, paid work and my book into just 3.5 hours a day.

It becomes more and more obvious that in moving into the van, I stepped into a situation that Thor had created – a situation which worked for *him*. I expected it to work for me. But of course, it doesn't. We need to cocreate something based on both of our needs and feelings, on both of our journeys and paths in life. If that can't work, then we have to go our separate ways. Right now, it feels that pragmatic. The van, which, in reality, always *has* been too small, soon starts to *feel* too small for me. I'm coming back into my individuality, and it's abundantly clear that that needs space. I realise that the dream of freedom I was incubating when Jay left, nearly a year ago now, has moved on; now I'm incubating a different dream.

But it isn't yet clear what can replace that broken dream: the one of us travelling around, communing with nature, until we find somewhere more long-term to do our missions together. Part of me feels that I *have* found somewhere I want to live – Leela – at least part time, but I still didn't know how I'd cope with the relentless schedule there if I did it full time.

I'm stuck: I can't seem to move in the direction of leaving. Fear and budding grief do a dance inside me for weeks; I don't want to lose him or for us to move apart. Somehow it feels like if I leave the van, it will just be over between us. We discuss the different options endlessly: should we go to the lodge? Should we move to Leela completely?

Then one day, the waiting comes to an end. It's not a dramatic moment – much like the day I announced to Luke that I was leaving, it's just an ordinary day. Thor is sitting on the sofa, the way he usually does, and I look at him and think, *this is not right, that my whole day, my whole life centres around another person.* And it's crystal clear to me, right now, that this is not my vision of life or of relationship.

In the next days, another situation confirms my intuition that I need more freedom to govern my own life. Another trip to see Jay is coming up, and this time Thor is struggling to find a place to park up where I can easily get to a train station, complicated by the fact that there are bad weather predictions. He makes it clear that it's a hassle for him, and we get into an argument. "You just don't support me to see my son!" I accuse him.

My anger is a front for my guilt as the words of another Leela CEP resound in my head: "A child should be with his mother."

Now, I try to address it openly. "The thing is," I tell Thor, changing tone, "I do feel guilty – I feel like Jay's missing me and I need to see him as much as I can, even though it's really inconvenient."

"You're accusing me of not facilitating you seeing your son but actually you don't do that for me," Thor says, and I'm stunned. How is it possible for me, without my own transport, to support him with that? "And anyway," he goes on defensively, "I do facilitate it because I've just spent an hour trying to find a good park up on Google Maps so you can see him. And Jay chose not to be with us as a couple – he chose something different."

But the way I see it, Jay didn't truly know what he was choosing; he was too young. He thought he'd see me every two weeks.

The ridiculous-ness of the situation hits me in a lightning bolt of clarity. I'm not angry. But I know I am leaving, even though I have no idea where I will go.

*

My heart is thundering in my chest. This is going to be a big conversation. So much has been building up inside, and everything seems to hang in a frightening yet exhilarating suspension.

Will we end it?

At the very least, I want to hold to my new-found clarity: I need to move out. And although I've been having this thought since March, on and off, this is the first time I feel ready to take action on it rather than waiting for something to emerge. My time in the van is at an end, and the thought fills me with grief, but my excitement at the idea of having my own space is stronger, finally.

Sitting on Graham and Kristen's bed, where I'm staying for the weekend, I take some deep, steadying breaths as I dial his number. As soon as I hear his voice, I soften and the tears skirt around the edges of my own voice.

But somehow it comes out: "I want to start looking for my own place."

It's not as if this is a new concept between us. It's come up a few times. But it's never felt like things were actually moving forward in that direction.

His response is calm and measured, and my racing heart begins to ease up. "I keep trying to make it work by making more improvements to the van. For some reason, I haven't been able to direct my energies successfully to us finding a space where we can have two structures to live in. So, I just keep tweaking the van." His voice is half sorrowful, half humorous. It's true. He recently got noise-cancelling headphones so he could endure my typing more easily and adapted the bed to make it more mould-proof.

"So, it looks like the only solution is for you to take charge of your own life, so you can have your autonomy." His voice is gentle, not judgmental. Or maybe it's just because I've come to the same conclusion so it doesn't hurt in the way it would have if it were forced on me before I was ready.

Relief floods through my body.

And then he says it: "I feel relieved. I don't have to look after you anymore. I've been basically looking after you for a year. Making the van nice for you to live."

There's a long silence. Then I open my mouth and the words just fall out. "I read this article about the psychology of relationships recently ... that issues set in motion at the start of the relationship tend to repeat until they are resolved. Like, those issues set a tone or a template, even if the couple aren't thinking about what happened anymore. And when I read that, I thought about how when we first connected, you had to wait for me. First, when I was still with Dylan, and I felt I had to see that relationship through and not jump ship, and then when you and I did get together and you came down to Lewes with me, after a few days of connecting I asked you to wait at Firle Beacon 'cos I needed time to myself."

"Yes. It's true. And then after that, living in the van, I kept waiting for you near train stations, like they were magnets." After a pause, he goes on, "I want to be free to travel wherever I want in these next few days. I don't want to restrict where I go according to where you need to go. It's time for me to go on my own adventures again."

Although I'm sad, and I know that the implications of his desire will be inconvenience and expense when I need to visit Jay, I agree. What else can I do?

And yet, although his words are strong, I don't feel threatened. This is something that would have triggered me severely before. I remember feeling awful on our Wales trip last summer, when we were planning to move in together and he told me that he only wanted to be at my house 50% of the time. I was spun out for ages by that, having no idea that 50/50 was a perfect arrangement for me too. Not for my inner child, of course, who wants her nearest and dearest to be there at all times. But for the rest of me.

That evening, I take my next concrete action towards independence. I post on Facebook to say that I am moving out of the van and now looking for a caravan of my own to rent, or a cheap one to buy.

To my amazement, by the next morning, things are moving. There are two suggestions of places I can park up with a caravan, one offer of a caravan for sale, and then the perfect solution, because, let's face it, it will take me a while to save up for a caravan. It's from a woman named Kate who I met last year at a 5Rhythms workshop I was synchronistically invited to attend for free. At the time, we had a long, meaningful conversation about my planned van travels, her recent cancer battle and her upcoming wedding. Now, she responds to my post with, "If you're ever interested in being in North Dorset, let me know. You can stay in our campervan and there's room for your partner's van too."

It feels instantly right. Dorset is, of course, where we've been spending more time than any other county in the past five months, at Leela and surrounding park-ups. We've come to love it. I feel even more excited when Kate says that she and her husband are willing to work with whatever resources I have and have no set idea of price. I've looked at my budget and, frighteningly, all I can reliably afford to set aside with my fluctuating freelancer income is £100 a month – who would rent even a box to me for that?

But there's still a sense of rightness, a thread I know I must follow. When I go to bed at Kristen's that night, after Jay has gone home, I realise that I'm looking forward to an hour by myself to do whatever I want, to give myself and my inner child some love. *Fuck. I've been trying to give more love to someone else – Thor – than I've been giving to myself ... that was never going to work. It's insane.*

Now that I've made solid moves towards moving out, and declared my intention to Thor, I can face up to the fact that what was expected of me – to be so present, connected and loving with someone when I didn't have the space to do it for myself – was just not reasonable.

It is with both trust and trepidation that Thor and I set off to go and see Kate and her husband Rolf's place. All my insecurities about not having money and being put in a 'beggar' position yet again are up, and it doesn't help that I've just entered the vulnerable Autumn phase of my cycle. But Thor says, "Just be OK with being a beggar, because that's what you are. Don't be ashamed of it. It's the way it is. Just offer what you can, and if they don't accept it, that's OK. Keep looking."

*

We're back at the Wiltshire field where we've often parked up. The season shifting palpably into autumn seems to heighten my sense of being in transition. How I love this season. Going for a walk just before sunset, my boots crunch against recently fallen leaves as pheasants call repeatedly. The ground is fertile with the tree's discarded colours, rich and full of longing. We've just passed the portal of Samhain – the traditional Celtic New Year and the time when the veils between this world and the next are reputed to be thinnest.

I suddenly remember the other signs that change was coming: the cow we saw giving birth at Cadbury castle, only a few miles from here. It was so dramatic: we were walking through the trees on the path winding up to the Iron Age Hill Fort, one of our favourite spots, when suddenly we heard this plaintive *moo*. "Look," Thor grabbed my arm and got me to stop. There, through the remaining foliage, was a big hulking black shape – and a smaller one, a calf struggling to get up, over and over. Its mother was licking it and making this mournful sound.

"It shouldn't take that long," Thor spoke my thoughts aloud as we continued to watch, awe-struck. I worried that we were disturbing the newborn pair and when the mother looked at us a few times, I insisted we leave. I was half afraid she would hurt us in defense of her young.

I have no idea if the calf survived.

Did the hare and the cow mean new beginnings? New life? In the case of the cow, new life that may or may not be sustainable?

As I walk back to the van, it looks all cosy with the light in the window, illuminating Thor. I feel almost overcome by fondness towards him.

*

We find the house after driving through promising looking countryside: narrow lanes lined with high hedges, the hills and trees enclosing us. We arrive early, so we take a little walk up the road first. Although the nearest town, Sherborne, is an hour's walk away, I don't think this will be a problem when I have this much beauty on my doorstep. Besides, I've grown accustomed to rural isolation in my year in the van. Here, I'll have Kate and Rolf around, and I'm hoping I could occasionally catch a lift with them into town.

As we approach the driveway, we're greeted by the sounds of radio music and DIY where it looks like someone is working behind some tarpaulin on a wooden structure. "Whew, it's scruffy," Thor says with relief when he spots the campervan, a Peugeot with a yin-yang symbol on the door and a colourful painting of the chakras on the other side. We've been a bit nervous that it'll be 'posh' and difficult to maintain at that standard, and that his van would be out of place on their grounds.

We decide against disturbing the tarpaulin and I ring the doorbell of the cute cottage, feeling brave. A man in his 60's with bright eyes and grey hair in a topknot whips the door open to greet us. He radiates excitability and enthusiasm. "I'm Rolf. You must be Morgan," he says, holding out his hand to shake mine. I introduce Thor and he grabs his hand warmly. "Kate's just working on her artist studio in the garden. Let's go get her." As we follow in his wake, I glance at the garden, which is strewn with building materials. The lawn is full of vegetable beds and flowerpots and looks lovingly tended. The garden, thick with birdsong, is held in the bowl of the surrounding hills.

After meeting Kate, who's gruffer than I remember, but probably just because she's immersed in her building project, we go into the cottage for a cup of tea. It's rustic and charming, with low ceilings and flagstone floors. "Now. What do you need?" Rolf asks in a way I find kind but disconcertingly direct. I'm not used to being asked this outside of the context of intimate relationship.

"Well …." Unsure how to answer, I waffle about my internet access needs – my main concern, because of my work – and he confirms that he can easily wire me up. There's no phone signal, but I do most of my correspondence through What's App and Facebook anyway, and apparently the signal is better on the other side of the garden.

Thor comes in and explains about the skills he can offer in exchange for staying there, making it clear he won't be staying there all the time.

The next question soon comes: "What would *you* like to happen next?" Rolf is sitting in the armchair opposite me and leans forward.

"Well…" I trail off and look at Thor a bit helplessly.

"The thing is, I don't have much reliable income because I'm freelancing. The most I could pay is £100 a month, so I wondered if I could do some work in exchange?" I brace myself for outbursts of outrage.

"Sure. We need a lot of help in the garden at the moment, because Sheila's so busy with her studio. What do you think, Kate?"

"Yes. A couple of hours a day, five days a week?" she responds.

The relief floods me. "I can do that, yes."

*

TRANSITIONS

How strange that the vision we had all along, of finding somewhere where we could live in our two 'pods', eluded us when we sought it together – but now that we've taken individual paths, it's effortlessly flowing towards us.

But disengaging my modus operandi from Thor's is confusing and sad as well as liberating. The day I move out, Thor says to me, "Sunbum says he wants to stay here," in his 'little' voice, clutching the second unicorn he bought for me. "But I need him," I protest. "I need his masculine energy."

"But he wants to stay with me," he says, and bursts into tears. We hold each other and cry.

In the absence of his routines (lie in bed till eleven a.m., cuddle till twelve), I'm enjoying more solo walks and loving diving into productive work. But my Pusher quickly comes into full force, expecting me to achieve eight-hour workdays even though I am *crazy* tired and there is obviously a fair amount of grieving going on. My eyes leak whenever we hug, or when our respective routines don't allow us time to connect. Which is already seeming to be often.

Four days after the move, I pop by Thor's van to give him some spinach I've gathered in the garden for my dinner. Even though I know I should get on with work, I ask him if we can watch some TV together later – I'm feeling the need for some cuddle and chill-out time. When he says no, that he's just about to get on with work, the tears spring up, but I hide them.

I'm experiencing the other side of the coin: that he's no longer always available to me, in the way he found so hard in the van when I wasn't always up for connecting. I tell myself that we're just in an in-between phase now and have yet to sync up our schedules.

One morning, he texts me when I'm half an hour into working on my book, the first chance I've had to look at it in days. "Come and check out my comfy warm new duvet," he says, and I can't resist. But once in his van, I move through a gamut of emotions from numbness to sadness – the salt of my tears burning my eyes – to restless impatience to be on with my day, to full-blown anxiety as my skin begins to itch and my nose tickles. I resign myself to going back to 'my' van.

We do connect, sporadically, and his eyes look sad, too, at times, when he does look at me. I realise how he hasn't said "I love you" lately, even in reply to me. Why does this bother me so much? Why do I need him to look me in the eyes so much?

Another night, he comes over for dinner and hot chocolate and I rub his feet. It's cosy and lovely. But when he says he wants to go 'home' and sort out his van, which is in a mess, the sadness strangles my throat, even though part of me wants him to go too because I'm really tired. I express to him that I don't feel we've connected properly today and ask for a cuddle. He says yes and we both express our vulnerabilities together a bit.

New to sleeping alone in a van, I'm stalked by fears, stirred by the night noises. I'm afraid of feeling scared when Thor goes, like I did in the Barcombe cottage in December. One night, I'm lying awake feeling anxious when I hear his footsteps – he's come back to check that I have a window open for gas safety. Relief and happiness flood through me and I quickly fall asleep.

Something is niggling at me: is our relationship just based on comfort and snuggles? Is it helping me or holding me back? I don't even know if I can grow in it, anymore. Now that all the intensity of being cooped up in the van together and having to thrash everything out is gone, I wonder if there's anything left.

But there's no denying I still need Thor. He spends a whole day fixing my broken door which wouldn't shut properly. I can't avoid seeing what this means, that it would need a lot of force for me to close it properly, force that would damage it. The boundaries of my space are in question, and it feels very uncomfortable.

*

Being settled in one place feels new and strange. I keep thinking that now when people ask me where I live, I can say 'Dorset', even though it's temporary – although, in fact, it's the place I've been the most for the past few months. Being able to say that I actually live somewhere, that I have a home, feels so different to being a wanderer, and yet still I have the freedom to go off and travel whenever I want.

Thor and I start to find a new rhythm. When my gardening work hours overlap with his building work hours, there's a fresh pleasure in the easy companionship of working in parallel. I enjoy pushing a wheelbarrow of straw and glancing over to see him raking the path.

There are other anchor points: from the moment I arrived, I've been in love with the maple tree in front of my campervan, captivated by its full head of star-shaped red leaves that, as the autumn weeks dissolve into winter, progressively let go of their grip and drop into the ground. We clear the surrounding space of building and gardening debris and sit on the wooden bench that Thor has fixed so I can commune with the tree more often. I touch it and say, "The tree is happy we're here." And Thor says, "I know. A tree spirit lives there, and it's been communicating with you."

Later, I have a moment of pure contentment and rightness as I walk up to the vegetable bed I'm mulching to see the first quarter moon, having risen at four-fifteen p.m, and the sunset blushing the sky pink on the other side of the horizon.

Cosily inside the campervan at the end of each day, the sound of the wind is a 360 degree experience – much more immediate than in Thor's van, where there's only one, murky window to either side. Kate and Rolf go away for a few days, and we relax into the peace of being together on our own.

But once the novelty starts to wear off, the fears begin to buzz around: will it all turn shit, like things always do? Will I be lonely and alone? Will my pattern of being trapped and isolated just transfer itself to this new situation?

*

We're sitting in my van over hot chocolate on a Monday afternoon when Thor says, "It took me so long to get used to you being in the van and now you've left." I feel surprised; I didn't know it had been such a big process for him. But of course, it would have been. "The van feels so empty now. I have to get used to that emptiness again, the masculine emptiness, that you used to fill with your feminine energy and life."

It's true – there are only three books left on his once-crammed bookshelf and many of the pictures and decorations have gone. I realise it's taking him longer to adjust than me.

"I won't be cooking good meals because I can't be bothered. I'll miss your cooking," he smiles. I am both touched by that and pleased to be off the hook – sometimes cooking for two every night felt a bit oppressive. But then again, now I have to cook *and* wash up, whereas before, the washing up was his job.

"Tell me … what are the pros and cons for you, of living in the van and living here," Thor invites. But in the space I'm in – day twenty-nine of my cycle, liminal and floaty – I can't be that logical. "I can't do pros and cons," I laugh.

"OK, just waffle then," he smiles.

"OK. Well, I can listen to Joy Division without having to hear "What is that depressing shit?" I can type to my heart's content … I got to two thousand words in my book the other day when I wrote barely anything for weeks before that. But … I also feel sad. It's like we're a symbiotic organism that's been split apart. Yes, we can see each other anytime – but here's something bizarre about texting each other to arrange a meet up time when our vans – our 'two boxes' – are right next door to each other."

And there's another big, noticeable difference in my new, separate life: daily, verbal sharing isn't part of the architecture. Even though all the processing did sometimes do my head in, I miss us connecting in that way.

But I don't say this. I stick to the fairly superficial aspects: pro's – being able to work, sleep and eat when I want. The cons: not cuddling up at night, not having immediate on-hand help with technical or practical issues.

"Now your turn," I say.

"Well, I really can't see many cons at the moment. It all feels ideal really."

I gulp. It's ironic, to me, that I, the one who most obviously wanted to get away, and initiated this move, am grieving more visibly, while he's the one enjoying the space.

The tears are just under the surface, but I notice that I don't feel close enough to him right now to delve into the emotions of it all. I listen mutely as he goes on:

"Pros: I don't have to be around you when I find you irritating. I tend to either find you an absolutely amazing goddess or find you annoying and want to get away from you." I wince and try to hide it, since I know he finds it distracting from his share if I show emotion. But part of me resents having to be archetypally 'masculine' in my holding of space, when it's more natural for me to nod, smile and grimace as I respond to what's being shared. I don't particularly get much from his blank listening face when I share, however much 'presence' he's in.

But then he drops deeper: "I can see now how impossible it was for you to want me when we lived together. Now, you have the space to come towards me. In the van, I was always seeking that from you, and you were trying to get your space from me. My need was running things. There's also more give and take possible now … I can feel the equality in that, that I couldn't feel before."

Hearing this, I feel my heart lighten. I've often feared he'd leave due to my not giving enough. Finally, he's seeing what I always said: that I can give if there's space for me to give in.

I had started to demonise myself for being too 'push-pull' in a pathological way, when really, I just needed space to feel my own self, my energy, my aura – my needs and feelings. My astrologer had been right all along. "Rolf," he goes on, "was like "Wow, a year together in the van – I couldn't do that." And I realised that it's not many people who could, and that there's no one in my life I could have done that with, and the relationship still survive."

Now the tears are coming.

*

For a while, I've been in that in-between phase where I've yet to really land in my own essence again. But I knew it was coming: that delicious feeling where I flow from one thing of my choosing to the next, the feeling I used to get on weekends when Jay went to Luke's.

This sublime state unexpectedly visits with wings of grace when I'm cooking dinner the night after our pros and cons discussion. This is a dinner I've invited Thor to, but he declined, which made me sad. Suddenly it hits me, as I stir the stew: Why would I want him here? I can work while the food cooks, I can listen to my favourite podcast, Medicine Tales, all about herbal remedies and ancestral connection and plant teachers. I learn that there are many different ways of finding the Green Path, as it's called – that it's about finding your own relationship with the plants and that this doesn't have to look like training as an herbalist.

I sing, I float, I let my mind explore, and I don't have to explain myself to anyone.

*

On the 'con's' side, it's an abrupt goodbye to being a Princess. Suddenly, I have to do the kind of practical tasks that Thor would always take care of, like filling up with washing water. One morning, I wake in the throes of intense period pain and there's no water left. There's a build-up of filthy washing up and it feels unbearable to have to go outside and hook up the hose. I also need to fill up with drinking water and empty my toilet into the septic tank. It's a humbling process.

*

I've been in my new home for nearly four weeks now, almost a moon cycle. After getting through a few teething problems – leaking roof, water tank leak onto the carpet, gas & electric hiccups, and, last, but not least, injuring my back, making gardening work impossible for several days – I'm feeling settled and content. I'm learning a lot about gardening, enjoying the chance to get outside every day and engage with the cycle of the seasons: putting vegetable beds to sleep for the winter, sowing seeds, harvesting dandelion roots and celery.

Thor and I now see each other on average once a week: quality time rather than having each other 'on tap'. My grief has settled, and I find the new arrangement suits me, even though I miss him. I'm deeply aware that everything is always changing. I've tapped into the local community and found a way to get to a 5Rhythms class in Glastonbury; I can see the Tor from one of the many beautiful walks right on my doorstep and feel the sacred energy of the place. There's a river right behind the house where I commune with the trees and the fairies.

I know the adventure is far from over.

THEATRE OF TREES

They are beginning to gather.

Thor's guitar starts gently, almost imperceptibly, and at first no-one notices, preoccupied as they are by decorating Amir, a chubby wizard type who grins in glee as children and adults alike place flowers all over him. Everyone is dressed colourfully, and the sun is blazing.

We are sitting underneath the magnolia tree at Osho Leela. We moved into the community full time three months ago, progressing from the Community Experience Program to the Team Leader Program, with a resultant ramp-up in responsibilities.

But today it's the Spring Easter Festival time and that is all that matters. I'm wearing a fuchsia-pink dress from the Theatre cupboard and a string of hippie beads. Thor is all in white, like John Lennon, and indeed I feel somewhat like his Yoko as my voice starts to join his delicate string-plucking: "By the grace ... of fallen daffodil spores." My nerves, which have gathered momentum throughout the day, now disintegrate into pure joy as I follow the notes and begin to lead the folk who are gathering under the magnolia for the closing ceremony of the festival, leading them towards:

"The Oak."

Along the way, we pass a gambolling Biodanza teacher who ritualistically raises his hat to us beside the reeds. He's been planted there as part of the Theatre of Trees.

Is this really happening? I cannot believe I have all these people following me. I'm no longer singing, but Thor is still improvising on his guitar, gentle, lilting tones as we all process to the line of oaks at the bottom of the field, where I have found such solace in the intensity of the past months.

I stand in front of the Oak and wait for everyone to be still. I read out my Oak poem from my pink unicorn notebook:

Watching the spaces between the dance of the leaves
As they play the wind's song
I sink into the arms of the oak tree
Her moss-covered lower limbs
Half merged with the earth
Strong and decisive, yet soft
And yielding to the soil

Showing me how to root
My self in my soul's clear knowing
In the ways words cannot touch
In the life that silence holds
I sit in a circle of all my relations:
Soil creatures and birds and 2-leggeds
Fire tenders, all holding their part of the whole

We progress, poem by poem, to the stand of birches leaning on a hill, to the willow grove where my friend Sian had her heart broken at a sexuality festival, and finally to the eight yews.

As everyone arrives in the yew enclosure, filling the cathedral-like space with sunlight streaming through the leaves, we begin to sing a song we improvised a few days earlier: "Listen directly", based on a poem I'd written at Into the Wild.

Listen direct
Listen directly
To the guardian of the underworld
Buzzards circling, taking the wind
Crows sounding their discoveries
Constant caress of leaves with air
Invisible yet so divine
Listen direct, listen directly

Channelling earth, conducting fire
Distilling through water

Don't let the energy go
Follow what it knows
The portal made clear
The portal made clear

If you listen, listen direct
Listen underneath your feet
Like an elephant sensing rain
Listen like the buzzard to the wind currents,
So deeply that you are one

Listen to the tree sap, to the fly's legs, to the bee's hum
To the drinking of nectar that makes it all run
Listen

I invite everyone to join in with the refrain, "Listen, listen directly" and as the sound reverberates through the trees, my heart explodes in my chest even as tears start to form at the back of my throat. I look around and see a man sitting silently, eyes closed, deeply inside; a woman with three blonde children, eyes shining as they sing along; one of the Osho Leela directors, leaning against a tree, smiling warmly at us.

I know the yews are vibrating with us. I sense that this has been waited for, a long time.

ABOUT THE AUTHOR

Morgan Khalsa is a neurodiverse womb creatrix, poet, author, singer/songwriter, and mother-of-one. Her previous book, 'Wild Motherhood' (as Morgan Nichols), explores how mothers can stay connected to their creative and spiritual paths through the intensity of the motherhood journey. She has been offering writing and creativity workshops as well as mentoring for fourteen years, and now creates soulcrafted songs and inspiration for nature connection, creativity and devotion. You can find her on khalsamorgan.com.

Printed in Great Britain
by Amazon